Global Shanghai, 1850–2010

G000036925

"This is a wonderfully entertaining and informative study of one of the most dynamic, yet enigmatic, cities of the world. Drawing upon an impressive array of primary and secondary sources, Wasserstrom presents a Shanghai that throughout its modern history has struggled with its twin identities as both Chinese and cosmopolitan. Grounded in serious research as well as extensive personal experience, *Global Shanghai* is a highly readable book that will be welcomed by scholars and the general public alike."

Elizabeth J. Perry, Henry Rosovsky Professor of Government,
Harvard University, author of *Shanghai on Strike*

"*Global Shanghai* ranges widely and entertainingly over the multi-coloured history of one of the world's most exciting cities."

John Gittings, author of *The Changing Face of China:*
From Mao to market

"Jeffrey Wasserstrom is a historian with a sense of not only the past but the present. He is surely right to call Shanghai's present-day transformation a 're-globalization.' As he deftly reconnects the city with its cosmopolitan past, he treats us to illuminating juxtapositions of fact and myth, historical detail and personal observation, Shanghai as it was and Shanghai as travellers and writers have imaginatively portrayed it. His book will inform and engage the general reader no less than the specialist."

Lynn Pan, author of *Shanghai Style:*
Art and design between the wars

This book explores the play of international forces and international ideas about Shanghai, looking backward as far as its transformation into a subdivided treaty port in the 1840s, and looking forward to its upcoming hosting of China's first World's Fair, the 2010 Expo. As such, *Global Shanghai* is a lively and informative read for students and scholars of Chinese studies and urban studies and anyone interested in the history of Shanghai.

Jeffrey N. Wasserstrom is a Professor of History at the University of California, Irvine, USA.

ASIA'S TRANSFORMATIONS

Edited by Mark Selden, Binghamton and Cornell Universities, USA

The books in this series explore the political, social, economic and cultural consequences of Asia's transformations in the twentieth and twenty-first centuries. The series emphasizes the tumultuous interplay of local, national, regional and global forces as Asia bids to become the hub of the world economy. While focussing on the contemporary, it also looks back to analyse the antecedents of Asia's contested rise.

This series comprises several strands:

Asia's Transformations
Asia's Transformations aims to address the needs of students and teachers. Titles include:

Debating Human Rights
Critical essays from the United States and Asia
Edited by Peter Van Ness

Hong Kong's History
State and society under colonial rule
Edited by Tak-Wing Ngo

Japan's Comfort Women
Sexual slavery and prostitution during World War II and the US occupation
Yuki Tanaka

Opium, Empire and the Global Political Economy
Carl A. Trocki

Chinese Society
Change, conflict and resistance
Edited by Elizabeth J. Perry and Mark Selden

Mao's Children in the New China
Voices from the Red Guard generation
Yarong Jiang and David Ashley

Remaking the Chinese State
Strategies, society and security
Edited by Chien-min Chao and Bruce J. Dickson

Korean Society
Civil society, democracy and the state
Edited by Charles K. Armstrong

The Making of Modern Korea
Adrian Buzo

The Resurgence of East Asia
500, 150 and 50 year perspectives
Edited by Giovanni Arrighi, Takeshi Hamashita and Mark Selden

Chinese Society, second edition
Change, conflict and resistance
Edited by Elizabeth J. Perry and Mark Selden

Ethnicity in Asia
Edited by Colin Mackerras

The Battle for Asia
From decolonization to globalization
Mark T. Berger

State and Society in 21st Century China
Edited by Peter Hays Gries and Stanley Rosen

Japan's Quiet Transformation
Social change and civil society in the 21st century
Jeff Kingston

Confronting the Bush Doctrine
Critical views from the Asia-Pacific
Edited by Mel Gurtov and Peter Van Ness

China in War and Revolution, 1895–1949
Peter Zarrow

The Future of US–Korean Relations
The imbalance of power
Edited by John Feffer

Working in China
Ethnographies of labor and workplace transformations
Edited by Ching Kwan Lee

Korean Society, second edition
Civil society, democracy and the state
Edited by Charles K. Armstrong

Singapore
The state and the culture of excess
Souchou Yao

Pan-Asianism in Modern Japanese History
Colonialism, regionalism and borders
Edited by Sven Saaler and J. Victor Koschmann

The Making of Modern Korea,
Second edition
Adrian Buzo

Re-writing Culture in Taiwan
Edited by Fang-long Shih, Stuart Thompson, and Paul-François Tremlett

Asia's Great Cities
Each volume aims to capture the heartbeat of the contemporary city from multiple perspectives emblematic of the authors' own deep familiarity with the distinctive faces of the city, its history, society, culture, politics and economics, and its evolving position in national, regional and global frameworks. While most volumes emphasize urban developments since the Second World War, some pay close attention to the legacy of the longue durée in shaping the contemporary. Thematic and comparative volumes address such themes as urbanization, economic and financial linkages, architecture and space, wealth and power, gendered relationships, planning and anarchy, and ethnographies in national and regional perspective. Titles include:

Bangkok
Place, practice and representation
Marc Askew

Hong Kong
Global city
Stephen Chiu and Tai-Lok Lui

Representing Calcutta
Modernity, nationalism and the colonial uncanny
Swati Chattopadhyay

Singapore
Wealth, power and the culture of control
Carl A. Trocki

The City in South Asia
James Heitzman

Global Shanghai, 1850–2010
A history in fragments
Jeffrey N. Wasserstrom

Asia.com is a series which focusses on the ways in which new information and communication technologies are influencing politics, society and culture in Asia. Titles include:

Japanese Cybercultures
Edited by Mark McLelland and Nanette Gottlieb

Asia.com
Asia encounters the Internet
Edited by K. C. Ho, Randolph Kluver and Kenneth C. C. Yang

The Internet in Indonesia's New Democracy
David T. Hill and Krishna Sen

Chinese Cyberspaces
Technological changes and political effects
Edited by Jens Damm and Simona Thomas

Mobile Media in the Asia-Pacific
Gender and the art of being mobile
Larissa Hjorth

Democracy in Occupied Japan
The U.S. occupation and Japanese politics and society
Edited by Mark E. Caprio and Yoneyuki Sugita

Globalization, Culture and Society in Laos
Boike Rehbein

Transcultural Japan
At the borderlands of race, gender, and identity
Edited by David Blake Willis and Stephen Murphy-Shigematsu

Post-Conflict Heritage, Post-Colonial Tourism
Culture, politics and development at Angkor
Tim Winter

Education and Reform in China
Emily Hannum and Albert Park

Writing Okinawa
Narrative acts of identity and resistance
Davinder L. Bhowmik

* Now available in paperback

Critical Asian Scholarship
Critical Asian Scholarship is a series intended to showcase the most important individual contributions to scholarship in Asian Studies. Each of the volumes presents a leading Asian scholar addressing themes that are central to his or her most significant and lasting contribution to Asian Studies. The series is committed to the rich variety of research and writing on Asia, and is not restricted to any particular discipline, theoretical approach or geographical expertise.

Southeast Asia
A testament
George McT. Kahin

Women and the Family in Chinese History
Patricia Buckley Ebrey

China Unbound
Evolving perspectives on the Chinese past
Paul A. Cohen

China's Past, China's Future
Energy, food, environment
Vaclav Smil

The Chinese State in Ming Society
Timothy Brook

China, East Asia and the Global Economy
Regional and Historical Perspectives
Takeshi Hamashita
Edited by Mark Selden and Linda Grove

Global Shanghai, 1850–2010

A history in fragments

Jeffrey N. Wasserstrom

Routledge
Taylor & Francis Group

LONDON AND NEW YORK

First published 2009
by Routledge
2 Park Square, Milton Park, Abingdon, Oxon, OX14 4RN

Simultaneously published in the USA and Canada
by Routledge
270 Madison Ave, New York NY 10016

Routledge is an imprint of the Taylor & Francis Group, an informa business

Transferred to Digital Printing 2010

Typeset in Times New Roman
by Keystroke, 28 High Street, Tettenhall, Wolverhampton

British Library Cataloguing in Publication Data
A catalogue record for this book is available from the British Library

Library of Congress Cataloging in Publication Data
Wasserstrom, Jeffrey N.
Global Shanghai, 1850 – 2010 : a history in fragments / Jeffrey N. Wasserstrom.
p. cm. — (Asia's transformations)
[etc.]
1. Shanghai (China)—History—19th Century. 2. Shanghai (China)—History—20th Century.
3. Shanghai (China)—History—21st Century. I. Title.
DS796.S257W37 2008
951′.132—dc22
2008023710

ISBN10: 0–415–21327–4 (hbk)
ISBN10: 0–415–21328–2 (pbk)
ISBN10: 0–203–38032–0 (ebk)

ISBN13: 978–0–415–21327–1 (hbk)
ISBN13: 978–0–415–21328–8 (pbk)
ISBN13: 978–0–203–38032–1 (ebk)

For Yilin, Xinyong, and Lynn,
who showed me so many parts of their city
and told me so many of its stories.

Contents

Figures

Acknowledgments

This book has been a long time in the making, so it is no surprise that I have accumulated a great many debts in the course of its creation. I want to begin by thanking the many Shanghai residents—the three old friends named on the dedication page, plus Yan Yiming, Liu Ding, Iris Qin, Anna Greenspan, Li Tiangang, Chen Danyan, Laurie Duthie, Duncan Hewitt, Greg Chapman, Graham Earnshaw, Zhang Jishun, and scores of people with whom I only had brief conversations in passing—who told me tales about their city and answered my questions. Individually and collectively they taught me an enormous amount about Shanghai's past, present, and future. I also owe a large debt of gratitude to Mark Selden, whose patience and prodding made sure that this book did not fall by the wayside, and whose detailed comments made me think harder about big issues and refine my use of language. Without his alternately patient and exasperated help, this would be a much lesser book—and might still be unfinished. I am grateful that neither he nor any of the many good people I've worked with at Routledge ever lost faith in this project or grew annoyed with me, as I followed the winding path toward its completion.

I am also grateful to a variety of people who read and provided thoughtful advice regarding part or all of the manuscript. Kate Merkel-Hess gave the whole thing a crucial reading at the very end. Elizabeth Perry, Nathan Wood, Harriet Evans, Soren Clausen, Paul Cohen, Robert Bickers, and Lynn Pan gave me important feedback earlier on, saving me from errors and nudging me in useful new directions. I benefited from feedback on what would become individual chapters given by audiences at events sponsored by or held at Indiana University, several Taipei academic institutions, three different University of California campuses (Irvine, Santa Barbara, and San Diego), the Shanghai Foreign Correspondents Club, and London's School of Oriental and African Studies.

This project also benefited from many conversations with colleagues at Indiana University (where I began this book), the University of California, San Diego (where I taught for a year as my thinking about the project was just taking shape), and the University of California, Irvine (where I finished it). Too many friends at those institutions helped me to name each individually. But special mention, for listening to my ideas and telling me what they thought of them, needs to be made of Jeff Veidlinger, Sue Tuohy, Mike Grossberg, Jeff Gould, Nick Cullather, Ken Pomeranz, and Tom Keirstead.

I also want to thank Yomi Braester, Daniel Fried, Carolyn Cartier, Bryna Goodman, Michael Schoenhals, Yeh Wen-hsin, Andrew Field, Ye Xiaoqing, Patricia Stranahan, Sherm Cochran, Susan Glosser, Elizabeth Sinn, Hsiung Ping-chen, Josh Fogel, Ruth Rogaski, Marie-Claire Bergère, and Barbara Mittler for sharing their thoughts and findings on Chinese cities with me; John and Aelfthryth Gittings for providing wonderful hospitality to me, in a perfect setting, during my 2002 stay in Shanghai; and Geremie Barmé and Jonathan Spence for being supportive of the project in ways they have probably forgotten—but I haven't.

I learned invaluable things about Shanghai from collaborating on an essay with Robert Bickers. I gained new insights into urban history and urban theory from stimulating workshops organized by Vanessa Schwartz and Philip Ethington (on "urban icons"), John Logan (on comparing Chinese cities), Elizabeth Sinn (on Hong Kong and Shanghai), and Christian Henriot and Yeh Wen-hsin (on Shanghai during World War II). And co-teaching memorable courses with Maria Bucur, Tom Gieryn, and Deidre Lynch not only taught me much of pedagogic value, but also contributed in various and sometimes surprising ways to making this book what it is.

None of those singled out above should be held responsible for any of the views expressed on, errors made in, or stylistic decisions shaping pages that follow. But those pages would be much less interesting to read, I am sure, if I had not encountered the people named above, and if I had not been lucky enough to have had a series of wonderful formal and informal mentors throughout my graduate school years and beyond. Many of these are mentioned in the preceding paragraphs; others include Lynn Hunt, Woody and Rubie Watson, Kumble R. Subbaswamy, and Marilyn Young. A final one deserves a sentence all his own—indeed much more—and I only wish I had finished this in time for him to see it whole. This is the late Frederic Wakeman, whose passion for Shanghai as a place and whose gift for crafting historical narratives that conveyed excitement about whatever subject he was addressing continue to inspire me.

Finally, I want to thank Anne—for many things, including taking on the challenging teaching assignment that provided us with what remain my most unforgettable Shanghai accommodations. And Sam and Gina—again for many things, including asking me just often enough as first children and then teenagers when I would finally finish that book I'd been talking about and working on for as long as they could remember.

Introduction

Shanghai, the Paris of the East! Shanghai, the New York of the West!
Shanghai, the most cosmopolitan city in the world, the fishing village on a
mudflat which almost literally overnight became a great metropolis . . .
Cosmopolitan Shanghai, city of amazing paradoxes . . . A vast brilliantly hued
cycloramic, panoramic mural of the best and the worst of Orient and Occident.

All About Shanghai and Environs, a 1934 guide
(reprinted in Hong Kong by Oxford University Press in 1983)

A decade of stellar achievements

The Shanghai Star is 10 years old this week. Over the decade it has charted the
transformation of Shanghai from a third world backwater into the world's
most dynamic metropolis . . . Over these 10 years the number of high-rise
buildings in Puxi [West Shanghai] has increased more than tenfold, while
Pudong [East Shanghai] has emerged out of swampy farmland to become one
of the most spectacular cityscapes on Earth.

The Shanghai Star, November 11, 2002

A central goal of this book is to assess Shanghai's past and present claims that it
qualifies as a "global city," a term about which much more will be said below. But
it is worth taking some time at the outset to ask a more basic question about this
giant metropolis that is continually making international headlines and soon will
be even more of a focus of global attention when the 2010 World Expo takes place
there: at what point did Shanghai first become a *city*, period?[1] The answer to this
question is complicated, and answering it takes us back to a time when Hangzhou
and Suzhou, now urban satellites to Shanghai's neon-lit sun, were by far the most
famous urban communities in the Lower Yangzi (Jiangnan) region.[2] Exploring
stories of Shanghai's origins will also introduce features of the local past worth
keeping in mind, while highlighting the degree to which urban legends and fairy
tale visions of Shanghai's wondrous transformations have long colored and
distorted (and continue to color and distort) local and global views of the city.

One standard way to answer the question of when Shanghai first became a city
is to look back as far as the Yuan Dynasty (1279–1368). This approach has gained

the official endorsement of the Chinese Communist Party (CCP), which singles out 1291 as the key point of origin. That was the year when the place name "Shanghai" was first used in official documents to refer to an administrative center that stood by the muddy Huangpu River, just upstream from where that small waterway joined the mighty Yangzi. This explains why in 1991 celebrations were held to mark the seven-hundredth anniversary of the founding of the metropolis.[3]

The main alternative approach, which depends upon what might be called the "Fishing Village Myth," places the start of Shanghai's history as an urban center in the 1840s, when Westerners first began to live in the port. According to this vision of Shanghai's origins, prior to the Opium War (1839–1842) nothing worth calling a city existed where the metropolis of today stands. This notion, first promulgated by Shanghailanders (as Britons and Americans who set up residence by the Huangpu came to be known), glosses over the many pre-Opium War moves toward urbanization that by the 1830s had made Shanghai much more than a "village," no matter how broadly one defines that term. Villages do not typically have central walled districts, but Shanghai had one from the sixteenth century on, after fortifications were built to protect the port from Japanese pirates. Villages do not serve as major transshipment points for goods circulating between countries, but Shanghai had done just this for centuries before the Opium War, thanks largely to a favorable location near the Yangzi River Delta that made it a natural pivot point for trade between China and Southeast Asia. Villages do not, as Shanghai did by the 1830s, have populations of a quarter of a million people and central

Figure I.1 The Huangpu River, 2004

Source: Author's photograph

districts with elaborate gardens, temples, guildhalls, academies, and government offices.

When does Shanghai's birthday fall according to this second tradition? Not sometime in 1291 but in 1843, on November 17 to be exact, the day that a diplomatic accord transformed Shanghai and four other Chinese communities into special "treaty ports" open to foreign trade and settlement. To drive home their vision of 1843 as the crucial point of origin, in 1893 Shanghailanders held a Victorian-style "Jubilee"—complete with parades, speeches, and fireworks and other "illuminations"—to mark the passage of the city's first fifty years.[4]

All commentators on Shanghai's past acknowledge that the implementation of the Treaty of Nanjing (the agreement China's rulers were forced to sign after being defeated by the British in the Opium War) constituted a major turning point in local history, marking as it did the start of a century of dramatic changes. During the hundred years following the arrival of the first Western settlers, the city's physical size would quickly double and then continue to expand, while its population increased ten-fold, hitting one million by the early 1900s, tripling again by the 1930s.[5] During that time as well, the city would take on a dramatically new shape, as it was divided into two foreign-run districts, an International Settlement that was largely self-governing and a French Concession run in a more conventionally colonial manner, and a separately administered Chinese Municipality. And, last but not least, during that period, the word "Shanghai" would go from being one that conjured up few distinctive connotations in either the Chinese or international imagination, to one that was among the most widely recognized place names on earth, as well as one whose very utterance evoked powerful positive and negative images, domestically and globally.[6]

Still, there are very different implications of saying that the Treaty of Nanjing started an important new chapter in the history of a city that was already a major hub of regional trade, on the one hand, and saying that it transformed a fishing village into the international city that is Shanghai, on the other. Tales of origin are always important to communities, but perhaps particularly significant for cities. In contrast to nations, often imagined to be timeless entities, an urban center is typically ascribed a particular moment of origin. It is natural, therefore, that even the seemingly simple act of picking a birthday for Shanghai is fraught with meaning. Most significantly, to place it in 1843 encourages us to think of the foreign presence as a natural, indeed decisive, part of the local past.

Looking back to 1291, by contrast, lays the groundwork for the tale of a protean Chinese city, which first evolved from a village into an urban center, then for a time, for better or for worse, was subdivided and run partly by foreigners, before becoming at last the sprawling metropolis of fifteen million plus inhabitants that it is today. According to this approach, which can be embraced by those who see 1843 as marking either a catastrophic or at least partially beneficial turning point in local fortunes, Shanghai may be a "young" city in Chinese terms, but one that by 1893 had a history of more than half a millennium not just half a century. Only an 1843 birthday fits comfortably with the notion, so central to the self-conception of Shanghailanders, that Westerners had come to an unpromising "city of reeds" and transformed it, "as by enchantment" (to use a phrase from a Jubilee text), into a wonderful metropolis.[7]

Fairy tales

There are, as we will see, many myths that distort our vision of Shanghai's past and present, but the notion that it was a mere "fishing village" before 1843 is the one that has retained the most stubborn hold on the international imagination, even though it is contradicted by the work of many historians who have detailed the existence of quintessentially urban phenomena prior to that time. One curious thing about the story of foreigners creating something from nothing in an almost magical way is that, had Shanghai truly been merely a "fishing village" in 1842, the British would not have been so eager to have it become one of the new treaty ports. And just how far from being simply a "village" it was by the 1830s shows through in this British travel account from the time:

> No other town with which I am acquainted possesses such advantages: it is the great gate – the principal entrance, in fact – to the Chinese empire . . . [T]he tide ebbs and flows a great distance inland, thus assisting the natives in the transmission of their exports to Shanghae, or their imports to the most distant parts of the country. The port of Shanghae swarms with boats of all sizes . . .[8]

Why has the myth of post-1843 Shanghai as an entity created from scratch proved so tenacious? One reason is that the land ceded to the British to build on after the Opium War was literally a mudflat just north of the walled city. It was on this reclaimed land by the Huangpu that some of the great landmarks of the treaty-port era, including the long line of neo-classical buildings dating from the 1910s through 1930s that still stands along the waterfront (in the famous district known as the Bund) and continues to grace postcards, would be built. Hence, there was a basis for what Robert Bickers, today's leading historian of Shanghai's Britons, has dubbed "mudflattism"—even though, as he notes, the Shanghailanders often misleadingly wrote (and acted) as though the International Settlement, which evolved out of that original British enclave, was the whole city, not just one part of a many-faceted metropolis.[9]

A second allure of the Fishing Village Myth lies in the fact that, prior to the 1840s, only a handful of people living outside of China, or indeed in parts of the country other than the Jiangnan (Lower Yangzi) region, had seen Shanghai with their own eyes or had any distinctive impression of it, yet by the 1930s it would become one of the most famous and infamous cities in the world. Its streets and buildings would be featured in Hollywood movies starring everyone from Marlene Dietrich to Shirley Temple, and uttering its name would conjure up a host of exotic images associated with danger and decadence, cosmopolitanism and excitement. Its name would even have made the unusual jump from a Chinese term for a place to an English verb—to "shanghai" someone coming to mean to kidnap them and force them into service, a nod to the port's association with shady activities of various sorts. Going so quickly from international obscurity to global fame and infamy fit nicely then—and still fits nicely now—with a vision of the place itself moving rapidly from mere village to modern metropolis.

There is a third factor that helps explain the hold of the something-from-nothing vision of the city's past—and, ironically, Shanghai's current rulers have contributed to this. Namely, the post-treaty-port incarnations of the city have often been presented as the result of astonishing transformations, in which the metropolis became quickly something that no one would have expected it to become. The CCP has claimed, not just once but twice now, that the Chinese people, under its leadership, have performed such a magic trick with the city.

This happened first in the Maoist era (1949–1976), when the tale was told of the city being wondrously remade into a socialist utopia. The transformation was said to have begun with the coming of the People's Liberation Army, which "liberated" a local population that for more than a century had suffered under and valiantly struggled against various kinds of domination by foreign and local oppressors—struggled and resisted, that is, if they were not bourgeois "running dogs" of the imperialists, collaborators with the Japanese, or lackeys of Generalissimo Chiang Kai-shek. Once incorporated into the newly founded People's Republic of China in 1949, according to this tale, the city became a thoroughly different place, a "New Shanghai" that was infinitely purer (by being devoid of foreign enclaves), more egalitarian (shown by the absence of slums and beggars), and more of an industrial powerhouse (symbolized by new ship-building plants and factories) than it had been during the treaty-port century (1843–1943), the years of partial or full Japanese military occupation (1937–1945), and the period when the Generalissimo's corrupt Nationalist Party ran the whole metropolis (1945–1949).

According to CCP texts, as we will see in a later chapter, while Old Shanghai may have been a "paradise for adventurers" (as some Shanghailanders insisted), it had been a "living hell" for ordinary Chinese. New Shanghai, by contrast, was—or was rapidly en route to becoming—a true people's paradise. To underscore this vision of transformation for the better, guidebooks of the time routinely referred to individual buildings and open spaces as having been "reborn" (literally, gaining a *xinsheng* or "new life") in 1949.[10]

More recently, as the second epigraph to this chapter illustrates, the build-up of Pudong, which now boasts some of the tallest buildings in the world, has been touted as triggering a transformation of Shanghai at least as astounding as any it has seen before. Once again, tales are being told of a completely revamped "New Shanghai" taking shape, though this time around assuming the form of a futuristic metropolis marked not by egalitarianism but by a "spectacular cityscape" of towering buildings, with edifices rising as if by magic on what until recently were unpromising pieces of "swampy" riverfront land, albeit this time just east rather than just west of the river. The imagery in play near the Huangpu now, according to Tsung-yi Michelle Huang, in her insightful recent analysis of urban change in several turn-of-the-millennium East Asian cities, is a variant on the Sleeping

Beauty fairy tale: a once lively and then for a time dormant metropolis re-awakening.[11] One thing that makes this ironic, from the historian's point of view, is that Sleeping Beauty also provided a framework for some Shanghailander commentaries on the transformation that China underwent in the wake of the Treaty of Nanjing. Consider, for example, the following line from *The History of Shanghai*, a 1921 work commissioned by the Shanghai Municipal Council (SMC) that ran the International Settlement (and was at the time a body with only foreign members): "Most fortunate was it for China that the Fairy Prince, who came to awaken her from her long sleep, came with the best and kindliest intentions."[12]

Real and imagined Shanghais

[N]othing in Shanghai was the least like the picture I had formed of it . . . Yet I am convinced that there exists a Shanghai corresponding to the city of our dreams; perhaps excelling it . . .

Jean Cocteau, 1936[13]

Fairy tales that treat Shanghai as the site of miraculous transformations, coupled with the attraction the city held late in the treaty-port era and once again holds for novelists and filmmakers (André Malraux and Joseph von Sternberg between the two World Wars, cyberpunk pioneer Neal Stephenson and directors like Wong Kar-wai now), have helped turn the metropolis into a special sort of urban center in the international imagination. What urban theorist Michael Sorkin said about late-twentieth-century Los Angeles holds true equally for contemporary Shanghai: that it has been represented and misrepresented so many ways in so many different sorts of media that it has become "virtually unviewable save through the fictive scrim of its mythologizers."[14] It is a very rare first-time visitor to Shanghai who arrives unburdened by prior expectations. As a result, one of the main questions raised by an initial encounter with the city is whether the diverse images of it to which a visitor has been exposed in advance—via novels and newspapers, photographs, films and folklore, and most recently websites—have or have not done it justice.

One reason I stress this phenomenon here is a personal one: the roots of this book lie, in part, in the reaction that I had to Shanghai during my first visits to it in the 1980s. One thing I remember vividly about my first two stays in the city (I lived there from August 1986 until July 1987 and returned for a brief visit in 1988) is how let down I was by the contrast between the drab city I found, on the one hand, and the exciting one I had conjured up in my imagination, on the other. And one reason I drew attention above to the prevalence of fairy tale visions of Shanghai is that subsequent return visits to the city have shown me first-hand just how seductive it can be to think of the tale of the city today as a variant on the "Sleeping Beauty" bedtime story. This is because one thing that has struck me powerfully during recent trips back to the city is that, in some ways, Shanghai is starting to seem more like the exciting place I imagined I would find than the one I actually lived in twenty years ago.

Figure I.2 The cover of a Shanghai Municipal Tourism Administration publication (no
    date given, but internal evidence suggests 1986)

Source: Author's collection

I realize now that my expectations before my first two visits were shaped unduly
by some notoriously unreliable kinds of representations, including Hollywood
movies and old guidebooks, each of which, focussing on the early 1900s, portrayed
Shanghai as an anything-goes sort of city that pulsated with a special kind of
energy. Intellectually, I knew that Shanghai, like all other parts of China, had

changed enormously since the first decades of the twentieth-century. Yet I continued to fantasize that traces of the unusual vitality and robust international flavor of Old Shanghai would still be apparent in the New Shanghai to which I traveled. And support for this notion was provided by guides to the metropolis of then-recent vintage, which insisted that Shanghai in the 1980s still deserved the title of "most cosmopolitan city" in China. This phrase just did not seem to fit the city I first encountered. Shanghai circa 1986 was certainly livelier and definitely had a more international air than many Chinese urban centers, but the gray terrain I encountered struck me as that of neither the country's most dynamic nor its most international metropolis, even though there were, to be sure, some inescapable physical reminders of the most cosmopolitan period in the city's past: the treaty-port century.

The most notable collection of these physical reminders of a cosmopolitan past lay in the waterfront embankment district known as the Bund, whose northern part formed in treaty-port times the eastern edge of the International Settlement and whose southern part formed then the eastern edge of the French Concession. Nearly all of this district's treaty-port-era landmarks could still be seen in the 1980s. It was on trips to the Bund in 1986, for example, that I first saw the Custom House (with its giant clock modeled on Big Ben), an iconic edifice that will be discussed below in Chapter 4 (a look back to the year 1925, when work on the structure began) and Chapter 7 (a look at what the competition between this and other old symbols for the city and soaring structures like the Pearl of the Orient Tower that now stands across the river from it in Pudong can tell us about contemporary Shanghai). And it was on ventures to the Bund that same year that I first ate *xiaolongbao* (small basket dumplings) in, and admired the view from, the restaurant on the eighth floor of the pyramid-roofed Peace Hotel (née the Cathay), a place where, guidebooks dutifully recount, Noel Coward stayed while writing *Private Lives*.

Additional reminders of Shanghai's cosmopolitan heritage when I first familiarized myself with the city included other culinary landmarks. In the former French Concession, the menu of "The Red House" restaurant (formerly "Chez Louis") contained dishes of European origin, and nearby was the Jing'an bakery, which according to local lore, had never stopped making croissants, even when criticism of Western influence reached its height during the Cultural Revolution (1966–1976). I regret now never having discovered whether the borscht at the former was any good in the 1980s. But bread and pastries from the latter became a staple part of our diet when my wife and I lived at Fudan University for eleven months in the mid-to-late 1980s, even though acquiring them required a long bike ride to the center of the city.

Still, aside from architectural remnants of a bygone era and some culinary artifacts—including a dish of hybrid Russian and Western European derivation as well as purely local characteristics called *sela* (salad), which showed up on the menu even of some restaurants that served only "Chinese" food—Shanghai seemed anything but cosmopolitan in the 1980s.[15] If a cosmopolitan place is defined as one where cultural influences from different parts of the world come together and intermingle in interesting ways, at a time when China was just tentatively opening to international influences, then Canton and Beijing fit the bill better than did Shanghai. And it was only when I reached Hong Kong, the site of a winter 1987 get-away, that I felt that I had finally come to a metropolis that closely resembled the Shanghai of my imagination.

Also missing from the city that I encountered when I first arrived in 1986 were traces of another important imagined Shanghai: the metropolis of revolutionary energy. In two very different periods, the 1910s–1930s (an era of radical nationalism and labor unrest) and the Cultural Revolution decade (an era of rhetorical and physical skirmishes of many kinds), the city had distinguished itself as a volatile hub of radical activity. When I first arrived, there were plaques on the streets and displays in museums reminding one of the great political events of the pre-Communist era—the strikes by workers and patriotic demonstrations by students in years of struggle such as 1919 and 1924–1927—that had earned the city its world reputation as a hotbed of radical activity.[16] And there were monuments as well to radical organizations that had been founded there (the CCP itself held one of its first meetings in the French Concession) and radical writers who had made the city their home (including Mao Dun, Ye Shengtao, and Lu Xun, China's most revered twentieth-century author). Other than these markers and displays, though, there was little about Shanghai, as I first encountered it, which flagged it as a place where political passions had once, or could again, run high.

Mid-way through my first stay in the city, however, in December 1986, a brief series of student demonstrations broke out, which showed me that I had been foolish to assume that passionate political engagements were only part of Shanghai's past. As I watched marchers follow old demonstration routes and demand, as their predecessors once had, an end to corruption, less governmental interference in their lives, and a more open political system—I felt an intense and unexpected connection to one of the Shanghais I had imagined before my arrival, the one that I had come to the city to study, as my dissertation focussed on patterns of popular unrest in the city between 1919 and 1949.[17] And the conversations I had with students in 1987—youths who in many cases would later take part in the historic and longer-lived upheaval of 1989 that may have been centered in Beijing but brought hundreds of thousands of marchers to Shanghai streets—confirmed my feeling of ties between historical and contemporary concerns. Their curiosity about Western political ideas, for example, resonated with that of their counterparts at the same universities during the early decades of the twentieth century.

The Shanghai illusion

It might be tempting to conclude that the disappointment I felt with Shanghai in the 1980s, tempered though it became after the protest wave, is a distinctively contemporary sort of let-down, one that could only come in an era when various forms of mass media continually bombard us with images of the world's most celebrated and notorious cities. This would, however, be a mistake. It is true that many contemporary encounters with celebrated real places leave first-time visitors feeling let down. And it is true that powerful media, such as television and cinema (and most recently the internet), play a crucial role in the process of creating expectations real places are hard-pressed to satisfy. Still, the general phenomenon is not completely novel. It is, instead, one with roots reaching back well beyond not just my own first arrival in Shanghai but also Cocteau's visit there half-a-century before that.

Mark Twain, for example, had a lot to say about the way travelers of a pre-cinematic age could be and often were discomfited by the lack of fit between their preconceived images of particular cities and their experience of seeing these places first-hand. This theme runs through *Innocents Abroad*, Twain's humorous account of his 1867 trip to Europe and the "Holy Land," which was published in 1869 and for decades afterwards remained the author's best-selling work of non-fiction.[18] Twain makes it clear in this book that, before setting off across the Atlantic, he and his fellow travelers—who were all part of an early packaged tour—steeped themselves in images of the cities and rural locales they were about to see. In some cases, he claims, the engravings they viewed and books they read before leaving North America provided them with an accurate sense of what famous locations would be like when they reached them. Where many of the best-known cities of Europe and the Middle East were concerned, though, he ended up feeling that the places he expected to find had ceased to exist—or perhaps had never existed at all, except in the imaginations of writers and illustrators.[19]

Twain's book draws attention to the extent to which, well before the arrival of powerful new forms of mass media, those wishing to get an accurate view of the world's most celebrated cities had to create strategies for piercing through mystifying layers of representation. By the 1860s, *Innocents Abroad* makes clear, urban centers such as Rome and Cairo were, to borrow Sorkin's language, already "virtually unviewable" save through highly developed "fictive scrims"—even if, admittedly, they were scrims woven by illustrated popular histories, novels, and collections of engravings as opposed to the television shows and movies that dominate our consciousness today. Los Angeles, which was not yet either the biggest or the most frequently represented city on the California coast, was not in that category by 1867. Nor was Shanghai. But Shanghai was well on its way towards becoming just such a place even then, and had Twain made it there in the 1860s and 1870s, there are a variety of written accounts and a fair number of drawings of Shanghai that he could have read and looked at to prepare.[20]

Famous novels with Shanghai settings—such as Mao Dun's *Ziye* (Midnight) and *Hong* (Rainbow), André Malraux's *La Condition humaine* (Man's Fate), and Yokomitsu Riichi's *Shanghai*—had not yet been published.[21] Nor had English-language guidebooks begun to appear.[22] There were, however, several books (including popular histories of China with chapters on Shanghai) and many periodical articles, some with illustrations, that Twain could have seen.[23] If he had immersed himself in such texts (including some discussed in Chapter 1, which is devoted to the year 1850), would he have ended up feeling that the Shanghai he actually encountered lived up to, exceeded, or fell short of his expectations? There is, alas, no way to know. Twain would write interesting things about Chinese topics throughout his career, including commentaries that castigated foreigners for taking advantage of China's weakened state (and even went so far as to express strong sympathy for the anti-Christian insurgents known in the West as the Boxers), but he never made it to Shanghai or indeed any part of the country.[24]

One thing we can say, though, is that if Twain *had* gone to Shanghai in, say, the 1870s, and *had* ended up feeling misled by Shanghai's advance billing, he would not have been the first to claim that the accounts of that city available to Westerners were riddled with inaccuracies. A Briton living near the Huangpu had already done this in 1850 (as we will see in the next chapter), lamenting that his compatriots back in England had been exposed to a mixture of "wild exaggerations," "ill-digested statements," "amusing twaddle," and "malignant inventions" in the publications about Shanghai that had appeared during the previous dozen years.[25] The idea that one needs to be wary of the contrast between the real Shanghai that stands by the Huangpu and the Shanghai that many people imagine exists is, in short, a very old one. As a wonderful 1930s guidebook put it, one always needs to be wary of the "Shanghai illusion," which is "as phoney as a Hollywood opium joint."[26]

Questions without answers

One central question that this book poses is whether the most popular image of Shanghai today (that of a once-and-now-again global city of enormous potential, bustling with just the sort of energy that I failed to find in the 1980s) should be dismissed as equally ungrounded in reality. Or, stated differently, what other realms of experience does it conceal? This is worth asking in part because the metropolis has been the subject of a great deal of breathless commentary since the early 1990s, with local spokesmen and newspapers continually trumpeting it as a "city of the future" and the international press often following suit. The *New York Times Sunday Magazine* even used the headline "The Twenty-First Century Starts Here" for a 1996 story about Shanghai.[27] And in the first years of the new century, Shanghai's boosters have been taking old rhetorical traditions to dizzying new heights. Hyperbolic commentaries on Shanghai's reclaimed status as a global city and a great metropolis have become the order of the day. Several years ago, an officially sponsored Shanghai website even had a section devoted to local "miracles," which celebrated recent changes in such things as local forms of transportation (the city now has an advanced subway system as well as the fastest-on-earth Maglev).[28]

Two early twenty-first-century news stories contributed to this latest wave of intense boosterism by focussing international attention on Shanghai. The first of these broke in October 2001 and dealt with the APEC Summit, which took place in Pudong (East Shanghai), a district directly across from the Bund that is the site of frenetic construction that has transformed the once landmark-free eastern bank of the muddy Huangpu River. That international gathering brought major political leaders (such as Vladimir Putin and George W. Bush) and global economic heavyweights (such as Bill Gates) to the skyscrapers of Pudong (literally

"East of the Huangpu") where, among other things, they watched a spectacular display of fireworks (a technology that originated in China but has now gone global), the highpoint of which saw rockets set off from atop the old Western-style buildings of the Bund. (The fact that a fireworks company based in the United States had been hired to put on this spectacle was cited, incidentally, as one sign that in today's Shanghai, nothing but the best things available anywhere will do.)

The second story broke a little over a year later when word came that Shanghai's bid to host the 2010 International Exposition had been accepted. To have the contemporary equivalent to the exhibitions and World's Fairs of old held in their city, Shanghai's leaders claimed, was a fitting tribute to its re-emergence as a global metropolis of the first rank.[29] Boosters claim that this event, which some predict will bring 70 million visitors to the metropolis and which is being touted as the first World Expo ever held in a developing country, will do the kinds of things for the city that the Columbian Exhibition of 1893 did for Chicago and that various universal expositions of that same era did for the "capital of the nineteenth century," as cultural critic Walter Benjamin famously dubbed Paris.[30] With luck, this future event, the planned date for which provides this book with

Figure 3 An advertisement showing Shanghai (represented by the Pearl of the Orient Tower near the far left) as a world-class metropolis in the same league as cities such as London (represented by Big Ben) and New York (represented by the Empire State Building). Photograph taken at the Pudong Airport in 2004 when the poster was the first thing seen upon arrival on a United Airlines flight. It was still in the same location at least as late as March 2007

Source: Author's photograph

its chronological endpoint, could even, the most passionate supporters of the city suggest, give Shanghai a basis for claiming a right to be called the cultural "capital" of a different era which is already being dubbed by some the Chinese century.

Are the boosters right? Or is all this hype just an updated "Shanghai illusion," and one that is just as phoney as any of its many predecessors? In the 1930s, Christopher Isherwood claimed that, while the large and imposing buildings of the Bund were certainly impressive at first glance, Old Shanghai merely had the "façade of a great city," not all the makings of one.[31] Could the same claim be made about the newest New Shanghai (the term "New Shanghai" has been used for different purposes for many decades) that now stands by the Huangpu? In spite of the five-star hotels, state-of-the-art airport and stunning train station, excellent new municipal library, museums and theatre complex and so on, are there still things missing from New Shanghai that would need to be there for it to be truly a great city? In an earlier period, Shanghai was not just a centerpiece of imperialism and hub of economic activity and consumer culture. It was also a major site of political, literary, and cinematic experimentation, with many of China's best and most daring artists and writers growing up near or going to live near the Huangpu. Are there signs of renewed political and cultural dynamism in New Shanghai, or just signs of economic resurgence? Is the internationalization taking place now contributing to more than just the flow into the metropolis of foreign investment dollars, upscale Japanese restaurants, German luxury cars, Korean movies, and Parisian clothing fashions? Who gains, and who loses by Shanghai's current race to develop?

One aim of this book is to put questions such as these into a meaningful historical perspective, by offering first a series of snapshots of individual years and then a final analytical chapter that takes up themes associated with the newest of the various "New" Shanghais—the city of today. My goal is not, however, to provide definitive answers to these questions. This is in part because I am pulled in two directions. There is ample reason to be suspicious of Shanghai's new boosters, since I know how easy it is to be taken in by this urban center's "city myths" (to borrow a term that Mike Davis has used to described powerful and persistent stories that are told about and can help shape the future of a metropolis).[32] And I continue to look in vain for clear signs that Shanghai is catching up with, let alone passing, Beijing as a site of political and cultural experimentation.

On the other hand, though, I have recently come to appreciate the danger of underestimating this protean metropolis. This is in no small part because of what has happened during my recent trips to the city, half a dozen over the last dozen years. Namely, as already mentioned, each time I have arrived, I have found, much to my surprise, that the city that surrounds me keeps looking less and less like the city I got to know in the 1980s (both for better and for worse—there is more excitement but also more beggars, streets are not nearly as safe, and the divide between rich and poor is much starker), and more and more like that which I conjured up before first crossing the Pacific.

What I find when I go back and what I imagined I would find in the city in 1986 are not a perfect match by any means. The Shanghai of my imagination circa 1985 did not include freeways, for example, or the gargantuan Pearl of the Orient Tower, each of which is now part of the cityscape. Nor did my imagination then have room for branches of Tony Roma's Italian food chain with bathroom walls adorned with sepia-toned photographs of "Old Shanghai." Nor did I conjure up in my mind anything like the "bizarre villa" and rock clubs that Shanghai writer Mian Mian mentions in a tellingly titled essay, "Illusionary City that Belongs to the World"—a piece, contributed to *Time*'s Asia edition in 1999, that takes the form of an extended riff on the theme of "magical" elements of the past re-appearing in a Shanghai undergoing rapid transformations that are both hurtling it forward into an uncertain future and making it more like its former self.[33]

Still, the metropolis I have encountered on my most recent stays near the Huangpu has been one that is very lively, more like Hong Kong circa 1986 than Shanghai of that year, and feels indeed like the "most cosmopolitan" city on the mainland. The city now has the kinds of public spaces—new, nicely landscaped public parks in the heart of the metropolis, cafés, avant-garde bookstores, expanding universities and so on—in which it is possible at least that the kinds of conversations are taking place and connections being forged that could, over time, make Shanghai a hub for political or cultural experimentation. It is also, though, now a place with more of the social fissures and exclusionary spaces that marked the dark side of Old Shanghai than the metropolis I lived in late in the 1980s.

A quick tour of the book

This book is partially an effort to explore the history of the "Shanghai illusion" and the history of local city myths, but it also probes other related histories. One of these is that of an urban center where people of flesh-and-blood have lived and died, worked and raised families, made and lost fortunes, and organized revolutionary groups or struggled to crush movements for change. Another is that of a process: globalization, defined here broadly and simply to mean the rapid development of an ever more tightly interconnected world.

To chart these overlapping histories, the book mainly comprises chapters that offer "snapshots" of the life and times of Shanghai in a series of individual years. These focus on Shanghai at particular moments, while also on occasion sketching in quickly things that had happened in the city since the year discussed in the preceding chapter. More specifically, the book provides snapshots in turn of 1850, 1875, 1900, 1925, 1950, 1975, and 2000. The goal of each of these chapters is not to provide a set of stories that, when taken together, will provide a comprehensive narrative of the metropolis as it changed over time, but rather to present a series of illuminating windows onto the local past. Just as anyone visiting a city and pointing a camera knows that only some things will end up inside the frame, so too with these chapters am I aware that many events and people who might have been discussed will be left out of the story.

I do hedge my bets somewhat in two ways, though, in these chapters. First, I sometimes briefly discuss parts of the local landscape that I thought about focussing on before, metaphorically, pointing my camera in a different direction. Thus, for example, while focussing mainly on an outburst of popular unrest in my "snapshot" of 1925, I take some time to ruminate on the fact that two Russian émigrés made their mark on the local publishing scene that year, an indication of the growing significance within Shanghai of people who had come there to flee the Bolsheviks. And, second, I occasionally mention things that occurred a bit before or a bit after the chosen year. Thus, for example, in taking up 1875, I look at the global tours that a pair of famous figures (the real Thomas Cook and the fictional Phileas Fogg) took just before our snapshot year, asking whether or not they stopped in Shanghai and, if so, what they thought of the place.

In choosing the years to zero in on, a relatively arbitrary method has been used, based on intervals of twenty-five years. The result is that some years of obvious importance in the history of China, the history of globalization, or the history of Shanghai are scrutinized. The year 1900 was, for example, definitely a turning point for China, the year that the Boxer insurgents killed a small number of missionaries and a much larger number of Chinese Christians and for fifty-five days held foreigners hostage in Beijing—events whose repercussions for Shanghai are discussed in Chapter 3. It also seems, at least from an early twenty-first-century vantage point, to have marked an important transitional moment in the history of globalization. This is because in 1900 a multinational force, consisting of soldiers from three different continents, ended up carrying out brutal campaigns of reprisal and looting in Beijing after the hostages were freed. This was an unprecedented event at the time, at least when it came to the range of countries represented in the Boxer suppression campaign, but there are eerie parallels to the multinational "peace-keeping" coalitions of the present, some of which, like that of 1900, have been criticized harshly for the violent acts they have committed in the name of restoring "order" and stamping out a threat.

In other cases, though, there is nothing about a chosen year that sets it apart. This is true, for example, of 1875. In chapters on such years, the challenge is to show how examining even "years of no significance" (to play on the title of a study of Ming China by Ray Huang) can illuminate general patterns.[34] To do this in the case of 1875, for example, I focus on maps. Why? Because that year saw the publication of the first map that paid relatively equal attention to the Chinese-run parts of Shanghai and the city's foreign enclaves, and that treated these districts as part of a single whole. It was also around 1875, I suggest (and this is where the look at the itineraries of globetrotters comes in), that Shanghai began, in a metaphorical sense, to make its way onto the map internationally.

The book's final chapter, "Ten Theses on Twenty-first-Century Shanghai," which closes the book (aside from a "Suggestions for Further Reading" essay), assesses trends in Shanghai as a place and a subject of global fascination during the first years of this new century, and speculates on where the metropolis might be headed. Particular attention is paid to the year 2010, when the World Expo will be held in the city. Even here, though, I do not abandon completely a concern with history, as I try to tease out the similarities and differences between the latest discourses on Shanghai's future and those that circulated during earlier periods. Among other things, I stress that this is not the first time that people have expected great things of Shanghai, but that there is at least one novel aspect to the predictions being made. Previously, when the city's future prospects were extolled, the claim was that it might catch up with Paris or New York. Now there are those who enthuse (or worry) that it will *surpass* them—and note that in one way, the number of skyscrapers it contains, not to mention the scores of others now rising, it already has.

Points of origin revisited

Before moving on to our first snapshot of an individual year, a question that may have formed in the minds of some readers needs to be addressed: Why choose 1850 as the starting point for a book on "global" Shanghai? This date may seem an anachronistically early one to some readers. After all, recent commentaries on Shanghai (especially by journalists) and on globalization (especially by social scientists) have tended to focus intently on the recent past. When history comes into play, it is often only that of the past several decades or at most the last century that is considered. On the other hand, some readers may wonder, after my concern with debunking the Fishing Village Myth, why I do not push the Shanghai story back beyond the Opium War. To begin as late as 1850 may seem to them to fall into the trap of presenting Shanghai as a foreign creation, rather than a city that began as and now once again is a Chinese metropolis.

I will get to the attractions of 1850 in particular later, but before that will wrestle with the general question of why sometime in the mid-1800s. Let me begin by taking up my reason for eschewing a starting point much further back in time, such as 1291 or the sixteenth-century creation of the city wall, which no longer stands around the oldest section of Shanghai, though the contours of its former route are still easy to see on maps. The fallacies of the Fishing Village Myth notwithstanding, it makes sense to begin the tale of *Shanghai* with developments that occurred many centuries ago but not to start the story of *Global Shanghai* then. Yes, Shanghai was a commercial and even an international city well before the middle of the nineteenth century, thanks to its links to trade between China and Southeast Asia, the challenges to the city posed by Japanese pirates, and so on. And, yes, as some world historians have recently stressed, there were phenomena with parallels to globalization occurring well before the Opium War broke out in China.[35] Still, it would be misleading to pretend that Shanghai was central to global as opposed to regional flows back in Marco Polo's day (the Italian adventurer's book, incidentally, raves about the glories of Hangzhou and Suzhou, but nowhere mentions the humbler port near those two great urban centers that is the subject of this book), during the Ming Dynasty (1368–1644), or even during the century and a half following the Manchu conquest of China and establishment of the Qing Dynasty (1644–1911).

Shanghai may, in other words, have recently entered its eighth century as a city, but it has hardly been an urban center of global significance for hundreds of years.

Prior to the 1840s, though it already had the potential to serve as China's major gateway to the world, it played a much more minor part in trade with distant lands than did Canton and Macao, the two cities through which all trade with the West was then routed. In addition, though it certainly qualified as a "city" centuries before the Opium War began, it was as late as the 1830s still far from the most internationally famous one in China—indeed it was still not even the best-known urban center of the Jiangnan region. As had been true in Marco Polo's day, both Suzhou and Hangzhou were much more famous, which explains why "Little Su" and "Little Hang" were nicknames for Shanghai.[36] Given that one key concern of this book is Shanghai's status as a globally renowned city as well as an international hub, we cannot go back too far.

The next issue to take up is why, if 1291 or even 1830 is too early a starting point, we need to bother going back beyond the early 1900s. Was Shanghai "global" at any point in the nineteenth century, in the sense not just of being intensively linked to the wider world via trade but of having grand ambitions and having a name that enjoyed global recognition? This question arises due to the strong tendency in popular commentary on the city, both inside and outside of China, to stress that its first great era of international celebrity and notoriety came in the 1920s and 1930s. Dislodging the notion that Shanghai only became global early in the twentieth century requires showing that from the early 1870s through the early 1880s the city already had both global fame and global ambitions.

Shanghais of the mind, 1871–1882

The year 1871 was not particularly important in the development of Shanghai as a physical place, but it was noteworthy when it comes to historiography (a thirty-two volume local history of Shanghai was published that year) and, more important for us here, to its evolution into a global symbol: the Oxford English Dictionary singles it out as the year during which "to shanghai" began to appear in newspapers. Another thing that makes 1871 a special year for Shanghai-the-symbol is that it witnessed the publication of the very first work of fiction by an internationally famous writer in which the place name "Shanghai" appeared. The author was Mark Twain. And the work was *Goldsmith's Friend Abroad Again*, an epistolary novel that follows the adventures and troubles of a Chinese immigrant to the United States. Though Twain never made it to China, as already noted, he seems to have had Shanghai enough on his mind by the start of the 1870s to choose it as the point of departure for his fictional character, Ah Song Hi. Most of the letters in *Goldsmith's Friend Abroad Again* are presented as having been written on the other side of the Pacific, but the first one, in which Ah Song Hi describes his reason for leaving China and his hopes for America, is presented as having been written in Shanghai.[37]

An even more interesting milestone relating to fiction came in 1879, when Jules Verne published a novel that uses Shanghai as the main setting. This book, *Les Tribulations d'un chinois en Chine*, which was translated into English in 1880 and published as *Tribulations of a Chinaman in China*, is interesting for our purposes for two reasons. First, Verne's choice of Shanghai as a setting testifies to the city's growing fame. Second, the central character, a Chinese resident of the port named "Kin-Fo," has distinctively cosmopolitan tastes, forward-looking ideas, and a fondness for the latest technological marvels. Within his home, "electric bells connected the rooms" and the furniture took a hybrid form, to make the most of all "that Chinese fancy, added to European comfort, could offer." The "progressive Kin-Fo" even used "phonography, recently brought to the highest degree of perfection by Edison," in his correspondence.[38] Chinese in general are portrayed in this novel, as in so many Western works of the time, as far too enamored of tradition and generally resistant to progress for their own good. But late nineteenth-century Shanghai becomes, via Kin-Fo, what local boosters would so often later claim it was: a place where, in contrast to most parts of China, modernity was often welcomed and to which those Chinese with their eyes on the future rather than the past were drawn.

While Twain and Verne's texts both support the notion that Shanghai's rise to importance as an international symbol was well underway by the final half of the nineteenth century, newspapers rather than novels provide the best evidence that this was also a period when local residents began to imagine that it was destined to become (though it certainly was not yet) one of the world's great cities. More specifically, we can look to the *North China Herald*, a publication about which much more will be said in the following chapter. The 1881 issues of this periodical are filled with evidence that the main features of the Shanghai city myth (of a port rocketing to greatness) had fallen into place by that year. Consider, for example, a February 22 editorial on the theme of "Municipal Progress," which states that "every ten years of the life of Shanghai present improvements that would seem incredible if we could be shown them at the beginning instead of the end of the decade." The author then muses that, if "Sir George Balfour, the first English consul here, could pay us a visit, he would probably be slow to believe that this could be the Settlement that he marked out in the paddy fields some forty years ago." And Shanghai's capacity for surprising us has not reached an endpoint by any means, the editorial continues, since "if one of us could be shown a picture of Shanghai in 1921"—forty years into the future—he would probably "turn away laughing at the credulity of the artist." It is "difficult to over-rate the importance in the world that Shanghai will at no distant period assume," the writer insisted, and if things continued in the pattern set by the recent past, "Shanghai must become one of the greatest cities in Asia."[39]

Looking backward to 1850

Let me end this Introduction with some general comments on two things: the value of looking backward more than a century for better understanding contemporary Shanghai, and the special relevance of 1850 as a starting point, for a book concerned with global flows. Perhaps the biggest problem with taking an overly present-minded approach to this particular city as it wrestles with globalization— or, as I put it in a later chapter, goes through a process of *reglobalization*—is that this leads us to overlook revealing analogies between current debates and nineteenth-century ones.

Take, for example, recent arguments over whether Shanghai, a port city near the Yangzi Delta, is destined to displace Hong Kong, its main Pearl River Delta competitor, as the most important "global city" in China. These echo closely, albeit with slightly different terminology ("global city" is a term of very recent vintage), discussions of the mid-to-late 1800s about the shifting relationship between Shanghai and Canton as international hubs.[40] Or consider debates over whether the "New Shanghai" of today is best seen as a direct descendant of the "Old Shanghai" of the early 1900s, or as something that owes little or no debt to any predecessor. This kind of query has a long history, and the modifier "new" began to be to be used in front of Shanghai in 1854.[41]

Another contemporary debate that has a history reaching back beyond 1900, if not quite to the 1850s, is that of whether Shanghai is the kind of city in which a World's Fair should be held. A version of this question was first asked in 1881, when plans were afoot—albeit ultimately abandoned as impractical—to bring Shanghai "in line with London and Paris and Vienna, Philadelphia, Sydney and Melbourne, in having an exhibition [by the Huangpu] of the arts and industry of all nations." Such an exhibition was promoted then, as the 2010 one is being promoted now, as an event that would bring sightseers as well as products from different lands to the city, and would symbolize the fact that Shanghai had come of age as an urban center.[42]

Yet another contemporary debate that has long historical resonances involves the politics of exclusion, the power relations that determine who does and does not have access to the most desirable parts of the metropolis. When detractors as opposed to boosters describe recent changes in Shanghai, one common theme is the way that some people are being left behind economically or are physically marginalized by the consumer revolution and urban development programs. The city presents an increasingly attractive façade to the world, and some new spaces, such as the parks in the central districts, are open to all. But consider the way that one of the new recreation grounds built in Pudong as part of a beautification drive that preceded the Asia-Pacific Economic Cooperation (APEC) Summit came into being and now is used. It stands on land that was expropriated from longtime local residents who had no option but to take the government's offer of new lodging far from the city center—meaning that they not only had to move to make way for the park, but now complain of living such a distance from it that they effectively cannot even use it.[43]

The discontent that arises from this sort of relocation does not have exact parallels in the mid-to-late 1800s, since development then often involved building on reclaimed swampland, but it does call to mind some phenomena that stretch back into the first half of the treaty-port era. A notable case in point is the long debate, which began in the 1880s and lasted until the 1920s, over whether or not Chinese residents of the city would be allowed to use the International Settlement's finest park, the waterfront Public Garden. This recreation area, now known as Huangpu Gongyuan (Huangpu Park), was not, as a widely believed urban legend has it, one that had at its front gate a sign saying "No Dogs or Chinese Allowed." It did, nonetheless, throughout much of the late Qing period and the first part of the Republican era (1912–1949), have rules prohibiting all Chinese other than servants from entering. This was periodically a source of complaint, until a change of regulations was introduced in 1928 that did away with this rule, but simultaneously introduced a small new use fee, which made it equally hard for working-class and indigent members of all nationalities (there was by then a large, mostly poor White Russian community) to take advantage of the grounds.

If looking backward more than a century benefits our understanding of Shanghai, it also usefully encourages us to appreciate the degree to which globalization is a process with a history. There are definitely ways in which specific recently developed technologies of communication (such as the world wide web) and transportation (such as jets) have altered global flows. And there is no question that people, ideas, diseases, and fashions are now moving across more borders more rapidly than ever. And yet, one can often hear in the present echoes of very old debates, including those from the mid-1800s. Consider, for example, the following excerpts from a speech that Queen Victoria's consort, Prince Albert, gave in the middle of the nineteenth century:

> Nobody . . . who has paid any attention to the particular features of our present era, will doubt for a moment that we are living in a period of wonderful transition . . . The distances which separated the different nations and parts of the globe are gradually vanishing before the achievement of modern invention, and we can traverse them with incredible ease . . . thought is communicated with the rapidity and even by the power of lightning . . . the products of all quarters of the globe are placed at our disposal.[44]

If his optimism is readily recognizable to a twenty-first-century reader, so too is the concern voiced in a piece called "The Exhibition Plague" that appeared in the comic magazine *Punch* (taking the form of a letter from an "anxious wife and mother") in the same year that Prince Albert gave his speech. If visitors from all parts of the world come to Britain for the great event scheduled to be held the next year, the author of the letter fretted, local people would surely be subjected to a litany of diseases associated with foreigners. She then provided a list of new ailments that would make their way to Britain: dropsy (from Holland), the black jaundice (from America), the mumps (from Greece), and something called the "King's Evil" (from Naples).[45]

It seems fitting to end this Introduction with those two texts, as each was published in 1850—the year that is the focus of the next chapter. Without further ado, then, let us move to Shanghai events that took place and Shanghai works that appeared around the time that Prince Albert was enthusing and *Punch*'s imaginary "wife and mother" was fretting about what the Crystal Palace Exhibition scheduled to take place in 1851 would do to the capital city of the country that had just defeated the Qing in the Opium War, thereby gaining full control of Hong Kong and a foothold for its traders and missionaries in five Chinese treaty ports.

1 1850: The birth of a newspaper

"*The North China Herald*" is the name of a new weekly paper commenced on the 3rd inst, at Shánghái, [by] Mr. Henry Shearman, publisher and proprietor. This new sheet has started into life a full grown newspaper—advertisements, occurrences, editorials, and all, as if it had emerged out of a box of types all ready to hand. Its typographical appearance is creditable, and we have no doubt the foreign community at Shánghái will support the efforts of the editor to make known the capabilities of that port and region.

"Journal of Occurrences," *The Chinese Repository*,
August 1850

As noted above, a good case can be made for treating 1850 as marking a turning point in the history of what we now call globalization—or constituting at least a watershed of sorts in the discourse surrounding the global circulation of goods, people, information, and ideas. This is because, although the Crystal Palace Exhibition did not open until 1851, it was in 1850 that plans for it solidified and extravagant claims began to be made for it as a fitting symbol of the knitting together of the world that had recently been taking place, while also having the potential to spur further shrinking of the globe. But was 1850 a special year for Shanghai? Or, rather, was it a special year when it comes to the play of international forces in Shanghai, which is the main focus of this book?

At first glance, the answer would seem to be a simple one: No.[1] The middle years of the nineteenth century certainly saw many local developments of great importance, both for the local Chinese population and for the foreigners who began to live and work just north of the old walled city on the unpromising plots of muddy land set aside for their use by the Treaty of Nanjing. But most of the big events took place either just before or just after 1850. It was in the mid-1840s, for example, that the first foreigners linked to countries other than Britain began to arrive. And it was in the final years of that decade that local French residents set up a "concession" of their own.

Turning to the 1850s, it was not at the very start but part of the way into this decade that the most dramatic developments occurred. It was then that the British and American settlements, which tended to function as a combined unit, and the separate French Concession were all transformed by an influx of Chinese residents.

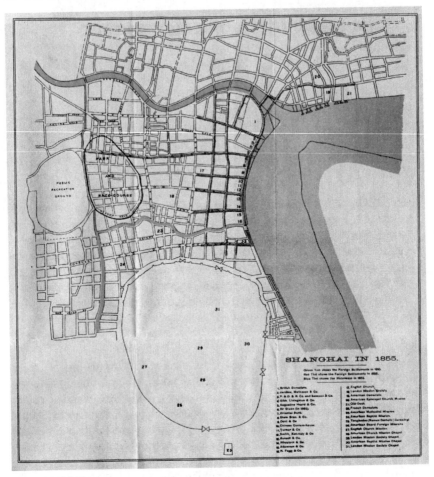

Figure 1.1 Map of the city in 1855

Source: From F.L. Hawks Pott, *A Short History of Shanghai* (Shanghai: Kelly & Walsh, 1928)

They poured into the foreign-run districts to escape the social turmoil generated by a series of revolts that centered in the countryside but spilled over into urban areas, including the Chinese-run part of Shanghai. This changed forever the nature of the foreign-run districts, which previously had been home only to citizens and subjects of distant lands and Chinese servants. From that point on, they would always have more Chinese than non-Chinese living within their borders. It was also in the early-to-mid 1850s that the local foreign community faced its first threat of invasion, when it seemed for a time that the violence of the Small Sword Rebels and the millenarian, quasi-Christian Taiping would not stay outside of the new settlements.

There was, however, one event that, in retrospect, marks 1850 as a turning point in Shanghai's centuries-long history as the site of international flows: the founding of the *North China Herald* (sometimes spelled with a hyphen, as the *North-China Herald*) described in the quote that opens this chapter. In modern times, one defining feature of any city with claims to global centrality has been that it has press organs that allow locals to know what is going on in the wider world, and, almost equally importantly (as the comments in *The Chinese Repository* suggest), allow outsiders in that wider world to know about the locale. The *North China Herald*, the first local publication that aimed to connect Shanghai to distant lands, is thus a fitting subject for this snapshot chapter.[2]

Shanghailanders through the prism of the press

Seeing, that our port has been opened to the commerce of western nations, for the past six years; the time has we think arrived, when the publication of a paper may be deemed not uncalled for.

"Address to the Public," *North China Herald*, August 3, 1850

This awkwardly worded, oddly punctuated paragraph appeared in the inaugural issue of the publication of interest to us here. It was a periodical that would have a good run, lasting just over a century, and would serve for nearly all of that period as a major source of information for and about the Anglophone residents of the British and American settlements (later merged to form the International Settlement) known as Shanghailanders. It would also come to function as a key vehicle for the expression and dissemination of the opinions of this group. Or, to be more precise, while the letters from readers it published would showcase many different sorts of viewpoint (offered up by local Chinese as well as foreign readers), the newspaper's editorials would express the views of a certain sort of Shanghailander.

What sort exactly? They were Shanghailanders about whom several things could be said. They came from and maintained ties with Britain (though there were certainly some American Shanghailanders with similar views). They thought of the name "Shanghai" as standing primarily or exclusively for the city's foreign-run districts. They thought that the part of Shanghai they lived in deserved the nickname "Model Settlement," which began to be used in the *North China Herald* at the end of the 1850s, according to Robert Bickers, the leading scholar of the Shanghailanders.[3] And they thought, even long after the influx of Chinese described above had changed the population make-up of the foreign-run districts, that the only fully legitimate residents of these districts were nationals of countries other than China.

In addition, the kind of Shanghailanders for whom the *Herald* spoke typically viewed their "eastern home" (a term for Shanghai that showed up regularly in the pages of this newspaper from the very beginning) as a place to which loyalty was due.[4] It was not just a city they were passing through, in other words. And they felt few qualms about taking advantage of local structures of foreign privilege, since they thought of the Shanghai that mattered to them as something that had been built by Westerners such as themselves. Even after Chinese residents were paying a large percentage of Settlement taxes, the sort of Shanghailanders for whom the *Herald* spoke clung to the notion that only foreigners were full-fledged citizens with rights, such as that of having a say in how the taxes they paid were spent. "Native residents," as they often called Chinese living in the enclaves, were considered at best "guests" allowed to reside in the Settlement due to goodwill on the part of the foreigners—a view that, for many of them, only began to shift in the 1930s, when common enmity toward Japan encouraged them to think in new ways.[5]

It is important to stress that during its very long career as Shanghai's leading English-language periodical, the *Herald* (and the affiliated *North China Daily News* established in 1864) represented the views of only some foreign residents. Why? Because the world beyond Shanghai sometimes made the mistake of assuming that these newspapers were the official organs of a homogeneous foreign community—or at least a homogeneous set of Anglophone Shanghailanders. This went along with and buttressed a more general and also erroneous assumption: that all foreigners in Shanghai thought the same way about basic matters. In fact, as recent scholarship by Bickers and many others has stressed, this was far from being the case.

There was, in fact, nothing homogeneous about the foreign community (or rather foreign *communities*) of Old Shanghai. For much of the time that the *North China Herald* was published, to begin with, many foreign residents of Shanghai were not Britons. And even among those Shanghailanders who did have ties to Britain, there was considerable diversity when it came to opinions about how the Settlement should be run and how Chinese residents should be treated.[6]

There were, for example, always some Britons who viewed Shanghai merely as a place to put in a few years, make money, and then move on. Hence there were British Shanghailanders who never viewed the Settlement as an "eastern home," but rather saw it as just a temporary posting.[7] There were also some Britons living by the Huangpu (at least by the late 1800s) who felt ambivalent about or were openly critical of the structure of foreign privilege that made Chinese residents of the enclaves feel like second-class citizens.

Within the local American community, there were many internal divisions as well, often along the same lines just described.[8] And the picture becomes still more complex when we bring in non-Anglophone Europeans (the French and Germans, for example), non-Chinese Asians (such as the Japanese), and foreigners who were neither unambiguously Western nor simply Asian (White Russian émigrés and Baghdadi Jews).[9]

There was, in sum, no single opinion about the nature of the city or about the legitimacy of treaty-port structures of privilege among local foreigners or even among those Anglophone ones who qualified as Shanghailanders (by the standard definition). Hence it is foolish to assume that one newspaper could speak for the cluster of overlapping communities that comprised foreign Shanghai. By the 1930s, reflecting this diversity, foreign readers could choose from dozens of dailies and weeklies. These came in varied languages (French from the late 1800s onward, then eventually German, Russian, and Japanese) and showcased widely varying viewpoints (among English-language periodicals alone, by the early 1900s there were those that were liberal, conservative, liberal on some issues yet conservative on others, and so on). The editorials in these publications would sometimes echo but sometimes directly contradict those put forth in the *Herald*.[10]

This said, when Henry Shearman founded this newspaper in 1850, the foreign community was not so variegated. (Among other things, the city did not yet have either Japanese or Russian residents, though it did already have Baghdadi Jews and Parsis living within its borders.) And the *Herald* was the only game in town when it came to the Western periodical press—a monopoly position that contrasted sharply with that of any Hong Kong periodical, since in that city there were already by 1850 several competing English-language newspapers.[11] This made it easy for outsiders to assume in 1850 that the *Herald* spoke for a single, unified foreign Shanghai, and it was easy for this assumption (partially justified at the time) to be carried forward into later periods—especially since the newspaper's publishers were delighted by the notion.

Indeed, when it first began publication, the newspaper could easily have been viewed as representing the views of the whole Anglophone population of coastal "north" China (a vague term often used in the 1800s to refer to everything above Canton). And it is also worth noting that the *Herald* was initially not just the only foreign periodical operating in the northern treaty ports, but the sole newspaper of any sort published in these cities. This is because, as of 1850, there were no Chinese-language periodicals based in Shanghai, let alone in places such as Tianjin and Ningbo.

The situation would become very different within a few decades, by which point there would be several Chinese-language dailies and weeklies in Shanghai alone, including such important and long-lasting ones as the *Shen Pao* (a newspaper launched in 1872 that we will return to in the next chapter).[12] But in 1850 the founding of the first local Chinese-language periodical (a supplement to the *Herald* called *Shanghai Xinbao*, made up of translations from the English-language edition) still lay more than a decade in the future. Also still to come was the founding of various other foreign-language weeklies (two American-run ones, *Celestial Empire* and *China Weekly Review*, for example) and of several English-language dailies (the *Shanghai Evening Post*, the *China Press*, the *Shanghai Times*, etc.) that would eventually vie for Anglophone readers with the *North China Daily News*.[13]

The simple fact that the *North China Herald* was the first local newspaper would be enough of a reason to focus on two of its early issues (its first number and its last 1850 edition which appeared December 28) in this chapter, as I will below. And there are other points that make this periodical especially worthy of our attention. One is that the *Herald* would eventually become the heart of a publishing empire that included not just the aforementioned affiliated daily and Chinese-language supplement but also books, pamphlets, and assorted official and semi-official documents of broad public interest that would shape world images of Shanghai and China. Another is that, again in time, the *Herald* and even the building on the Bund that housed it would take on important symbolic dimensions. The newspaper would earn a famous nickname ("Old Lady of the Bund") and come to be celebrated by some local residents, who either agreed with its editorials or simply admired other things about it, such as the wonderful political cartoons that it carried in the 1920s and 1930s.

Both the weekly *Herald* and the *North China Daily News* would, in other quarters, however, eventually come to be reviled for epitomizing the parochialism, decadence, and conservatism that characterized foreign Shanghai at its worst. It is worth noting that right up until its final days, the Herald empire's publications remained controversial. Indeed, they provoked contentious discussion even after the publishing house went out of business. One reason is that between the time that the Communists took control of the city (in 1949) and the time the whole operation was shut down (in 1951), the *North China Daily News* ran a famous column that compared Shanghai to a giant "dye-vat" capable of altering any political organization's coloration. The implication that the Communists in charge of the city would lose their redness before Shanghai lost its capitalist nature appalled the new rulers of the metropolis. And the "dye-vat" image was discussed and criticized in various literary and propagandistic works that appeared in the 1950s and beyond.[14] It is worth pointing out that, over the course of its nearly century-long history, the *Herald* would leave many marks on the political history of Old Shanghai. It is not just that arguments over key issues of local significance (such as the struggle over whether the Chinese should be allowed a voice in the municipal councils of the two enclaves) were played out in its pages. It is also that, because outsiders tended to assume that this newspaper spoke for the Shanghailanders generally, the *Herald* even helped shape international policies toward the city.

It is also worth noting that the newspaper would influence the city's historiography in many ways. The *Herald*'s publishing house issued several standard works of local history, some of which (such as a pair of volumes by Russian émigré A. M. Kotenev) continue to be cited. In addition, though no issue of the *Herald* has appeared for more than half a century, in a sense it continues to shape Shanghai historiography by serving as an archive. This is because scholars, especially in the West (myself very much included), have long relied and continue to rely heavily on this weekly. (One reason may be that it is available on micro-film at many libraries and was conveniently indexed at six-month intervals during most of its existence; another is that it was the most widely distributed English language Chinese newspaper of its day.) We find in it not just details about local events but also a window onto a particular Shanghailander worldview. In fact, thanks to its letters pages and translations or summaries of Chinese publications, it even provides insights into the views of local residents whose opinions contrast sharply with those of its publisher.

In light of all of this, it seems safe to say that the *Herald*'s founding was one of the most important local events, if not *the* most important local event, of 1850. It is no accident that one of the first chapters in the most comprehensive general history of Shanghai newspapers looks closely at the early issues of the *Herald*.[15] And it is fitting that this exploration of "Global Shanghai" should follow that work's lead, especially since the *Herald* was an important definer and purveyor of various Shanghai city myths.

The state of the city when the newspaper arrived

Before focussing on the content of two of the *Herald*'s early issues, something needs to be said about the kind of city that existed by the Huangpu when its first issues appeared. A general sense of Shanghai prior to and on the eve of the *Herald*'s inaugural issue can be patched together from a variety of works, including Chinese and foreign language histories of the city produced between the late 1800s and the present, many of which make use of gazetteers and other primary sources from an earlier time. Also helpful are detailed reports on Shanghai that appeared in the 1830s and 1840s in Hong Kong-based and Canton-based periodicals and in book-length travelers' accounts.[16]

What do these varied sources tell us? They tell us that, for centuries, the term "Shanghai" had been used to refer to a port by the Huangpu River. They tell us that this urban center first served as the capital of a district or county (*xian*) and then in 1725 became the capital of a circuit (*dao*), meaning that it had its own intendant (*daotai*). And they tell us that Shanghai became a community of increasing economic significance, social complexity and political importance in the late eighteenth and early nineteenth centuries. We discover from these sources as well that Shanghai, while still a purely Chinese city early in the 1800s, was by no means completely isolated from international currents prior to the Opium War. Interactions with foreigners and foreign lands were already affecting Shanghai in several distinct ways before it became a treaty port. One important kind of interaction took the form of the periodic attacks by Japanese pirates that inspired local residents to build large city walls in the 1530s.[17]

A second important form of interaction with foreigners involved religion. The Jesuits' presence in China in the sixteenth and seventeenth centuries led to the conversion of a local notable, Paul Xu. At least one Western priest (an Italian) lived in Shanghai for a time (two years, according to some accounts) early in the 1600s.[18] And there were some 135 chapels in the Shanghai area in the middle of the seventeenth century.[19]

A third form of pre-Opium War interaction between the Chinese in Shanghai and foreigners took the form of early nineteenth-century visits by a few traveling merchants and ministers. They came to the port as part of an effort to discover which Chinese cities had the greatest potential to serve as effective bases for operation, should the Chinese government ever decide, or be forced, to allow foreigners to live in or work from places other than Canton and Macao.

Then, last but far from least, there was a fourth form of pre-Opium War international activity: namely, via trade. Shanghai was a major trans-shipment point of goods flowing between China and non-Western foreign countries, a lynchpin in the trade routes that tied hinterland provinces of China to Southeast Asia.

All of these things were significant parts of the history of early Shanghai. And they should be kept in mind, even though none of them made that urban center an "international city," for this was something it only became when the Treaty of Nanjing formally opened it to British trade and settlement.

One thing to remain cognizant of, then, is that when the first issues of the *Herald* appeared, Shanghai had been an international city, as opposed to simply a Chinese port with varied links to the outside world, for less than seven years. This makes quite remarkable Shearman's decision to launch not just a small newsletter but a "full grown newspaper"—as the Canton-based *Chinese Repository* put it.[20]

What sort of foreigners—the main audience for this new "full grown newspaper"—lived in Shanghai in 1850, and how did they live? We know that most of the two hundred or so foreigners in residence (the number fluctuated between 150 and 210) resided close to the Huangpu, on its western bank. We also know that most of them were subjects of the British Empire, which is no surprise given that Britain was the foreign signatory of the Treaty of Nanjing. There were also a smaller number of French and American residents—France and the United States being the first two countries to force China to extend treaty-port privileges to their citizens.

When the first British Shanghailanders arrived, they established a line of warehouses and other buildings (including a consulate that sometimes doubled as a church) along the waterfront. They then began to develop a second patch of ground just in-land from there. Merchants and missionaries from the United States, meanwhile, either lived in the British zone or established themselves just north of Suzhou Creek. In addition, there was already by 1850 a fairly clear divide between the Anglophone and Francophone foreign districts. A French Concession was formally established in 1849, just to the south of the original British district and just to the north of the old walled city—even though fewer than a dozen citizens of France were living in Shanghai at the time.[21]

We know a few other things about the Westerners living in Shanghai circa 1850. There was a very high male-to-female ratio within the small band of foreigners living in both the British and American areas and in the French Concession.[22] And business was taking off in a dramatic fashion, as two statistics relating to Shanghai's position vis-à-vis Canton's illustrate. In 1844, 95 percent of all goods bound for Britain were shipped from Canton and only 12.5 percent from Shanghai, but by 1849 the percentages were 51.7 percent and 40 percent, respectively. And total export ratios tell a similar tale, with Canton moving from handling 88.7 percent to 61.7 percent and Shanghai moving from handling 11.1 percent to handling 37.1 percent.[23] Finally, we know one more thing: that the total population of all of the foreign communities combined was tiny compared to that of the local Chinese population (as of 1852, more than 99 percent of Shanghai residents were in the old walled city and districts other than the enclaves).

We do not know just how many Chinese lived in Shanghai when the first issue of the *Herald* appeared. The likely number is somewhere between more than a third to just over half a million. It is difficult to be more precise because at that point census figures still sometimes gave numbers not of individuals but of households and used the same place name, Shanghai, to refer to territories of widely varying sizes.[24]

It is worth noting, as may already be clear from the vagueness of the above statements, that patching together a comprehensive picture of Shanghai *circa* 1850 is no easy matter. Relatively few works about Shanghai were published in the early to mid-1800s. In time, it would become one of the most-written-about cities in all of Asia, indeed the world. But this was definitely not true at that point. In Chinese, there were gazetteers and a few miscellaneous works, but nothing like the voluminous texts (from poetry to detailed descriptive works) that focussed on Suzhou and Hangzhou. In foreign languages, much more was published on Canton than on Shanghai.

This meant that a Westerner setting out for Shanghai who wanted to know what to expect had limited options before the *Herald* began its long run. He (and our imagined traveler was very likely to be a man) could try to find a recent brief account of the new treaty ports in a British or North American periodical. Or better yet he could track down a copy of one of a pair of books that detailed a rare pre-Opium War Shanghai stop in the city by a British ship. The most often-cited is Hugh Hamilton Lindsay's *Report of proceedings on a voyage to the northern parts of China, in the ship Lord Amherst: extracted from papers printed by order of the House of Commons relating to trade with China* (London, 1833). The other is Charles Gutzlaff's *Journal of two voyages along the coast of China in 1831 and 1832; the first in a Chinese junk, the second in the British ship Lord Amherst: with notices of Corea, Lewchew, &c.* (New York, 1833).

Alternately, our imagined traveler could look for one of the handful of recent books on China that included some discussion of Shanghai. The most famous of these was Robert Fortune's *Three Years' Wandering Among the Northern Provinces of China* (London, 1847). And, last of all, he could spend some time perusing the *Chinese Repository*, an important source on foreign activities along the China coast in this period, which was published by and primarily for missionaries. In addition to miscellaneous short pieces (such as the notice about the *Herald*'s launch), this journal carried several reports on Shanghai *circa* 1850, as well as reviews of books dealing with the city.

This final course of action would be the best or at least most efficient of all, in part because our traveler would find in the *Repository* discussions of and excerpts from the aforementioned works by Lindsay, Gutzlaff and Fortune. For example, in the April 1834 issue, he would find a joint review of the two books on the Lord Amherst's visit. He would encounter there Lindsay's oft-repeated claim that Shanghai was already in the early 1830s the "principal emporium of eastern Asia," a port through which four hundred junks (some coming from as far away as Siam) might pass in a single week.

Even more useful to the prospective foreign visitor would be the lengthy article (36 pages long) devoted exclusively to the city that appeared in the November 1847 issue of the *Repository*—along with a map of the urban center. This article is generally cited just by its short title, "Description of Shánghái." Its full title, though, gives a clearer sense of the range of issues it addresses: "Description of Shánghái; its position; early history; walls; gates; canals and ditches; pools and wells; streets; houses; government officials and incumbents; custom-houses;

military forces; literary institutions; common schools; religious institutions; Chinghwáng miáu; Buddhists, &c.; benevolent institutions; burying grounds; the trades and handicrafts; commerce, foreign and domestic; cotton; tea; silk; woolen stuffs; manufactures; ship-building; commercial houses; suburbs; the Foreign Factories and residents; real estate; climate; population; and Christian missions."

Our Shanghai-bound traveler would learn from this text many things. For example, that he should expect to find a city with "narrow and very irregular" streets, averaging about six feet in width, that were "flagged or paved with stone, or laid with brick or broken tiles" (pp. 540–541). That he should be ready to see houses (of the Chinese population) that "vary in size and quality from beggarly hovels, only a few feet square, covered with tiles and thatch, to large and commodious habitations extending over several acres" (p. 541). Some of these, the author stated, "any people" would deem comfortable, but the "great majority, say nine tenths of the whole," were "such as few Europeans would like to inhabit." Why? Because they were "low, damp and dark, and contracted and close, as to be both very hot and very unhealthy" (p. 542). The exteriors tended to be made of "dark walls, unglazed windows, and heavy roofs surmounted by a long line of tiles" (p. 543).

When it comes to economic matters, as opposed to the look of the streets and dwellings, our traveler would learn that Shanghai had long been and remained a place with "numerous and thrifty, and sometimes extensive" trades and handicrafts. Cotton played a particularly large role in the "domestic if not in the foreign commerce" of the city, he would discover, with each of "the branches" of its production ("cultivating, spinning, weaving, &c.") carried out in "the simplest manner" (pp. 560–561). "There are no immense farms, nor any great manufacturing establishments. The work is all done single-handed; a few plants here, and a few threads there are seen; and from these dribblets, comes the grand total of this valuable product" (p. 561). In general, according to this text, Shanghai was still a place where manufactures were "few in number, very limited in quantity, and of no superior quality," as well as a place where ship-building was one of the few thriving industries (p. 563).

When this report was written, it seems, Shanghai was home to just over one hundred foreign residents (though this number was growing "every month," p. 563). This helps explain why, in contrast to so many later works in English, this one focusses so largely on the Chinese districts of the city, with only the final pages (pp. 563–565) given over to description of the foreign sections. From those pages, our Shanghai-bound traveler would learn that thirty foreign houses had sprung up near the British consular grounds by the Huangpu, and that many more buildings, including a church, were being built. He would also find out that the value of real estate in Shanghai, as in other treaty ports, had been "greatly enhanced" (even "trebled" in some cases) by the city's opening to foreign trade and "the establishment of a European town." And he would learn that representatives of several missionary groups were active there.

Two other informative, though less comprehensive, reports that might have been of interest to our prospective foreign visitor appeared in the *Repository* in July

1849 and February 1850. These took the form of letters from Shanghailanders, one identified by name (E.C. Bridgman), the other simply by a *nom de plume* (Spectator).

The letters deal in part with missionary concerns, which is to be expected as the *Repository* was largely devoted to assessing efforts to convert the Chinese to Christianity. Still, each writer draws attention to some significant points about the city during the year or so prior to the launching of the *North China Herald*. Bridgman, for instance, describes Shanghai as having "superior advantages" over other Chinese urban centers as a "mart for trade" as well as a "field for missionary enterprise." Because of this, he claimed, it deserved more attention than it had been accorded, presumably by foreign writers. The most noteworthy thing about Shanghai, in his view, was its "central position, by which it has easy communication with immense agricultural regions of great fertility, whose inhabitants are peaceful and passionately fond of traffic."

"Spectator," for his part, stresses the heterogeneity of the Chinese population. It contained, he writes, large numbers of immigrants from various parts of the empire, with the "worst" being the "Canton men," followed closely in "badness" by those from Fujian, and the most agreeable being those from nearby Ningbo. He also notes the widely varied estimates of how many Chinese lived in Shanghai, saying that he had heard claims that ranged from less than two hundred thousand to half a million. Two things were clear, he wrote. The size of the city was "increasing, both in the extent of its business and number of its inhabitants." And due to recent crop failures, the "number of distressed people has been, and is still very great."

The first and last 1850 editions

One of the most valuable things about the early issues of the *Herald* is that they allow us to add meat to the bare bones picture of the local scene provided by population figures and the like. For example, in the same "Address to the Public" quoted earlier, we learn that even as early as 1850 some Shanghailanders were already concerned about two things that would worry their counterparts in much later parts of the treaty-port era: the way their community was being represented abroad, and how Western activities in China in general were being understood back home.

A main stated goal of the newspaper, according to its publisher, was to counteract mistaken views that had taken hold in Britain. These mistaken views were due to the "wild exaggerations," "ill-digested statements," "amusing twaddle," and "malignant inventions" of certain people (and he was ready to name names) who had recently published English-language reports on the city. Shearman insisted that writers such as Fortune (a purveyor of "amusing twaddle") and Gutzlaff (he of the "wild exaggerations") had got many things wrong about both Shanghai and China. And this made it difficult for Shanghailanders to "arouse public opinion in England, and to direct it in aid of our peculiar relations with the Chinese Empire." More particularly, it was crucial for London to understand that, in order to make the most of Shanghai's economic potential (and help spread Christendom as well as trade throughout China), the gains made via the Treaty of Nanjing needed to be built upon, not left alone. Diplomatic energy needed to be exerted to open inland territories to Western traders and missionaries. This statement shows just how early a common Shanghailander complaint of the first decades of the 1900s was being made: it was hard to get the right kind of support from London.[25]

It is particularly interesting to note the presence in the list of people who supposedly did not understand Shanghai or China the names of Fortune and Gutzlaff. The former was a Scottish botanist who had visited Shanghai soon after its formal opening to foreign trade. The latter was one of the few Westerners to visit the port during the decade preceding the Opium War, and someone who wrote so glowingly of the city's potential that his words helped convince the British to call for Shanghai's opening.

Both Fortune and Gutzlaff's views of Shanghai would be reprinted over and over again in standard guides to and potted histories of the city through the 1800s and early 1900s—indeed they still show up in new works of the sort today. Hence it is no minor matter that the *Herald* should dismiss them so caustically, and their dismissal underscores the need to think of foreigners in China as having, from the start, divergent viewpoints.

It seems fitting to end our discussion of the first issue of the newspaper with reference to one other thing revealed by the early issues of the newspaper: some Shanghailanders were convinced—again at what might strike us as an unusually early point in time—that their city was destined for greatness. They were pleased that it had begun to rival Canton for the title of the China coast's most important port. They were convinced, though, that, as Shearman put it, if only the "British Government" would "exert her influence at the Court of Peking, to extend the facilities of trade with the interior," it could be much more. An essential characteristic of Shanghailander city myths, the idea that enormous changes had been effected, yet that the future was even rosier, was thus present from the beginning. There were, in Shearman's eyes, no limits to what this "new and important mart," this "centre of civilisation," could become. "Canton," the publisher acknowledged, "has been the cradle of our commerce with this wonderful country." Shanghai, however, was scheduled to surpass it. According to Shearman, "it is the destiny of Shanghae to become the permanent emporium of trade between [China] and all nations of the world."[26]

Shearman struck an even more boastful tone in his December 28 end-of-the-year issue. "Where but half a dozen years ago were nought but straggling cottages and paddy fields," he wrote in his opening editorial for that final 1850 edition, "is now a large and rapidly growing emporium of commerce." This development he viewed as "a triumphant instance of the enterprise and indomitable energy of the Anglo-Saxon race"—another theme that would continually reappear in the works produced by foreign boosters of the city in later decades. "Let us look onwards," he continued, "and it needs no spirit of prophecy to enable us to see that Shanghai is rapidly leaving her sister ports behind, and will soon be the first port in China." This city would, he was sure, in a statement that might in the case of another metropolis have been remembered merely for its hubris but here is truly prescient, "ultimately attain such an importance compared with which its present position is as naught."[27]

2   1875: Putting the city on the map

> Shanghai is now a major commercial port, and the city is booming with
> Chinese and foreigners, "hips touch hips and shoulders rub shoulders," private
> and public interests alike congregate.
>
> Li Fengbao (as translated by Catherine Vance Yeh), 1875[1]

The year 1875 is described above as having been a "year of no significance"
in Shanghai's history, or at least in its history as a global city. For this reason, it
would be appropriate, I claim, to devote a snapshot chapter on that year to a pair
of interrelated side issues, both associated with maps. And this is what I do below.
One of the side issues has a local focus: the way the city was represented on an
actual map produced in Shanghai—the map that inspired Li Fengbao to write
about the increasing interconnections between Chinese and foreigners in the treaty
port. The other side issue linked to mapping has a more global twist. I will explore
toward the end of the chapter whether we can say that, as of 1875, Shanghai was
"on the map" of international travelers. That is, was it by then a place that
globetrotters based far from China knew about and thought worth a visit.

But before getting to maps, real or metaphorical, it is worth explaining why
the "year of no significance" description seems apt—albeit perhaps a bit of an
overstatement. One source of support for this idea comes from the chronology that
Marie-Claire Bergère, a leading French Sinologist, appends to her *Histoire de
Shanghai*, one of the best general surveys of the city's modern period available
in any language.[2] She lists no major turning point occurrence for the year 1875.
Moreover, though she has something to say about, for example, the years 1863,
1864, 1865, 1866 and 1869, as well as about 1882 and 1883, she omits any
mention of turning point developments for most of the entire decade of the 1870s.
The reader is taken in this appendix directly from 1870 (which earns a mention
for being the time when Shanghai, Hong Kong and London became linked to one
another by telegraph) straight up to 1879 (when St. John's University, which
would have a long run as one of the city's premiere educational institutions, was
founded).[3]

To skip so swiftly through the 1870s is to gloss over several events of that
decade that played important roles in the development of the city, the growth of its
international reputation, or the expansion of its links to the wider world. Of

Figure 2.1 Wax statue of a boy hawking the *Shen Pao* newspaper on the streets in the late
1800s or early 1900s

Source: Author's photograph taken in 2000 at the Shanghai History Museum located in the base of the
Pearl of the Orient Tower

particular note among 1870s phenomena was the rise to prominence of the first local Chinese language publishing empire, which was founded by a Briton named Ernest Major. According to Rudolf Wagner, the scholar who has written most extensively and illuminatingly about Major, the publisher of *Shen Pao* (as noted in the previous chapter, Shanghai's first Chinese-language newspaper), was one of those relatively rare Shanghailanders who moved regularly and easily between Sinophone and Anglophone local circles, writing letters in English to the *North China Herald* one day and editorials in Chinese for his own newspaper, which had been launched in 1872, the next.[4] His publishing concern was not like that of missionaries, who tried in essence to translate a Western message into a different language, for he employed mainly Chinese writers, editors and illustrators, and his publication presented a view of both local and international events that was much more that of a certain type of local Chinese resident (the sort most open to foreign ideas) than of any group of Westerners.[5]

Another key 1870s development was the rising importance within Shanghai of publications that brought images of the wider world to the city. Here, again, Major is a key player in the story. He is mostly remembered now as the founder of *Shen Pao* and various affiliated text-driven periodicals and books, but from around the time of our current snapshot year, his company also had a busy lithographic studio attached to it, which employed skilled artists and turned out materials made up purely of images or of images accompanied by a small amount of accompanying text. It was not until the 1880s that he would start his most famous illustrated periodical, *Dianshizhai huabao* (Dianshizhai Pictorial), a magazine that used a distinctive style of line drawing that linked it to Chinese artistic traditions, but which was modeled largely after comparable Western periodicals of the time such as *The Graphic* and above all the *Illustrated London News* (a work to which more than a few Shanghailanders subscribed, as we learn from a *North China Herald* story published in our snapshot year that refers to the growing popularity of giving sample copies of it away as gifts when traveling to other parts of China).[6]

The tale of *Dianshizhai huabao* itself—a fascinating work through which local Chinese residents could armchair travel to other parts of the world to get a glimpse of the wondrous aspects of European cities, and through which Chinese living beyond Shanghai could armchair travel to the International Settlement to catch a glimpse of such oddities on display there as roller coaster rides and ballroom dances—takes us beyond the 1870s (we will revisit them in the next chapter), but the story of *Shen Pao* illustrated materials can be taken back nearly to our current snapshot year.[7] In 1876, according to Wagner, the organization created a "sensation" by publishing a map of a "height of 110 and width of 155 cm and meant to be hung on the wall, [which] was the first map of East Asia done on the basis of geographic surveys with a modern projection technique and all the place names in Chinese," meaning that it enabled *Shen Pao* readers to "locate the places mentioned in the news," "get an optical impression of China's place" in the region, see the "world cut up into nation-states," and "travel through East Asia with the eyes and fingers—and all this without needing any English." And in 1877, Major launched a short-lived precursor to the *Dianshizhai*, the *Huanying huabao* (Global Illustrated).[8]

The 1870s were noteworthy for more than just shifts in the world of Chinese language publications. This decade also saw, in 1874, the arrival in Shanghai of an import from Japan that would eventually become an iconic mode of transportation in both that city and Beijing: the rickshaw.[9] It saw as well the opening of the city's first museum and first newspaper run by Chinese residents.[10]

If a good case may be made for Bergère moving too swiftly through the 1870s as a decade, there is less reason to think that she has skipped too lightly over 1875 itself—for none of the things listed above took place in precisely that year. It is not surprising, therefore, that 1875 is passed over even in chronologies of major Shanghai events which mention multiple events of significance in the 1870s. A recent comprehensive history of the city compiled by members of the prestigious Shanghai Academy of Social Sciences, for example, includes multiple entries on the 1870s in its appendix on *Shanghai dashiji* (Shanghai's Big Events), yet none on our snapshot year.[11] It points readers first to two major occurrences of 1872: the founding of *Shen Pao* and the departure from Shanghai of a pioneering group of thirty Chinese men heading to the United States to study. The next 1870s stop in this chronology is 1874, which is noted not for the arrival of the rickshaw but for a conflict—the first of several—that arose between members of the Ningbo Native Place Society and the French Concession authorities over pieces of land that both sought to control. Then readers are taken to 1876, the year China's first railroad went into operation near Shanghai, something that was eagerly welcomed by some *Shanghairen* (literally, people of Shanghai, a common term, along with Shanghainese, for Chinese residents of the city) as a sign of progress, criticized harshly by others as a geomantic disruption to the country's *fengshui*, and treated by still others simply as just yet another addition to a long list of exotic treaty-port occurrences.[12]

Is there nothing, then, to be said for 1875 itself, other than that it saw the publication of the first map showing the Chinese and Western districts of the city as a single entity? Not quite. The year did witness another publishing milestone of sorts: the issue of an early booklet on the city's history as an international urban center, which may not have been the very first effort to take stock of the local foreign community, but was the first to provide a detailed look at many issues, particularly the character of local public and associational life among the Shanghailanders. Written by H. Lang and based on a lecture he had given, it was titled *Shanghai Considered Socially*, and issued by a local religious press.[13]

Looking beyond Shanghai to events that had implications for the presence of international actors within China, 1875 stands out as the year of the Margary Affair, which involved the murder of an interpreter for the British mission and sent shockwaves through the foreign communities of all of the treaty ports.[14] The killing of Augustus R. Margary was much on the minds of Shanghailanders, even though the murder took place far away in Southwestern China, and the event eventually left its mark on Shanghai via a local memorial monument erected to the victim in 1880.[15]

Another thing that generated interest and either concern or amusement among local foreigners in 1875 was a memorandum on Shanghai's future as a port penned by Robert Hart, an Ulsterman who was perhaps the most influential Westerner in China at the time. Hart, who headed the Imperial Maritime Customs Service, a quasi-colonial institution that was technically an arm of the Chinese state yet manned largely by foreign employees, warned that Shanghai might soon lose its prominence as a center of regional and international trade unless a dramatic change in dredging practices was made—and perhaps even if the steps he proposed were taken. He argued, in what turned out of course to be a far from prescient document, that it was getting so hard for ships to make their way up to the port from the Yangzi that its role in trade could easily, within a few years, be eclipsed by lesser ports near to it.[16]

We can also learn from a perusal of various issues of the *North China Herald* from 1875—and from a special "Retrospect of 1875" that ran in the same newspaper early in 1876—that Shanghailanders were also worried about or interested in other things in our snapshot year, including the following:

1   whether the city had developed to the point that it merited a Cathedral to serve its Anglican population;[17]
3   whether plans for opening up a tramway would be put into operation;
4   increases in the cost of sending telegrams;
5   the building of an impressive new headquarters for the Hongkong and Shanghai Bank (the company back then spelled and today still spells "Hong Kong" as one word in its name), on the same spot on the Bund where a less grand building that served the same purpose had previously stood.[18]

This indicates that much was going on in Shanghai in 1875, but a close reading of the *Herald*'s retrospective article in particular still gives one a sense of a twelve-month period of little, if perhaps not quite "no," significance. Though Shanghai in the late 1800s is routinely called, for good reason, a boomtown, so rapidly did its economy grow (as trade increased and the textile industry began to take off), that particular year was one when the *Herald* had to admit commerce was sluggish. And though the new Hongkong and Shanghai Bank headquarters was an important addition to the Bund and a decided improvement in terms of its grandeur over the structure it replaced, the *Herald* begins its comments on the edifice by describing it as the only notable public building erected that year.[19] All in all, then, we can understand why Bergère and the Shanghai Academy of Social Sciences scholars decided to skip over our snapshot year.

Mapping a cosmopolitan metropolis

Having concluded our brief overview of the year's major events—or lack thereof—let us return to maps in general, and more specifically to the quotation used to open this chapter. It is taken from the "Introduction" that Li (who would later serve as China's ambassador to Germany) wrote to accompany an 1875 map compiled by two Shanghai residents, Feng Zhouru and Xu Yuchang. This cartographic portrayal of the city was a very special one, according to literary specialist Catherine Vance Yeh, who reproduces and analyzes it in a fascinating essay on Shanghai maps.[20] What made it special, she argues, is that it broke with tradition in several ways. For example, unlike previous Chinese maps, it included a careful and accurate representation of the city's foreign-run districts. And in contrast to Western maps that both prior to and after 1875 often either ignored Shanghai's Chinese-run areas completely, showed only parts of them at the edge of the page, or showed them fully but rendered them as lacking in all points of interest, Feng and Xu treated the old walled city, the International Settlement, and the French Concession in an integrated and equal fashion.

The map thus marked, in Yeh's words, a "watershed in the representation of Shanghai." It was a text that approached the city as a "greater unit" made up of disparate parts, something that was highly unusual at the time, no matter what medium was being used to approach the city. Li argued, in his introductory commentary, that a "major commercial port" needed to be made legible to merchants and other interested parties. A map such as Feng and Xu's was hence of great value. And it is of value to us here as well, in part because it provides a starting point for a consideration of some of the ways that Shanghai had changed in the two and a half decades that followed 1850.

One thing that made an integrated map so useful in 1875 was that during the preceding years the distinction between the foreign-run and Chinese-run parts of Shanghai had become much less pronounced. This was because a series of rebellions and revolts that began in 1853 and continued up through 1864 had altered the structure of the city. When it came to administrative and legal matters, there were still important things that separated the British and American enclaves (now governed by a single Municipal Council but not yet referred to as simply the "International Settlement") from the French Concession (which had initially been part of the new multinational unit, then decided to go its own way), and that separated both of these from the old walled city under Chinese control. And there were physical differences to note (the lay-out of streets, housing styles, and so forth) as one walked from one part of the city to another. But it was no longer true that the population mix one encountered changed radically as one passed in and out of different parts of Shanghai.

In the very early 1850s, the only Chinese residents of the Western-run districts were household servants and followers of Catholicism.[21] A local secret society rebellion, known as the Small Swords Uprising, however, sent many local Chinese rushing into the foreign-run districts in 1853 and 1854, seeking protection from the insurgents. And large numbers of Chinese streamed into all parts of Shanghai in the late 1850s and early 1860s when the much larger Taiping Uprising (1848–1864) (a millenarian rising, led by a man who claimed to be Christ's younger brother, that almost succeeded in toppling the Qing Dynasty) moved into the region. By 1875, the official fiction still held that only foreigners could make their homes inside the foreign-run enclaves but both had majority Chinese populations. This had many ramifications, including that of increasing the proliferation of hybrid, Sino-Western architectural forms.

An 1870 census of the International Settlement shows just how radically the proportions of foreign to Chinese residents shifted in the wake of the uprisings of the 1850s and 1860s. It also shows, in some cases in wonderful detail, how variegated the population of this enclave had become in other ways as the time when Feng and Xu's map appeared approached. According to this census, the results of which Lang included in *Shanghai Considered Socially*, the total foreign population (in the Settlement) stood at 2,767 in 1870. This means that it had increased more than ten-fold since 1850, an impressive rise. But the number of Chinese residents in this enclave had risen still more rapidly, soaring from perhaps a couple of dozen in 1850 to 58,981 in 1870, meaning that by then they outnumbered foreigners in the enclave by a ratio of well over 20 to 1.[22]

In terms of other forms of diversity, this census tells us that, within the foreign community, some twenty different nationalities, as opposed to just several, were now represented. Among this group, the largest contingents came from Britain (1,338, but 114 of those were members of the Royal Navy stationed temporarily in Shanghai), France (379, with 335 in the Navy), the United States (352), and Germany (165). A sizable contingent of Indians and Malays (grouped together in the census) lived in the Settlement by that point (152), as did a fair number of Portuguese (108), and Spaniards (56). Rounding out the population were 39 Prussians, 29 Japanese, 23 Swedes, 16 Danes, and handfuls of Mexicans, Greeks, Italians, Norwegians, and Austrians. One thing that remained constant from 1850 to 1870 was that the overwhelming majority of local foreigners were male; more families arrived each year, but there were still only 321 women who were not Chinese, meaning that there were about nine foreign males for every foreign female.[23]

One other intriguing nugget this census provides, which gives us a sense of the economic and social as opposed to demographic or physical terrain, is a list of foreign occupational groups. We see from this that in the Settlement the range of jobs done by foreigners had widened dramatically in recent decades to the point where some seventy different kinds of occupations could be listed. In 1850 the enclave was home primarily just to missionaries, seamen, servants, merchants and clerks, as well as people working for a few miscellaneous enterprises (such as the city's one newspaper), but in 1870 the Settlement had everything from auctioneers (2) to watchmakers (7) and hair dressers (3) to tailors (7). It also, curiously, had equal numbers of dentists and professors of astronomy (1 apiece).[24] This suggests that the Settlement had by the 1870s become in two ways at least much more like the old walled city: it was a district in which most residents were Chinese and in which a wide range of businesses operated.

One thing that is not revealed by this census, which gives many more details about foreigners than about Chinese, is the extent to which lives within the enclaves and the old walled city had become intertwined, making the time ripe for the appearance of an integrated map like Feng and Xu's. Many foreign residents continued to spend their days primarily in the Settlement and the Concession in the 1870s, viewing an excursion into the Chinese-run parts of the city as a venture into an exotic and, to the mind of some, aesthetically unpleasant region.[25] Some of the only Westerners who went to the walled city with any regularity were mission-aries. This may explain why so many foreign maps left the old walled city as uncharted territory, or presented it as a district whose only points of interest were churches. But the situation was quite different for local Chinese.

There were doubtless some Chinese residents of the International Settlement and French Concession who tended to stay within the borders of the enclaves, and there were certainly some Chinese who rarely left the old walled district. But many native residents (especially those with money to spend) found it natural to move regularly between different parts of the city. They would simply go from whichever district they lived in to whichever district happened to have shops that stocked the goods they wanted to buy, businesses that offered the services they wanted to make use of, housed the temple or church in which they wanted to worship, or contained the meeting halls of the associations to which they belonged. It mattered little that this might require them to cross the border between administrative districts (borders that were policed only in rare times of crisis), and that it might mean entering or leaving the walled city.

One way to illustrate the lesser importance of the lines between districts in Chinese as opposed to foreign lives—and hence the greater use native residents had for mental and actual maps that included all parts of the city—is to compare and contrast the role of native-place ties and associations for Western and non-Western residents of Shanghai. The port was, in 1875 as in earlier and later periods, a city of immigrants. And as in many cities of immigrants, much social life was organized around institutions that catered to people who had come from a given place originally or shared other regionally defined cultural traits (such as a common language). This meant that, for foreigners, there were clubs where people of specific nationalities gathered, social groups that catered to people who spoke a common language (such as English or French), restaurants that specialized in dishes from particular distant lands, and so forth.

Similarly, for local Chinese, regionally defined benevolent associations—known as *huiguan* or *gongsuo* (guilds) or as *tongxianghui* (native-place societies)—that served migrants from particular provinces or cities were an important part of the local landscape. Indeed, since Shanghai was a city of Chinese migrants before the foreign-run enclaves were founded, some of these benevolent associations were very well established by 1875: twelve pre-dated the Opium War, two traced their roots back to the 1750s.[26] There were also teahouses and restaurants that specialized in providing food and drink from particular regions. One attraction of frequenting these places, as well as of belonging to a *tongxianghui*, was simply that it provided a setting in which sojourners from a given part of China could converse freely with others in their native dialect.

Even though there were parallels here between the situation of foreigners and Chinese newcomers to Shanghai, there was also an important difference—and this brings us back to issues of geography. Namely, a displaced Briton would find all of the clubs and stores that catered to him (it was still, as noted above, usually "him," not "her") within the Settlement. A Frenchman, meanwhile, would find most of the things that reminded him of home within the Concession. Each of these two imagined Westerners might have need of a map that showed him both foreign-run enclaves, but they would not necessarily see the point of one that also included the Chinese-run parts of the city. To produce documents called maps of "Shanghai" that showed only the foreign-run districts, as Westerners did throughout the treaty-port era, was thus both an act of cartographic imperialism and a utilitarian reflection of the boundaries within which immigrants from the West found the things they wanted and needed.

The situation of Chinese sojourners who had come to Shanghai from other parts of the country was quite different. A Cantonese resident, for example, might well live in the Settlement but be drawn to the old walled city when seeking out people or products from his native place.[27] He might buy cloth or silk in the French Concession, take it to a Chinese tailor who had set up shop in the Settlement, then wear his new clothes to an event held at the main building of the Canton guild in the walled city. Similarly, he might like to spend his holidays visiting a temple or a teashop in that oldest part of Shanghai.[28] There were neighborhoods within Shanghai in which many Chinese from a given region lived (informal "enclaves" of a sort), and those residing in such districts might find fewer reasons to venture across the borders between the city's main parts. Nevertheless, it remained much more likely that Chinese as opposed to foreign residents of the city would be drawn to venture into different sections of the metropolis on a fairly regular basis.[29]

Was Shanghai on the global map in 1875?

Having dealt a bit with a local work of cartography, let us ponder briefly another sense in which a city can be "put on the map," in a more metaphoric sense. This phrase refers to a place's fame. In 1850, as we have seen, some Shanghailanders at least were clearly already eager to have their "eastern home" seen as an important locale; not just a site of economic activity (though definitely that) but also something more. By the 1930s it had certainly become a metropolis of inter-national renown and notoriety, which was on the mental map of many people living far from the Huangpu and considered a desirable stopping-off point for the cosmopolitan globetrotter.[30] But had it reached that status in 1875, the year that interests us now?

The best answer is probably a simple though ambivalent one: almost. Let us consider, as evidence, some famous actual and fictional global journeys of the time, beginning with that of Thomas Cook, who did so much to help invent mass tourism in the West. In late 1872 and early 1873, he took an extended trip to Asia and North America (among other regions), during the course of which he sent letters to *The Times* (London) and assorted other periodicals (the *Temperance Record*, for example). These letters were initially published separately in these various venues and then subsequently they were collectively issued as a book. This work, *Letters from the Sea and from Foreign Lands Descriptive of a Tour Round the World*, which first appeared in 1873 and has recently been reissued, also included some additional materials (such as announcements of upcoming trips).[31]

The most interesting things about this work, for our purposes, are the following: Cook chose Shanghai as one of the stops for his tour and mentioned the city in two of his letters; he advertised it as one of the places those subscribing to a future "Round the World Tour" sponsored by his company would visit; but he only stayed in the city a short time and was disparaging about it in one of his letters.[32] For him, it seems, Shanghai was "on the map," but just barely. It was worth a visit, but twenty-four hours there "quite satisfied" him, he wrote to *The Times* (letter dated February 13, 1873). He "hastily visited the old Chinese city, which presented a strange contrast to the [Japanese] cities we had just left." Why? Because it was so much less appealing a place in which to spend time, being made up of "[n]arrow, filthy, and offensive streets" and filled with "pestering and festering beggars in every shape of hideous deformity."

According to Cook, the unpleasant "sights, sounds, and smells" of this part of Shanghai "cut short" his stay in the old walled district, to which he stated "no one paid a second visit"—meaning of course no foreigners—and hence the "chief part" of his group's "short stay at Shanghai was spent in the American, English, or French concessions." He had little to say about these sections, though he clearly implied that he found frequenting them less of a trial to his senses. One of the only things he wrote in the letter to *The Times* was that throughout Shanghai both modes of travel and "street sights" contrasted "very disadvantageously with Japanese arrangements and appearances." One other tidbit about Shanghai appears in a December 19, 1872 letter to a Mr. Rae of *The Temperance Record*. Here, Cook simply mentions that a temperance meeting had been the major news item in the first newspaper he saw in Shanghai.

Next let us turn to an even more famous book on global travel that appeared, like Cook's volume, early in the 1870s: *Around the World in Eighty Days* by novelist Jules Verne. Did Phileas Fogg stop in Shanghai? Almost. Verne has his hero miss a steamer that was to take him from Hong Kong to Yokohama via Shanghai, then charter a boat to try to catch up with the one he failed to board on time. This chartered boat, though, never quite reaches the city on the Huangpu, since the Yokohama-bound steamer passes it several miles downriver from Shanghai (which it has just left). Fogg manages to board it without ever getting even close enough to Shanghai to catch sight of its famous Bund. This means that the first city to be described in detail after Hong Kong in the novel is Yokohama—and indeed a lively and colorful scene in the novel is set in that Japanese treaty port, which has long been the one most frequently compared to Shanghai.

There has been some debate over whether Cook's famous tour influenced Verne when writing his novel. The letters and the serialized version of *Around the World in Eighty Days* appeared in periodicals simultaneously, so the influence was minimal at best, yet it is true that Cook's itinerary (which is close to Fogg's) was announced early enough (June 1872) to have come to Verne's attention. In any case, what matters most to us is that Verne published the China sections of Fogg's trip before Cook's letter describing Shanghai appeared in print. Thus the novelist's decision to have his character stop short of spending in that city even the twenty-four hours that Cook allotted to it on his tour had nothing to do with the famous travel agent's negative impression.[33]

Reading the two books side by side, though, does give us an interesting window onto a topic of continual interest to residents of Shanghai and of the Hong Kong and Canton region from the 1840s on: the relative attractions and competing positions of these two parts of the China coast. By 1860, according to the edition of *Encyclopedia Britannica* issued that year, Shanghai had firmly established itself as "next to Canton, the most important of the five ports that were opened to foreign trade by the treaty of 1843."[34] But what does reading Cook and Verne tell us about the relative attractions of Shanghai and its neighbors to the south, Canton and Hong Kong, in the 1870s?

Cook, for his part, describes Shanghai disdainfully. He then mentions in the same February 13, 1873, letter to *The Times* that his "worst miscalculation" (and one to be rectified in future trips) was that he budgeted too little time for Hong Kong. He had to content himself with "a glance at another edition of English life" (the Crown Colony), "without being able to see Canton, the Chinese city of all others to be seen."[35]

Jules Verne, meanwhile, mentions but does not describe Shanghai in *Around the World in Eighty Days* (though as noted above he would rectify this oversight in a later novel), yet presents Hong Kong in detail and says things about it that correspond closely with things that proud Shanghailanders liked to say about their Model Settlement (this term was already in circulation by the 1870s). For example, Hong Kong appears in *Around the World in Eighty Days* as a port on the rise, which is "bound to overtake" nearby Macao as the area's great center of international trade, and is already serving as the place through which "the majority of Chinese imports and exports pass."[36] Visions of Shanghai as a port that had attained commercial greatness and would continue to rise were, as we saw in the preceding chapter, a theme of an article in the very first issue of the *North China Herald*, and remained a favorite topic in that paper in the 1870s.[37]

Verne also says other things about Hong Kong that echo claims some Shanghailanders liked to make for the Model Settlement. For instance, he portrayed it as charmingly reminiscent of a British town in its physical layout. "Docks, hospitals, wharves, godowns, a Gothic Cathedral, a Government House, and surfaced roads—everything made you think that one of the many market towns in Kent or Surrey had passed right through the terrestrial sphere and popped out at this point in China, almost at the antipodes." Likening the city to Bombay, Calcutta, and Singapore, Verne mused on the existence of a "trail of British towns" that encircled the globe.[38]

British Shanghailanders who came across these passages might well have been envious that they had been written about the Crown Colony—a rival in not just economic terms but also other realms, including sports—as opposed to the Settlement.[39] After all, as texts such as the commemorative volumes issued to mark the 1893 celebration of the Shanghai Jubilee (held to celebrate fifty years of the foreign presence in the city), a common trope of Shanghailanders was to view their enclave as a piece of the civilized West that had been "dropped down" in the midst of a barbaric empire.[40] Some Britons had been arguing from nearly the moment they arrived by the Huangpu for the idea that their new home was part of just the sort of global "trail of British towns" on which Verne placed Hong Kong.

In addition, in the decades immediately preceding the publication of *Around the World in Eighty Days*, local residents had done several things to make the Settlement more closely resemble a "British town." By 1873, the enclave had amateur dramatic societies, sporting clubs (including ones devoted to hunting), a racetrack (the first had been created by the Bund in 1850, then new and improved ones had been opened inland in later years), and a library. It also had a police force and Municipal Council, each modeled on those then extant in Britain.[41] Last but not least it had, from 1867, a "Public Garden," something that, according to Victorian ideas about urban planning, needed to exist to serve as the "lungs" of a city. According to a 1921 history of Shanghai, this park had paths laid out by the "Municipal Engineer," and the first "Garden Committee" put in charge of it had even recommended that "for 200 pounds a year and second-class passage a gardener should be got from England" to maintain the grounds.[42] This text does not tell us, alas, whether the plan to employ such a gardener was realized (and if so, when exactly), but there is abundant evidence to show that over the course of its history the park came to contain more and more Victorian features. A bandstand was eventually even erected, so that the local Municipal Orchestra would have a place to play.[43]

Figure 2.2 The Shanghai Public Garden as it looked in the early 1900s

Source: Postcard in the author's collection

It may be tempting to conclude from the evidence just presented that there was a sharp contrast between the way proud local foreigners, on the one hand, and Westerners who were not Shanghailanders, on the other, viewed Shanghai's importance and attractiveness in the 1870s. There is ample proof in 1875 *North China Herald* articles that this newspaper still considered Shanghai a special place that was destined for greatness and already deserving of the "honest pride" that Shanghailanders felt in the "position it had attained." When the question came up in March of that year of whether Shanghai should have an Anglican Cathedral (one officially opened that May), the newspaper naturally enough responded affirmatively. Of course it should have this symbolic recognition of its stature. After all, "Shanghai is now, and is long likely to continue [to be] the foreign capital of North China, and as such it deserves an ecclesiastical as well as legal status."[44]

Did anyone other than Shanghailanders view the city as special? Neither Cook nor Verne did, but at least two travelers who arrived in the port around the same time that the former came with his touring party and the latter decided to have Fogg give the city a miss, had different ideas. E.K. Laird, whose *The Rambles of a Globetrotter* was published in our snapshot year, was one. Laird was very impressed by cities to the South, including Canton, which he thought "as superior to" other Chinese cities "for shops as Paris is to London."[45] But he also had a generally positive view of Shanghai—aside, that is, from its Chinese-run section, which he found "unbearable" during his short visit to it.[46] "The town," he writes, "is beautifully laid out with macadamized roads, and the buildings are quite palatial, reminding one of the marble palaces of Genoa." He also thought the cricket ground a "splendid" one, even if the caliber of the play during a match he saw "was not of the best."[47]

The other traveler of the period who stopped in Shanghai and found it much more interesting than did Cook was Le Baron de Hubner, an Anglophilic former French diplomat whose *A Ramble Round the World, 1871* was first issued in English in our snapshot year. We will end this chapter by looking at his positive impressions of the city—a city that he did not think lacked flaws but definitely considered a place worth more than twenty-four hours of a world traveler's time, and which he wrote of in ways of which the *North China Herald* and the Shanghailanders whose views it represented would surely have approved.

He begins his account of Shanghai on a downbeat note, acknowledging that there is "nothing in the scenery" along the Huangpu "that strikes the eye or speaks to the imagination" as you near the city. "Nevertheless, on the river, the animation increases" as one "nears the great metropolis." One begins to see "through a forest of masts," he writes, "the imposing buildings of the English town, the houses of the American quarter, and the flags of the different Consulates."[48] His account is not completely unlike Cook's, for de Hubner also deplores the smells he encounters in the old walled city (focussing particularly in his case on those emanating from both high-class and low-class restaurants), but he continually either softens the criticisms he makes or combines them with words of praise for local residents. For example, though eager to leave the walled city (an "untempting place"), he thinks it only fair to note that the "principal streets of Shanghai in the Chinese quarter are not worse than what one sees of this kind in the south of Europe." And he is filled with admiration for the evidence he sees in the Settlement of the "boldness, the perseverance, the elastic, energetic, indefatigable genius of the Anglo-Saxon race" (echoes of Sherman's comments in the early issues of the *Herald*). Who else but the British, he muses, could have managed against such odds to build a fine town in such an inhospitable setting, overcoming in the process everything from the problems posed by a miserable climate to the obstacles associated with Chinese bureaucratic obstinacy?

He is most positively struck by several things he attributes to the special characteristics of the Britons who (with some assistance from other foreigners and Chinese merchants) built Shanghai into the "great metropolis" that it had become. One is the shops "richly furnished with all English productions" found in the Settlement. He marvels at the ease with which, when in their midst, one can "fancy oneself in Oxford Street or the Strand."

De Hubner goes on to make a statement that is much like that Laird made about Canton—except that here Shanghai is linked to India's great cities. In terms of stores, he claims, "neither Yokohama nor any other European town in Asia, saving Calcutta and Bombay, can bear comparison to Shanghai." He is also impressed by the ability of foreigners in the Settlement, though not in the Concession (where officials have to continually refer affairs "to the foreign minister in Paris"), to manage their own affairs with a minimum of outside interference.

De Hubner sums up his impression of all of the wondrous things that the Shanghailanders have accomplished in a paragraph that is reminiscent of the *Herald* at its most fulsome. It reads as follows:

> The results of the English system have gone beyond one's expectations. Look at this town of palaces; count, if you can, the masts of the ships, with which the port is bustling; look at those great leviathans of steamers continually coming and going; examine the commercial statistics in any one of these large [trading] houses, and you cannot fail to admire the vigor, the energy, and the vitality of the Queen of the Yang-tse-kiang [Yangzi River] and of the Yellow Sea, and the strength of the link which binds the immense Celestial Empire to Europe, America, and Australia; and all this is the work of a handful of brave, enterprising men! Their country's cannon has opened the way for them; and the breach once made, they have established themselves so securely that it is not very probable that they will ever be dislodged.

Clearly, then, from as early as the 1870s, not all of foreign Shanghai's most enthusiastic boosters were Shanghailanders. Nor were Shangailanders the only ones who mistakenly assumed that Western control of part of the city could go on indefinitely.

1900: A year of fire and sword

A new chapter is to be opened in the history of foreign intercourse with
China. The closing pages of the last are being written in letters of blood, with
illustrations by fire and sword . . . The very name treaty port will gradually
die out when all [Chinese cities] are open alike [to foreign trade]. Little by
little China will be Westernised . . .

"The Future of the Treaty Ports," *North China Herald*,
November 14, 1900

The quarter-century following our last snapshot year saw Shanghai change
in many dramatic ways, often due to the arrival or increasing popularity of an
imported machine or technology. Some of the most obvious alterations of this
sort had to do with transportation. Rickshaws, just starting to make their mark in
our last snapshot year, were by 1900 regular modes of conveyance, and in the
foreign-run parts of the city still newer vehicles were regularly seen. The railway
line that provoked controversy and inspired curiosity in the 1870s was abandoned
after a few years in operation, but a new one was established successfully in 1898.
One of the many imported wonders that the *Dianshizhai* presented to readers living
in and far outside of Shanghai were horse-drawn buggies, while by 1900 some
Shanghailanders could be seen riding bicycles. The plans to have trams run
through Shanghai streets that were floated in the 1870s came to naught. But early
in the new century, trams finally arrived, and they quickly became almost as iconic
a form of Shanghai transportation as rickshaws—one reason that replicas of
them are almost as commonly seen as faux rickshaws in the "Old Shanghai"
displays that twenty-first-century visitors to the city encounter. Other changes
linked to technology included electric lighting gaining popularity in the foreign-run
districts (right around 1900) and the creation of the city's first extensive telephone
system allowing people at one hundred different stations to talk to one another
(in our snapshot year itself).[1]

Had the anti-Christian Boxers not laid siege to the foreign legations in Beijing
(in June of 1900) and a multinational band of soldiers (representing six European
powers, the United States, and Japan) not lifted that siege fifty-five days later,
and then begun brutal campaigns of reprisal (that would last well into 1901), a
theme for a snapshot of Shanghai in 1900 might well have been the coming of

these new technologies. Such a chapter could highlight the emphasis that Western travel writers of the day put on the presence of these technologies in arguing that the foreign-run parts of Shanghai seemed more like displaced pieces of the West than districts located in Asia. In a 1901 book, *China through the Stereoscope*, for example, the author lists many things that catch a traveler's eye upon arriving at the International Settlement that are "not Chinese," such as the "well-paved streets lined with shade trees" and the gazebo in the "beautiful public gardens," and then comes to "those tall posts bearing myriad wires that span the streets" and "tell of a busy, ceaseless enterprise that is not Chinese."[2]

Such a chapter could look as well at varied Chinese responses to how new technologies and a developed public works system allowed life to be lived in the Settlement and the French Concession. On the one hand, many Chinese commentators praised or simply marveled at streets that seemed amazingly smooth and well-lit (as early as 1872, the *Shen Pao* carried a limerick about gas lamps that ran "east and west," allowing "[r]unning fires beyond the skill of man" to race across the Settlement) and about the apparent miracle of tap water (an 1887 limerick spoke of a "black dragon, sucking Shanghai's water" and then making it "flow up" a "tall building").[3] On the other hand, the streets and public spaces of the enclaves were sometimes seen as dangerous places, in moral terms, where Chinese women who rode in buggies pulled by horses left themselves open to improper flirtatious advances by members of the opposite sex.[4]

Alternately, a theme for a snapshot of 1900, were it not a year of stories "written in blood" tied to the Boxers and the foreign invasion, could have been Shanghai's shift from being a city whose economy was dependent largely on trade to one where factory production and finance were also key. The Treaty of Shimonoseki, which China signed after its defeat in the first Sino-Japanese War of 1894–1895, made it much easier for foreigners to establish industrial plants in the country, and in its immediate wake many factories were established in Shanghai and other ports. Most of the new Shanghai factories seem to have been built across the river from the Bund in Pudong, which a 1900 article in the *North China Herald* described as containing a "steadily lengthening line of docks, mills, and various industries, studded with chimneys."[5] On the financial front, foreign banks and traditional Chinese banks had been significant parts of the local scene for decades. It was only in the late 1890s, however, that the first Western-style Chinese-run bank began operating near the Huangpu. Admittedly, economic developments of the sort just sketched out unfold over decades not months, making it easier for scholars to associate them with an extended period (in this case, running from the end of the first Sino-Japanese War to the start of World War I). Nevertheless, 1900 would serve as well as any other in this period as a focus for a discussion of the growing complexity of local business activity—Chinese, foreign, and Sino-foreign alike.[6]

Yet another option that might have proved attractive, were 1900 not a year of such a great crisis in Beijing that Shanghai could not help but be wrenched by it as well, would have been to structure a snapshot chapter around shifts in local demography and geography. The year 1900 was, for example, when the borders of

Figure 3.1 Advertisement from *The Hotel Metropole Guide to Shanghai*, 1901. The increase in the number of factories was matched by a rise in the number of commercial establishments, including those that allowed foreign, and also some elite Chinese women, to purchase dresses cut in the latest European fashions

the French Concession were extended to the west to provide additional space for housing (much of it for Chinese who wanted to live in the district) and for new commercial enterprises.

This expansion was important for its own sake and also because it followed on the heels of a similar (but much more dramatic) enlargement of the International Settlement to the east and to the west in 1899.[7] The year 1900 thus saw a foreign Shanghai take shape that was considerably larger than that which had existed since 1861, when the last major additions had been carried out. And the northern and eastern borders of this new foreign Shanghai—indeed all of the boundaries of the Settlement—would remain essentially unchanged until the end of the treaty-port era, though there would be continual struggle over the jurisdiction of some roads that began in the enclave and went beyond its borders. The only further formal expansion of foreign territory would come in 1914, when the French Concession would gain a large new tract of land to the south and west.[8] In addition, though precise figures are not available, it is possible that the total population of all of Shanghai first topped one million in 1900.[9] And it was near or at the turn of the century that there were, for the first time, fewer than two men for every woman in the Settlement. This suggests that while the enclave, and indeed the city as a whole, remained one that contained a disproportionate number of single men, it was also increasingly a place where families lived.[10]

A very different sort of approach to 1900, which again will not be pursued, would involve zeroing in on a contentious court case that made headlines. Often, when people have described Old Shanghai's legal arrangements as having been amazingly complex, they have had in mind the special ways that issues involving Chinese and foreign interests were handled. This is understandable. The most dramatic conflicts associated with Shanghai law cases, such as a 1905 case that sparked a riot, involved the "Mixed Court" (which Westerners often portrayed as fair, but Chinese frequently complained was anything but).[11] The 1900 court case I have in mind, though, shows how complicated things could get within the Settlement even when Chinese were not involved. The case pitted electrician E.E. Porter (who had fitted up his own house so that it could be lit by electricity) against the Shanghai Municipal Council (SMC) (which had recently bought out the Shanghai Electric Light Company, becoming the sole supplier of electricity). The plaintiff was angry that the Council, which usually took charge of fitting houses for electricity, refused to provide him with current. The case was tried in a "Court of Consuls" presided over by the American Consul-General, with British and German Consul-Generals also serving as judges. The plaintiff won the case, since the judges found unpersuasive the SMC's claim that public safety, not an interest in asserting a monopoly, had been its primary concern. The Council's failure to even inspect Porter's house before deciding that supplying him with current would be dangerous clearly worked against the defense.[12]

Finally, had 1900 been a less eventful year, it would have been tempting to organize this chapter around an exchange (in the form of a letter to the editor and an editorial written in response) that took place in the pages of the *North China Herald* on March 21. This is an exchange that illustrates nicely the way that two different types of Shanghailanders envisioned the place and proper status of Chinese living in the Settlement. Both the letter (which first appeared in the *North China Daily News* and then was reprinted in the *Herald*) and the editorial (written exclusively for the issue of the *Herald* in which the letter was republished) bore the same title: "The Franchise at Shanghai." This is, however, slightly misleading. Yes, each dealt with a voting issue (which foreigners should be granted the franchise in municipal elections). But, as we will see, each devoted attention as well to the question of whether the SMC was doing enough to improve the quality of life of the enclave's largest block of non-voters: Chinese residents of the Settlement.

The letter, signed "C.B.," took issue with the fact that all power in the Settlement lay in the hands of a small set of foreigners. These "representatives of wealth and class" formed an "oligarchy" insensitive to the burden that even a small tax increase could be to Shanghailanders of the middling sorts. C.B. went on to chide these oligarchs for their "entire lack of consideration for the lowest class of workers among the Chinese." He thought more should be done for the "thousands of poor natives in the settlements, who help by hard toil to build up and maintain the commercial greatness of Shanghai." After all, these Chinese did as much for the city, in their way, as did "the banker or merchant, broker or official, and the taxes contributed by them amount to a large sum. Why, C.B. wondered, "[c]ould not some of the money derived from taxation be used" to ameliorate their hardships? The SMC could "provide shelters on the streets for protection of the coolies against the extremes of climate." It could establish "good lodging houses in which" workers "could get a bath, and a clean and healthy bed for a small payment." Or it could set up a "convalescent home" for over-worked rickshaw pullers.

C.B. ended with a call to "widen the franchise" (only a small percentage of foreign residents qualified to vote in SMC elections), so that a fuller expression of the "public opinion of this very large foreign community" could be heard.[13] The implicit assumption here is that less well-off foreigners would naturally be more supportive than rich ones when it came to channeling more funds toward social welfare programs for Chinese workers.[14]

How did the *Herald*'s editors respond? They began by calling C.B.'s a "very temperate letter" (a nod to the fact that many critics of the SMC used harsher words), but then proceeded to counter each of his claims. They thought it not unreasonable that only 711 men could vote, since the "foreign population" stood at just "6,000 men, women, and children, including Japanese." Yes, something short of full "manhood suffrage" existed in the Settlement, since there were roughly 2,500 adult male foreigners. But, they pointed out, "hardly anywhere," even at the end of the nineteenth century, was "the municipal franchise" much more extensive. Moreover, far from jealously guarding their control over the voting process (as C.B. claimed), the so-called "oligarchs" had, the *Herald* insisted, continually worked to broaden the electorate.

The editors cited, to back up this last claim, developments that had taken place two decades previously, at a point "when the franchise was very much more restricted." At that time, the alleged "representatives of wealth and class" had "spontaneously provided in the Revised Land Regulations" (the main code of Settlement life) "for a very material reduction in the qualification for the franchise."

The editors thought it "hardly necessary to controvert" the charge of SMC neglect of the needs of Chinese laborers, since "the ameliorations and amenities of civilization which taxation provides benefit the poor proportionally more than they do the rich." But they nevertheless went on to "controvert" it in some detail. Surely, they insisted, it "is more important to the poor wayfarers, the jinricshaman [rickshaw puller], the carrying coolie, the wheel-barrowman, that the streets should be smooth and clean, well-lighted and well-policed, than it is to the wealthy man in his carriage." And as for such things as the creation of "lodging-houses," while these might be excellent projects, they were ones best left to private philanthropists. They also pointed out that, based on the evidence of Britain in the wake of the Reform Act, there was little reason to think that a broader electorate would "change the general course of the municipal administration of Shanghai to any appreciable extent." There were, it seemed to them, always likely to be about as many conservatives amongst the lower as amongst the upper classes.[15]

In the shadows of the Boxer Crisis

All of the developments and texts described above draw attention to interesting dimensions of Shanghai *circa* 1900, but the local effects and after-effects of the conflagration in North China were so significant that focussing on them here makes sense. The siege of the foreign legations and the military campaigns of first salvation and then revenge comprised one of the biggest international news stories of the year. And even though there was no fighting in Shanghai, this city inevitably felt the impact of the upheaval. So, let us turn now to the nature of that impact.

The first thing to stress is that the effects of the Boxer Crisis on the city were complicated. Just before and during the siege, local Westerners worried that they might be in danger. Around the same time, though, Chinese journalists writing in the *Shen Pao* expressed what turned out to be a more prescient concern: that "if the Boxer rebels" were not reined in and "taken to task" by the Chinese court, the foreign powers would muster large numbers of troops to "enter China, and within the twinkling of an eye, a scene of total destruction" would ensue.[16] There was intense grief among the Shanghailanders when rumors spread (that turned out to be false) of a massacre of all the hostages. Since Japanese as well as European and American hostages were held, concern about the plight of those held in Beijing was felt throughout the diverse foreign community. But as soon as the siege was lifted, optimism about the good (for foreigners) that might come from the tragedy asserted itself. Surely now, some Shanghailanders assumed, a complete opening up of China to traders and missionaries would be possible. Surely now, fewer scruples would be made about allowing foreign troops to march through the Settlement—despite a tradition of keeping the enclave neutral in military terms. Some even thought it possible that, with Beijing in ruins, Shanghai might become China's capital.[17]

There were still other, harder-to-categorize ways in which the crisis affected local life. For example—and this is an issue we will linger on—a debate broke out over whether or not public displays of relief and joy should be held, complete with "illuminations" and parades. Would this be seemly? Would it be safe? These questions were raised and argued about in the local press, showing yet again the danger of thinking of the still small foreign community in Shanghai as a completely unified entity—even in times of crisis. Some popular histories of the city have referred to the foreign reaction to the lifting of the siege and the freeing of the hostages, but in fact there was not one reaction but many.[18] This is revealed clearly by the widely divergent ideas expressed in the editorial and letters—many dealing with a proposed parade—that appeared in the *Herald* on August 29.

There was complete agreement among all contributors to that intriguing edition of the newspaper on two basic points: that it was a great relief that the siege had been lifted, and that it was comforting that a large contingent of foreign troops was now present in China. These writers, however, agreed about little else—including whether the crisis was rapidly coming to as satisfactory a conclusion as anyone could have hoped. The editors and some letter-writers took it for granted that the days of intense worry were finally over, and that the Boxer insurrection would be wrapped up in an efficient manner by the foreign powers. Some letter-writers, though, clearly thought it very likely that more trouble lay ahead. "The dying shrieks of ten thousand Chinese and foreign victims to barbarous treachery and savage hate are still ringing in our ears," one Shanghailander wrote, but already there were signs that the status quo would remain intact rather than be altered. This was because, he claimed, the "old spirit of compromise, which has ruled all Western intercourse with China in the past is insidiously stealing into our newspapers, our diplomacy, our overtures for peace, again." And hence it seemed likely that, as had happened before, the "guilty ones in high places" within the Chinese government would be spared, the only ones punished "common people" who had merely done what their rulers had "incited" them to do.[19] This was not the only letter-writer to insist that, unless harsh punishments were meted out to China's rulers, more horrific events like those that had just been seen were bound to occur. A letter entitled "How to Treat China," for example, endorsed the idea that only by "chopping off the heads" of a great many officials and partitioning the country would foreigners be safe in the future. Its author also claimed it was pure folly to "deal with barbarous hordes" as if they were an "enlightened people."[20]

Another thing that divided contributors to this issue of the *Herald* was their sense of how the local Chinese population felt about the Boxers—or, more particularly, whether Shanghai's "natives" might be prone, in certain circumstances such as a public gathering, to engage in anti-foreign violence.[21] The fear of what local Chinese might do to foreigners, if given the chance, brings us to one of the two main issues at play in the controversy over the proposal to hold celebrations (that never took place in the end) on the streets of Shanghai. (The other issue involved a pair of more generic questions: is it ever appropriate to express joy in the aftermath of an event in which many people had suffered, and if so how long a time of mourning should pass before such expressions are made? To some, as one letter-writer put it, something "more sober and more sorrowful" than a parade was owed to the victims of 1900.[22]) Let us look now, in some detail, at the letters that focussed on fear of what might happen if crowds were allowed to gather in Shanghai, and at some of the responses (in the form of a pair of editorials and a pair of letters) that these provoked.

A good place to start is with a letter signed "Lucellum," which begins with the author stating that "I have not met one person in favour of the proposed illuminations." Lucellum goes on to state several objections to the proposed celebration: seemliness, timing, even economics (the money spent on "thousands of paper lanterns" could be better saved to treat "heroes" wounded in the north). Most of all, though, Lucellum worried that bringing "large crowds into the settlements" at "this time of strained feelings" all around might lead to trouble. "No one will deny that the horrible outrages of the last three months and the fighting they have entailed have caused a very bitter race feeling, and there are those on both sides who would welcome a row."[23]

In contrast to Lucellum's even-handed reference to "bitter race feeling" on both sides, a letter from one Cecil Holliday dated August 26 was only concerned with the way Chinese residents would behave if a celebration was held. The foreign consuls and municipal councils—the celebration was to be a joint production of all of these—were violating a basic "axiom" of good governance by encouraging a "large concourse of persons" to gather at this particular time, Holliday claimed. It was foolish to hold a parade at the "very moment when the minds of our Chinese co-residents are inflamed and excited to the last degree" and "when the whole country is seething with hatred of the foreigners." Moreover, according to Holliday, the "most popular 'catch-penny' in the native city" was "a series of coloured prints representing the slaughter of foreign troops and the decapitation of foreign prisoners before high Chinese officials." Surely, at such a time, it made no sense to "hold a function that will bring, not hundreds or thousands, but tens, possibly even hundreds, of thousands of natives together to deluge the Settlement for many hours during the night." Why invite "a mob to come" and wreak havoc in the Settlement? He admitted that, if the celebrations were held, nothing might happen. But then it is "very possible to sit on an open barrel of gunpowder and smoke a pipe without anything happening." That is not, however, as he put it caustically, "usually considered a prudent proceeding."[24]

Now let us turn to some responses to Lucellum and Holliday that appeared in that same issue. The first thing to note is that a brief comment by the editors was appended to the latter's epistle, which showed that the *Herald* endorsed the plans for a parade. It read simply as follows: "With all respect for Mr. Holliday, who being in a responsible position is naturally anxious, we are entirely unable to share his apprehensions."[25]

Even more interesting are two letters defending the proposed celebrations, each signed "L.H.K." (one dated August 25, the other August 27) that appeared, respectively, between the letters by Lucellum and by Holliday and right after the brief editorial note just quoted. L.H.K.'s first letter did not refer to Lucellum's but did contradict that author's claim to have encountered no one in the community who supported the idea of holding a celebration. On the contrary, this writer argued, there was widespread enthusiasm for staging a parade among all but a few "morbid" souls eager to "spoil our joy." Not just the Municipal Council but "the community" had decided to "rejoice" publicly over the course of recent events. And far from making it more likely that trouble would break out in Shanghai, according to L.H.K., holding a showy "fête," complete with illuminations and displays by the international troops by then present in the area, might have a "good effect upon the rowdies" within the native community. Such an event would put to rest at last misconceptions about the way things had turned out in Beijing. The real danger to the Settlement, this letter insisted, lay in the belief that foreign troops had been defeated as opposed to victorious up north—a belief that was kept alive via talk "in the teahouses" and "pictures sold in the city" that portrayed Chinese soldiers or Boxers as victorious. Adopting the "tearful listless attitude advocated by the objectors would, if adopted by the foreign community, lead the natives to think themselves right in surmising that the foreign troops were utterly beaten." L.H.K. pointed out that those whose "consciences or feelings" precluded them from joining in during the celebrations were free to just "stay away." No one would dream of interfering with their "arrangements or pleasures" (the ability of foreigners to do as they pleased as much as possible was something many Shanghailanders agreed was a basic right). But neither should they be able to prevent the festivities (sure to be "an immense success") from taking place without them.[26]

The same author's second letter—written in direct response to Holliday's epistle—repeated many of the same points but added some new twists. The most interesting one, for our purposes, comes in a paragraph that is designed to demonstrate that the event need not be quite the powder keg that Holliday suggests it was likely to be. (This paragraph also inadvertently reveals much about L.H.K.'s low opinion of many of Shanghai's Chinese residents.) Of course steps would, as they should, be taken to minimize not just the dangerous but also aesthetically unpleasant presence of large Chinese "mobs," this section of the letter stresses. After all, "nobody, the Consuls included, expected or wished in this hot weather to push their way through crowds of half-naked, filthy, vermin-covered coolies." It had been "taken for granted" that only "foreigners and well-dressed Chinese" would be allowed into certain areas during the event, and that a strong police and military presence would be on the scene to keep control of and intimidate native residents.[27]

As previous notes have indicated, the editors of the *Herald* held views very much like L.H.K.'s (though by 1900 they tended to avoid writing about Chinese residents in such explicitly demeaning ways). The editorials on the topic that appeared in that same August 29 edition illustrate this clearly, especially the second one (dated August 28). This began by stating that "as everybody knows" the "two Municipal Councils had arranged" for "illuminations to-night and a torchlight procession to celebrate the relief of Peking."

It was, however, "announced at the last minute that General Creagh, through and with the support of the British Consul-General, Mr. Pelham Warren, and without any consultation with or reference to the French authorities," had "obliged the Council [the SMC] to postpone" the event. No explanation had been offered, but there seemed "little doubt" that fear of an outbreak involving "local rowdies" was behind the decision. The postponement was a worrisome "false step," according to the *Herald*, since the Chinese might assume that the Daotai had "been successful in forbidding the celebration," and this notion would do "far more harm" to foreigners than "local rowdies" could have hoped to do.

What would the celebration have been like if it had taken place? And why did some Shanghailanders consider it so important to seize this moment to hold a public event—or at least avoid the appearance of having been scared out of going through with one once it was planned? To answer these questions, and place the various pieces from the August 29 issue of the *North China Herald* into context, it is important to look at a series of things that happened in the 1890s. The first event worthy of attention is the 1890 visit to Shanghai of their Royal Highnesses the Duke and Duchess of Connaught. For a city with strong ties to Britain, that was eager to establish itself as a world center, the arrival of a son of Queen Victoria and his wife was seen as highly significant. (It was viewed as even more important than the arrival in 1879 of General Ulysses S. Grant, during that former U.S. President's tour around the world.) It provided an opportunity for not just local Britons (though they played the leading role) but also other foreigners in Shanghai to make a positive impression on a pair of visiting dignitaries, who might, with luck, speak well of the city when they returned to Europe.

According to a commemorative album published by the *Shanghai Mercury*, many things were done to encourage the Duke and Duchess to view Shanghai in a positive light. Local leaders gave speeches that typically focussed on what had been accomplished in less that fifty years in the Settlement, and a new statue to a British hero, Sir Harry Parkes, was unveiled in the Public Garden. Different groups presented gifts to the visitors (for example, the local German community presented them with a "huge pagoda of flowers"), and sightseeing tours were arranged. In addition, they were treated to a lavish tiffin at the Shanghai Club, with a menu (reproduced in the commemorative volume, all in French of course) running to many courses. This was attended by leaders of the foreign business and diplomatic communities, their wives, and four Chinese: two Daotais (important local officials), a Magistrate Tsai (from the Mixed Court), and a translator (for one or both of the Daotais). In addition, the two Daotais played host at an evening event that included a Chinese banquet and theatrical performance.[28]

Judging from the admittedly unreliable source at hand (commemorative volumes are not known for their impartiality) all of these things made a positive impression on the Duke and Duchess. But the highlight for all came after the Chinese banquet was over when the royal couple was taken to "Messrs. Jardine, Matheson & Co.'s hong [trading company] to see the Fire Parade, Illuminations and Fireworks." The decorations and displays are described in great detail in the commemorative album. The Duke and Duchess were driven through a "tree-lined avenue" covered with "myriads of lanterns and lit up with coloured fires." The Public Garden, "at all times beautiful," was "rendered an enchanting blaze of

Figure 3.2 The Astor House, Shanghai, 1901. The Astor was where General Grant and other visiting dignitaries from the West often stayed and is probably the "Central Hotel" referred to below. Note the turbaned Sikh constable and the rickshaw in the frame; these were often included in shots of the city intended for Western viewers, not only because of their prevalence in central locations but also because photographers desired to convey succinctly that Shanghai had buildings that looked familiar yet also contained people and vehicles that flagged a location in Asia.

Source: Photograph from G. Waldo Browne's *China: The Country and Its People*, p. 296 (Boston: Dana Estes & Company)

bright colours," some from flowers but others from artifice, "as if nature and art were entering a friendly competition to outshine each other." The "Central Hotel" was "decorated with gas devices," some of them in the shape of the year's number "1870" (a precursor to the famed neon lights of 1930s Shanghai?). And a lively parade was staged by an international array of Fire Brigades, who marched along with the flags of different countries and roman candles and other fireworks going off in their midst. The writers of the volume insisted not just that this was the best display "ever seen in Shanghai" but also—and this reveals the ongoing concern with asserting their community's status as a world-class metropolis—a "spectacle worthy of any city, no matter how large, populous and wealthy."[29]

In this commemorative volume, pride was taken not simply in the beauty of the displays (to which Chinese contributed by making decorations and in some cases marching), but also the way the large numbers of native residents who came to watch the "greatest success that Shanghai has ever witnessed" behaved. "Where else but here," the writers for the *Shanghai Mercury* wondered, "could a crowd of some 200,000 persons be found to give so little trouble?" The police deserved praise for their exertions, but it was the calmness of the Chinese—who "on such occasions could well give a lesson to us Westerners in 'law and order'"—that stood out as one of the truly "remarkable features of a very remarkable day."[30]

Displays similar to those just described (though on a smaller scale) had been seen during Grant's visit and would be seen again a few years later during the Shanghai Jubilee of 1893—this time to accompany not a visit by a foreign dignitary but the passage of a local turning point. There were some differences that time around. For example, a highlight in 1893—again according to commemorative albums—was the launching of particularly creative fireworks by Japanese groups. And of course different mottoes and slogans were spelled out on the streets: in place of 1890's "Young Shanghai welcomes the Scion of Old England," for example, there was 1893's "In what region of the earth is not Shanghai known?" One thing that was constant, however, was the keen participation of Chinese residents in the celebrations, both as participants (some made decorations) and as observers (filling the crowds of parade routes).

There were some signs of tension in 1893, and a reference to ill-feeling even made its way into a generally rosy commemorative text, in the form of an allusion to a Chinese language newspaper that had suggested that only *hanjian* (traitors) embraced the emblems of other countries. (This had been a criticism of a Chinese painter who had put a Western flag on his door, a form of "fulsome flattery" to foreigners.) In addition, a parade by Chinese guilds scheduled to be part of the festivities never took place—though this was due to conflicts between different native-place groups, not with foreigners. And, when the Jubilee Oration was delivered, Chinese were kept back behind a police cordon—symbolizing that even at moments of supposed general community solidarity, distinctions were drawn. Nevertheless, as with the Royal Visit, the Jubilee was thought to show that local Chinese could contribute to the success of festivals organized by foreigners. 200,000 people "turned out" and all of them were "orderly and good-natured"— so much so that "there was not a single charge recorded at the Police Stations," proving the "amenability of the Chinese native when he comes under the influence of firm and friendly control."[31]

These comments on the festivities of 1890 and 1893 give a taste of what might have taken place in 1900 had the celebration gone ahead as planned. They also give a sense of why it might have been construed by some as symbolic of a loss of confidence as well as of a change in the character of local Sino-foreign relations for the August fête to be canceled. The analysis could be extended via closer scrutiny of the 1893 festival. Or it could be extended via careful consideration of Grant's visit. That 1879 occasion had, like the Jubilee and the royal visit of 1890, been a time for "illuminations" (that locals claimed, as they seemed to each time a new celebration was held, exceeded anything seen in the city before) and a parade by firemen. It had been another time for celebratory speeches. (In one of these, a local businessman hoped Grant would "find something to interest" him in the Settlement, "a small commercial republic" that was "as cosmopolitan as the great country" that the former President had once governed.) And it had been an occasion when, as in 1890 and 1893, large crowds of Chinese locals gathered without incident (an estimated one hundred thousand, for example, lined the riverbank when the General first arrived).[32]

But as fascinating as celebratory events such as these (and others such as the marking of foreign national holidays and of Queen Victoria's Jubilees) are for shedding light on the texture of life in Shanghai in the late 1800s, we will now move in a different direction. Not all public events were so little marked by anger, resentment and tension as were these, after all, and it is important to provide some feel for how conflicts played themselves out on the streets just prior to 1900. One way to do this would be to focus on a riot that took place in 1898 and pitted sojourners from Ningbo against the authorities in charge of the French Concession. Sometimes called the "Coffin Riot," this event, like a similar one that broke out between the same two groups in 1874, was triggered by French plans to run a road through ground that the local Ningbo native-place society used for burial purposes.[33] Instead, though, since it was of greater concern to the *North China Herald's* Anglophone readers, whose views have been showcased above, we will look at the Wheelbarrow Riot of April 1897. This was clearly in the back of the minds of some, perhaps most, of the participants in the August 1900 debate over whether to hold a celebration in public.[34]

According to a standard short history of Shanghai by American Shanghailander and one-time St. John's University President F.L. Hawks Pott, the 1897 crisis developed as follows. Early in the year, the foreign Ratepayers (at their annual meeting) voted to authorize the SMC to "raise the price of wheelbarrow licenses." This triggered a strike by "wheelbarrow coolies" (Chinese who made their living using this still important competitor to rickshaws) when the new rate went into effect April 1. Then "for two or three days there were minor disturbances," followed on April 5 by a riot by a "mob" that had amassed in the French Concession and then begun "streaming into the International Settlement." The Shanghai Volunteers (a local militia) went into action and landing parties came ashore from two British ships and one American ship anchored in the harbor. Tensions remained high for several days, even though the "rioters were dispersed."[35]

The next key development came on April 6 when the SMC announced it had retracted the rate hike. Anger toward the Council now began to come from local Westerners. The SMC claimed that it had merely struck a deal with the Daotai in the interests of stability: the rate would go into effect, just not right away, and the Chinese official would guarantee that there would be no trouble when it did. Some foreign ratepayers cried foul, blaming the Council both for doing something that contradicted a decision that the larger group they were supposed to represent had made, and for giving local Chinese the impression that a riot could achieve results. A meeting was held at which a motion was put for all members of the SMC to resign; it passed unanimously; and the Council stepped down en masse.

How do we know that the Wheelbarrow Riot was in some people's minds when the debate on celebrating the end of the siege took place? Because of a comment in the *Herald* editorial "A False Step": "Only three years ago Shanghai was up in arms when the Council of that year gave in to the fear of local rowdies." And there was an irony here. In 1897, Cecil Holliday, who now called for a change of plans to ensure stability, had been "among the most indignant speakers at the indignation meeting" chastising the SMC.[36]

The *Herald*'s dismay over the canceled parade and the 1897 dispute will be interesting to keep in mind as we move forward in the next chapter to 1925— a year when there was a great deal of violence on the streets. It would be misleading, however, to leave 1900 behind without noting that the *Herald* recovered its sense of optimism before that year ended. The opening quotation to this chapter suggests as much. And so does its final editorial of 1900. Yes, the year coming to a close had been a dark one, but the "outlook for the new century" was "brighter." Why? Because the Chinese Government seemed certain to accept whatever peace conditions the foreign powers offered, and local Chinese merchants were "confidently expecting" 1901 to be "a good year for trade."[37]

4 1925: A city in the streets

The weather was unusually close and oppressive on May 31st 1925. At intervals a shower of close-dropped rain would come spilling down, as pitiless as the criminal bullets of the day before, when Shanghai, the great city of the East, had been the scene of a drama that had ripped away the mask of civilization to reveal the beast in man. Now, everything was quiet, and the tall Western-style buildings, which reared up against the sky and looked down unmoved on the boulevards that had yesterday run with blood and been strewn with bodies, seemed to be thinking: it's all past now . . .

[Later, though, Ni Huanzhi heard the sudden] "ding-ling-ling" of bicycles' bells as four or five cyclists came dashing through the heavy rain from west to east and flashed past. Small slips of paper scattered from the riders' hands, fluttering in the hundreds amidst the rain, and falling soaked to the ground in their hundreds. This was an order, the order to assemble, the order to take action! At once the groups of people clustered on the pavements sprang into life; from the sidestreets and alleyways students and workers poured out into the street and began distributing leaflets with the slogans "Help the workers," "Help the Arrested Students," "Take back the Concessions," "Down with the Imperialists," and others of the kind . . . at every street-corner and in front of every store there was someone making a speech to a crowd of citizens who had gathered around to listen . . . An expression of sorrow and anger combined on every face . . .

Ye Shengtao, Ni Huanzhi (a novel), 1929, Chapter 22[1]

There are two famous fictional accounts of the May 30th Movement, the most important Shanghai event of 1925, by leading Chinese writers who joined the Communist movement early on: one is Mao Dun's *Rainbow*, the other Ye Shengtao's *Ni Huanzhi*, the work of someone who is in the eyes of most critics a lesser writer. Still, it is Ye's account of the protests (in a novel named for its schoolteacher protagonist) that is quoted above and will remain of great focus here. Three things make it of particular interest for our purposes. First, its author, like Mao Dun, was an eyewitness to the May 30th struggle.[2] Second, a large segment of Ye's book details the events of 1925 (whereas just a small part of Mao Dun's does), and much attention is given to the fateful day of May 30 itself when members of the British-run Settlement police force fired into an angry but unarmed crowd. Third, and most crucially in light of this book's aims, it is only in Ye's novel that Shanghai as a physical place emerges as a key character, not just a setting where things happened.

This last point is revealed clearly in another passage from *Ni Huanzhi* translated below. The following basic things about the May 30th Movement should be kept in mind when reading it. The stage for the movement had been set by February 1925 strikes at Japanese-run textile mills—factories in which CCP activists had been particularly energetic organizers of unions. The struggle gained momentum in mid-May when a new round of strikes broke out and a fracas took place in which a Chinese worker, Gu Zhenghong, was killed by Japanese nationals. A mass memorial service for the martyr drew a crowd of more than a thousand people. Then, in the final days of May, radical students flooded into the Settlement to distribute pamphlets and give speeches calling for further actions of protest.

The main theme of the protesters was the unjust nature of imperialism, which they claimed harmed Chinese of all classes. The plight of workers in Japanese mills was given special attention, but other issues were brought into play. These included local issues, for example efforts by the Settlement authorities to control Chinese language publications within the enclave. Some of the student propagandists were arrested and taken to the Laozha Police Station. And it was outside that station that the crowds, made up mostly of workers, gathered on May 30 to demand the release of the students.

Figure 4.1 A monument to the worker heroes of the May 30th Movement, located on Nanjing Road

Source: Photograph taken by the author in 2002

Anger intensified as soon as news spread that the Settlement police had fired into a crowd of unarmed protesters (killing four immediately and wounding many others, some of whom would later die). It increased still further during the days that followed when there were additional clashes between protesters and groups of Settlement police (generally Chinese and Sikh constables taking orders from British officers). In early June, a boycott of Japanese and British goods and a *sanba* (triple stoppage: of market activity, labor, and classes) was launched. Here is Ye's description of how life in Shanghai (and Shanghai itself) then changed:

> All of Shanghai's *shimin* (citizens—literally "people of the city") were filled with anger and indignation. There was a great demand every morning for the broadsheets that had temporarily appeared [to carry strike news]. Acts of repression continued to occur, and one method of intimidation after another was employed [to try to break the strike]; as the news of these appeared, the anger and indignation cut deeper than ever into every heart. The gongs and drums became silent in the theatres, and the amusement parks had to close their gates—a sign that no one had a moment to spare for relaxation or amusement, now that a task rested on their shoulders that was infinitely more urgent than the need for such things.
>
> The trams had disappeared from the streets. The trams were the life-blood of the metropolis, and that blood was now still. The ships that came and went between Shanghai and all sorts of ports now stood motionless at their moorings. The ships were the city's organs of digestion and elimination, but now these organs were clogged. And if the stagnation of the circulatory system and of the means of intake and expulsion are not symptoms of death, what are they? This modern metropolis of world importance, Shanghai, which had been built up to its present stature through decades of painstaking work by a band of bloodsuckers, had suddenly become a dead Shanghai.[3]

It was above all the attention to Shanghai as a physical place in passages such as this that led me to choose *Ni Huanzhi* rather than *Rainbow* as a focus for this chapter. We will return at the end of this chapter to Ye's representation of Shanghai and the May 30th Movement. First, however, following the pattern set in the preceding chapter, a look at roads not taken. Let us consider things that might have been placed at the center of our snapshot had 1925 not been, like 1900, a year of blood and fire.

A 1925 miscellany

Aside from May 30th, what happened in 1925? Here is an admittedly idiosyncratic list of four occurrences emblematic of changes of the time:

1   A man who had once been the French Concession's most famous resident died.
2   A new publishing company was founded that would soon gain great fame.

3   A White Russian émigré completed a still-valuable study of Shanghai law and politics.
4   Work began on the Custom House, one of the Bund's signature buildings.

This list is not exhaustive. It passes over one of the 1925 developments that Bergère includes in the chronological appendix to *Histoire de Shanghai*: the birth of the local modernist movement in literature.[4] It does not mention that the world's first international ping pong competition was held in Shanghai.[5] It ignores a demographic milestone: the combined population of the foreign-run enclaves reached one million in 1925. It skips over the end, that January, of a war between regional militarists that had brought an estimated 200,000 refugees streaming into Shanghai. In addition, the list contains no reference to the anniversaries of two famous periodicals. The *North China Herald* turned seventy-five in 1925 (and, not surprisingly, published an editorial celebrating its longevity and grow-ing influence), while *Xin Qingnian* (New Youth), a radical journal known for its criticism of Confucian traditions and its support for literary experiments, turned ten.[6]

Each of these items left off my list could easily have found their way onto it. And the same could be said of some other developments or occurrences. For example, it was in 1925 (or perhaps just before that point: the data we have only list totals at five-year intervals) that a turning point came for Japanese residents of the Settlement. Namely, this group that had been tiny as recently as 1900 began, for the first time, to outnumber Britons by a two-to-one ratio; within a few years it would outnumber them three to one.[7]

Nevertheless, my original list of four events is sufficient for our purposes here. I will take them up in order, starting with the most enigmatically worded item: the death of the man who had been the French Concession's most famous resident.

A former President's days in Shanghai

The person I had in mind was Sun Yat-sen, who moved to the Concession in 1918, setting up house there with his second wife, the American-educated Song Qingling (whose sister, Song Meiling, would later marry Chiang Kai-shek). Due to the international reputation Sun had earned for his role in the 1911 Revolution and his brief tenure as the first President of the new Republic of China (in 1912), it seems safe to say that, from the moment he arrived, he was the Concession's most famous resident.

It is true that Sun died in Beijing and that his mausoleum now stands in Nanjing. It is also true that Sun had, in life and in death, important ties to still other Chinese urban centers. He was educated in Hong Kong, for example, and established his final political base in Canton in the early 1920s. Nevertheless, while Shanghai is not the only city that can lay claim to him, the city played an important role in the last phase of his life. His activities were often discussed in the Shanghai press, especially but not exclusively in those organs controlled by or strongly sympa-thetic to the Nationalist Party and/or the CCP. And the French Concession house in which he and Song Qingling lived has earned a place of honor on the itinerary that the CCP suggest be followed by all patriotic Chinese tourists, and all foreigners interested in revolutionary history. Sun's death on March 12 could thus have made an appropriate starting point for a consideration of Shanghai *circa* 1925. A snapshot organized around Sun could have used any one of several themes as a jumping-off point. For example, it could have focussed on the passionate commentary on the meaning of his life and work that appeared in the local press right after he died.

Surveying this commentary would have helped give the reader a good sense of the range of political viewpoints on display by 1925 in foreign and Chinese newspapers and magazines. There were articles in Chinese and other languages that praised Sun as a visionary who had taken the lead in transforming China into a Republic. But there were also editorials and commentaries—again in Chinese as well as other languages—which denounced him as a dangerous figure. Particularly worrisome in the eyes of denunciatory writers was his recent decision to have his Nationalist Party (GMD) work with the CCP and his growing coziness with advisors from the Soviet Union. (These moves by Sun had been inspired in part by Moscow's renunciation of all the privileges that Czarist Russia had gained via the unequal treaties of the 1800s and the Boxer Protocol of 1901.)

A second starting point for a snapshot chapter based on Sun could have been the mourning activities that took place in Shanghai in the wake of his death, which are detailed in a history of the city's student movement. The day after he died, this work claims, representatives of dozens of local radical groups gathered outside the fallen leader's Shanghai residence to express their grief. Then, on April 12, a mass memorial meeting drew a crowd of one hundred thousand people. Sponsors included "the Shanghai branch of the GMD, the National Student Union, the Shanghai Student Union," and also Shanghai University—an institution whose faculty included many people who were already or would soon emerge as leaders of the CCP. Speeches were delivered and then the throng marched through the city.[8]

Finally, and perhaps most fittingly given the purpose of this book, a chapter organized around the Nationalist Party leader could have used his time in Shanghai as an excuse to explore the ambivalent love–hate relationship that intellectuals of a certain type had with the city. The category of people I have in mind, one to which both Sun and Song definitely belonged, was made up of political activists and literary figures who might best be dubbed "cosmopolitan nationalists."

These were people about whom two things could be said. First, they were critical of imperialism and viewed the unequal treaties and the existence of foreign-run enclaves as a source of national humiliation. Second, however, they were anything but parochial or xenophobic. They had a familiarity with and fondness for foreign cultures, or at least specific elements of those cultures, many of them having spent time abroad as students or workers.

A very high percentage of these cosmopolitan nationalists lived in Shanghai for at least part of the first quarter of the twentieth century, while others such as Lu Xun (who settled in the city in 1927) moved there a short time after our snapshot year. These were people who had a degree of fluency in at least one foreign language. Some were converts to Christianity (as was Sun), while a few (such as Song) had been Christians from childhood. They were people who were likely to enjoy some or all of the following: Russian poetry, German classical music, American movies, Viennese-style cafés, French novels, and Japanese clothing styles. They would think nothing of attending or hosting a dinner that included people of varied nationalities, such as one at which Sun met a visiting John Dewey. And they might well relax by playing an imported game (Sun and Song liked croquet).[9]

Yet another thing that many cosmopolitan nationalists who lived for a time in Shanghai during this period had in common was admiration for a particular Western thinker. This might be the aforementioned Dewey, a great influence on Hu Shi (who studied with the American pragmatist at Columbia). It might be one of Dewey's British counterparts such as Bertrand Russell (who visited China in 1920, stopping in Shanghai to give a series of lectures) or Henry George (whose vision of socialism had a strong effect on Sun).[10] Or, of course, it might be the German Karl Marx or the Russian V.I. Lenin. This was the case with Qu Qiubai and Cai Hesen, to cite but two of many possible examples.

Qu, who taught at Shanghai University in the mid-1920s, was one of the first leaders of the CCP. He had gained fame early within radical circles, thanks to going to Russia right after the Bolsheviks took power and sending back a series of positive reports on life in the new system that were published in China. He also got a chance to meet Lenin himself while abroad. Qu, who developed a reputation as a suave dresser and generally was something of a dandy, regularly contributed political articles to *Xin Qingnian* and other CCP periodicals such as *Xiangdao Zhoubao* (the Guide Weekly). He was also an active translator of foreign works, including, most famously, a song, "L'Internationale," that had already begun to serve as the global anthem of the Communist movement. While at Shanghai University, Qu married Yang Zhihua, who became an important force within the local labor and women's movements.

Cai was very different from Qu in some ways but similar to him in others. Cai studied in France as opposed to Russia, and while there earned a reputation for being unconcerned with his personal appearance (allegedly only washing and changing his clothes occasionally). But like Qu he married someone who would become a major feminist voice within the CCP, Xiang Jingyu. According to Steve Smith, they met abroad and their 1920 "wedding photograph," taken in Montargis, shows the couple "sitting side by side, holding a copy of *Das Kapital*." After being kicked out of France for their role in a student protest, they settled in Shanghai, where Cai wrote regularly for many of the same journals to which Qu contributed.[11]

Shanghai, to people of the sort just described, whether or not they were Marxists or communists, was an alluring place to live for many reasons. One attraction of the metropolis was purely pragmatic. The division of the city into multiple jurisdictions meant that if one's activities (say, publishing a radical newspaper) attracted the attention of a given police force, one could easily move to another district and go on with what one had been doing. Another attraction was the ready availability of foreign products. For those who had developed a taste for Russian borscht, French bread, Austrian pastries, or Japanese sashimi, Shanghai was a very good place to live. Similarly, for those who liked to read Dickens and Zola and keep up with new work that was being written in Japan or translated into Japanese, Shanghai was the best Chinese city in which to reside.

In addition to this, if one wanted an opportunity to listen to speeches by, or perhaps even get a chance to meet, major foreign intellectual figures, it was advantageous to be located either in Beijing or in Shanghai. We have already seen that both Dewey and Russell passed through, but they were hardly isolated cases. For example, one of the most exciting Shanghai events of 1924 (for local intellectuals at least) was the arrival of the Indian philosopher and poet Rabindranath Tagore, who, like Russell, was a winner of the Nobel Prize. His stay in Shanghai began with a reception sponsored by local publishing houses and other groups that was attended by more than 1,200 people.[12] Many other cases could be cited to show just how firmly "on the map" for globetrotting intellectuals Shanghai had become by the mid-1920s. Famous visits by Shaw, Isherwood, Auden, and Coward would have to wait until the 1930s, but two renowned European novelists, Vicente Ibáñez (about whom more below) and Aldous Huxley, arrived in the mid-1920s.

Despite the allure Shanghai held for them as a place to live, many cosmopolitan nationalists fixed on it as a symbol of national humiliation in their writings. Consider a piece that Cai Hesen wrote in November 1923, exactly thirty years after the Jubilee festivities described in the last chapter. Foreigners were preparing to celebrate the eightieth anniversary of the implementation of the Treaty of Nanjing, Cai wrote, but this was not a joyous occasion for Shanghai's Chinese residents. Prior to 1843, "every stone and every blade of grass" in Shanghai had belonged to them, but now there were parks they couldn't even enter. Nor could Chinese vote or stand for office in the enclaves. Cai, a leader of the CCP, not surprisingly went on to introduce issues of class. A Chinese merchant who allowed a foreign-run body to use his taxes as it pleased, he said, was one who proved himself willing to be "the dog of the foreigners."[13]

A 1924 speech by Sun made similar points, without the class struggle angle but with the additional grievance thrown in that Chinese could not even enter the grounds of some leading Shanghai clubs. Sun argued that Shanghai's exclusionary rules proved that China's current status was best seen as "subcolonial" not merely "semi-colonial." In fully colonial Hong Kong, he argued, the Chinese were the "slaves" of one set of foreigners, but at least Britain showed some concern for its colonial subjects. In Shanghai's enclaves, the Chinese were simply the slaves of all foreigners. In Hong Kong, Sun claimed, he could enter all the parks. And he could also meet his foreign friends for dinner at the best clubs in that colonial metropolis.[14]

This divide between Shanghai's attractions as a place to live and its status as an emblem of national humiliation made the relationship between cosmopolitan nationalists and the city a complex and ambiguous one. This was especially true since most chose to live not in the Chinese-run part of the metropolis but in one of its enclaves. In general, the French-run part of the city seems to have appealed to them most of all. This was due to a combination of factors. One was the comparative laxness of the local authorities, which made the Concession a haven for gangsters and radicals alike.[15] Another was that cosmopolitan nationalists who had studied in Europe were likely to find it a particularly enticing part of the city.

This was probably true of Cai Yuanpei, for example, whose French Concession home has recently been added to the city's itinerary of revolutionary sites. Cai is best known as the one-time president of Beijing University but he also played key roles in Shanghai schools early in the 1900s. In addition, a recent work by Jonathan Spence tells us two other intriguing details about his life that substantiate his status as a cosmopolitan nationalist with Shanghai ties. First, Cai was studying philosophy in Germany when the 1911 Revolution broke out, but rushed home to serve the nation as the new Republic's first minister of education. Second, in 1927, while living in Shanghai, he officiated at the Chinese wedding ceremony (there was also a separate Christian one) of Chiang Kai-shek and Song Meiling, which was held in a local ballroom.[16]

There were also cosmopolitan nationalists who preferred to live in the International Settlement. The Hongkou section of the Settlement, which became known as "Little Tokyo," for example, was home to two renowned writers who have already been mentioned above. One was Mao Dun, who worked at Shanghai's famous Commercial Press in many capacities, including that of translator, in the early 1920s, and was among the relatively few famous cosmopolitan nationalists never to study abroad. The other was Lu Xun. Unlike Mao Dun, he never joined the CCP but rather tried to carve out an independent radical position that did not adhere to any single party line. And, again unlike his friend Mao Dun, he did study abroad, in Japan. One thing that seems to have drawn Lu Xun to that particular district, in fact, is that he had a large number of Japanese friends and he had spent a formative part of his youth in Tokyo. He apparently was especially fond of the area's Japanese bookstores, and Joshua Fogel tells us of a visit that the writer made to one of the most famous of these in Hongkou just two days after moving to Shanghai.[17]

The Hongkou houses in which these two writers lived in the 1920s have each been restored and preserved as sites for political and literary pilgrims. Other nearby sites are devoted to Lu Xun's memory, his tomb and a museum dedicated to the great iconoclastic author. Although only Mao Dun joined the CCP, it is his friend who has been sanctified more forcefully since 1949, as evidenced by the lack of a Mao Dun museum in Shanghai. The fact that Lu Xun wrote scathingly about the Nationalists and was a powerful critic of imperialism has made the CCP's lionization of him possible. And the consensus among many critics, Chinese, Japanese, and Western alike, that he was China's greatest twentieth-century writer has made it understandable.[18] The different evaluations of Mao Dun and Lu Xun are reflected in the greater attention paid to the latter's presence in Shanghai not merely in official tourism but also in some of the unofficial varieties that have now become prevalent. One anecdotal illustration of this comes from a visit I made to the city in June 2002. I saw no restaurants celebrating Mao Dun in Shanghai on that trip, but I dined at a new one in Pudong that serves dishes from Lu Xun's hometown (Shaoxing) and contains at its entrance a statue of the eponymous lead character of one of his best-known short stories (Kong Yiji).[19]

A publishing house, a book, and a building

The publishing house I had in mind for the second item on my list of four was one whose best-known product was Shanghai's most famous Republican-era pictorial magazine *Liangyou huabao* (The Friendly Companion). This magazine, which has recently attracted a great deal of attention from scholars interested in popular culture, did not begin its run until 1926. Nevertheless, as Leo Lee notes in *Shanghai Modern*, the publishing house that bore the same name as the magazine (and became the leading rival to the Commercial Press) was founded in 1925.[20]

Liangyou Press immediately began publishing works that, like the pictorial that became its flagship product, were devoted largely to fashion and popular entertainment. Its periodicals included movie magazines and books that were designed, at least in part, to make Shanghainese conversant with the elements of new *modeng* (modern) lifestyles and worldwide trends in the popular arts. The press's arrival on the Shanghai scene in 1925 is thus both fitting and revealing. Why? Because the mid-1920s were a time when the ongoing love affair between Shanghai's Chinese population and Hollywood films was taking off and local movie production was shifting into high gear. It was also a time when local Chinese with money to spend were starting in growing numbers to revel in activities such as ballroom dancing and jazz, wear European and Japanese fashions, and enjoy cafés. Liangyou was both a product of this new cosmopolitanism and a shaper of it. Liangyou publications, which often had words from foreign languages sprinkled through their texts and reprinted photographs from foreign newspapers, fit perfectly in this milieu.[21]

The important book by a White Russian émigré that appeared in 1925 (item three on my list) was Anatole Kotenev's *Shanghai: Its Mixed Court and Council*, which was published by the North China Herald. (This work has already been cited in the previous chapter as a basic source for the history of Shanghai legal affairs.) Kotenev, who served in the Shanghai Municipal Police for a time, went on to write other books that remain of use to this day, including *Shanghai: Its Municipality and the Chinese* (North China Herald publishers, 1927). That sequel of sorts to *Shanghai: Its Mixed Court and Council* contained a large section devoted to the May 30th bloodshed and the judicial reviews and trials as well as mass actions that followed that event.

Both of these two books were made up largely of official documents and excerpts from the press, as well as some narrative additions and interpretive comments by the author. Given the fact that the author was no friend of Bolshevism and was writing for a publisher that, as we have seen, tended to be supportive of the basic structures of foreign privilege, these Kotenev volumes are surprisingly even-handed and moderate in tone. The same could not be said for many other

North China Herald publications of the day, including a series of Red Scare pamphlets and a Chinese-language supplement, *Chengyan* (True Words). The latter was issued during the May 30th Movement and was devoted exclusively to denouncing all strike activities as the work of nefarious Soviet agents and unscrupulously opportunistic Chinese labor leaders.[22]

Just as the founding of the Liangyou publishing house could have been used as the starting point for a snapshot chapter on the increasing importance of new modes of entertainment, the Kotenev book could have been used as the starting point for one that surveyed the increasing importance in Shanghai of White Russians. In simple numbers, the increased presence within the enclaves of Russians (as of Japanese) was striking in the period in question. There were only 47 of them in the Settlement in 1900, for example, but 1,766 by 1925. In the French Concession, meanwhile, there were 210 Russians in 1920 but 1,403 by 1925 (and more than four times that number by 1932).[23]

One person who would certainly deserve mention in such a chapter would be the Russian émigré cartoonist Georgii Avksent'ievich Sapajnikoff, a former lieutenant in the Russian Imperial Army who used the *nom de plume* Sapajou. He came to Shanghai in 1920 but did not begin his famous stint at the *North China Daily News* and the *North China Herald* until our snapshot year. Some of his drawings dealt with political issues, but many (such as ones that portrayed cocktail parties) played upon and added new twists to standard Shanghailander visions of the city and its people.[24]

Leaving aside individuals, a snapshot chapter organized around the increasing presence of White Russians might dwell on the roles that young female émigrés played in Shanghai's nightlife, and in popular representations of that nightlife. The 1920s and 1930s are often seen as the heyday of Shanghai hedonism, and White Russian women (including the character "Shanghai Lil" whom Marlene Dietrich played in *Shanghai Express*) have long figured centrally in treatments of that aspect of the city's past. Here, for example, is novelist Vicente Ibáñez writing about a visit to Shanghai in the 1920s:

> Besides being famous throughout the Far East for its industries and the activity of its port, Shanghai represents to those who know the East a city of pleasure and reckless spending. The electric lights of its Fou-Tcheou [Fuzhou] Road shine brilliantly until dawn, and all night long its restaurants are open, and its cafés, and gambling houses, and other houses which I need not describe . . . There is nothing to be compared with a night on the famous avenue known as Fou-Tcheou Road. Here one may find women from all countries, and every language known. The Russian upheaval sent to Shanghai a great flood of red-haired, green-eyed women, emotional, neurotic, and semi-savage, all at the same time. European courtesans are here in great numbers, side by side with their Chinese competitors . . .[25]

One general theme for a chapter on White Russians, which would allow us to link the mark that Kotenev and Sapajou made with their publications and the activities of the "semi-savage" women of Ibáñez's imagination, is the way lines between "East" and "West" increasingly blurred during the early 1900s. The distinction had never been as clear in Shanghai as some Shanghailanders and Chinese officials would have us believe. This was due to the presence within the city from the 1840s on of groups whose members defied simple categorization along an east–west axis (such as Iraqi Jews and Sikhs who were turbaned subjects of the British Empire). There were also by the late 1800s a fair number of local residents (though how many is unclear) who were neither clearly Chinese nor clearly non-Chinese: Eurasian children with one Chinese parent. And, reflecting these and other cases of blurred boundaries, there was always a tension within the foreign-run enclaves over issues of social and cultural differentiation. This showed through in such ways as the rules stipulating that Japanese should be allowed access to some spaces that were off-limits to Chinese, but only if they wore Western clothing while in those areas. Still, the rapid increase in the size of the local Japanese population and the nearly simultaneous influx of large numbers of Russians in the 1920s changed the situation dramatically. Any illusion that there were clear and unambiguous dividing lines had to be abandoned.

In light of this, one way to think about White Russian writers of this era is that their works were in part an effort to assert or solidify their Shanghailander identity. This was a pressing issue because at the time there were some Shanghailanders who were concerned by the number of White Russians who had begun to fit into occupational and social niches that had previously been reserved for or taken up mostly by local Chinese. Once White Russians arrived on the scene, it was suddenly no longer the case that the beggars one saw on the streets were bound to be Chinese, since they could also be foreigners, even ones with relatively light skin. And there was also, as Ibáñez's account underscores, much more of a mixture of Europeans and non-Europeans in the many fields of entertainment and sex-work that proliferated in Shanghai.

These blurred boundaries opened up a new maneuvering space for members of the Shanghainese elite. They had been struggling for decades to convince foreigners to let their class trump their race in certain instances (so that, for example, "respectable" Chinese would be granted the access to public spaces that Westerners and non-Chinese Asians were allowed). Beginning in the 1920s, they could, and did, make the argument that, surely, they were more entitled to be treated as full-fledged citizens of the enclaves than the poorest (or least "respectable") of the new arrivals from Russia. A countervailing trend was that some émigrés, hoping to gain acceptance within the Shanghailander community, went to great lengths to demonstrate their own respectability. The cases of Sapajou (who became one of the rare members of the Shanghai Club who was neither Western European nor American) and Kotenev are relevant here.

Perhaps the most telling illustration of this phenomenon of all, however, involves another Russian who began publishing works about Shanghai a bit later. I am thinking here of I.I. Kounin, who is best known for a history of the Shanghai Volunteer Corps he wrote. One of his other publications took the form of that most quintessentially Victorian of works: a Jubilee commemorative album. He put together this volume to mark the 1938 diamond jubilee of the International Settlement (which had been founded in 1853).[26]

Finally, we come to the fourth item on my list: the building of the Custom House whose clock tower is a recognizable part of so many photographs of the Bund taken between the late 1920s and the present. Lynn Pan aptly describes this edifice as "[p]residing over the bustle of the Huangpu quayside," and tells us that it replaced an earlier Tudor-style Custom House [on the same spot] that had "looked as though it had been lifted straight out of England."[27]

According to a recent pictorial history of the Bund, work on the new Custom House began in 1925 and was mostly completed in 1927 with the final addition, in 1928, of a set of Greek Doric temple-style columns at its front entrance. This same book states that it contained the largest clock to be found anywhere in Asia.[28] Tour books of the 1930s and the present day alike routinely refer to it as one of Shanghai's most noteworthy examples of early twentieth-century architecture. And architectural histories of the city routinely single it out as one of the most impressive local buildings of its time.[29] Of particular interest for our purposes here is that nearly all the tall structures now associated with the Bund were built around this same time. Some were completed a little earlier in the 1910s or the

Figure 4.2 The Bund *circa* 1930. A classic framing of the waterfront, with the Winged Victory statue on the right (the only key landmark shown that is no longer in place), the half-shown domed Hongkong and Shanghai Bank on the far left, and the clock-towered Custom House and pyramid-topped Cathay Hotel between

Source: Postcard from the author's collection

first years of the 1920s, for instance the headquarters of the Hongkong and Shanghai Banking Corporation that stood beside the Custom House. Others would be completed later, for example the tallest part of what is now the Peace Hotel, which was known as the Cathay when it opened in 1929.[30]

Why is it so interesting to note that the foreign businessmen of the Settlement sponsored major construction projects not just before but also after 1925? Because this year is often singled out as marking the beginning of the end of the treaty-port system. The May 30th Movement, during which "Take Back the Concessions" became a central cry, is routinely said to illustrate the strength of Chinese nationalism. And it is often described as having rejuvenated the Nationalist Party and transformed the CCP from a minor to a major force in Chinese politics. These things may be true, but what the architectural history of the city shows is that even if the die was cast by 1925 this was not something that all Shanghailanders realized by any means. When they supported grand construction projects, they were hardly behaving like people who thought their days in the city were numbered.

We see here a classic illustration of the crucial difference that Paul Cohen has described between history as event, myth, and experience. In the long run, as *events* the radical protests of 1925 definitely had a profound impact on Shanghai (and indeed all of China). And, when turned into *myth*, they have often been presented as marking the crucial turning point in an epic struggle between good and evil, in which larger-than-life heroes figured prominently. Yet, in the realm of *experience*, things were different. Unlike today's historians, elite Shanghailanders of the day did not know what would happen in 1937, 1941, and 1949. As their buildings show, some viewed May 30th as representing an important challenge to their authority but hardly the beginning of the end of their way of life.[31]

May 30th reconsidered

> Yet what was dead [that June] was only the monstrous city itself. There was something present that was *not* dead, but was, rather, overflowing with the vitality of green shoots bursting forth in springtime. There was something increasing in vigor inside this corpse. This growing thing was a fervent devotion to the nation and a desire to sacrifice all one had in the service of the nation!
>
> Ye Shengtao, *Ni Huanzhi*[32]

This passage, which follows directly upon the last one quoted in the opening section of this chapter, takes us from the realm of experience into that of myth. More specifically, it introduces the dominant CCP vision of May 30th as a struggle that helped awaken the people of the nation to the injustices of class oppression and imperialism. This approach to May 30th as a combined class-based struggle and national struggle has informed innumerable works of hagiography and popular history produced in the PRC. And many of the best works of scholarship dealing with May 30th, by Chinese and Western scholars alike, have also stressed its pivotal role in the development of either the Chinese labor movement or Chinese mass nationalism.[33]

While the movement was unquestionably in large part about the meaning of class and about nationalism, in its local manifestations—related strikes and boycotts swept through all of China—it was also about what it meant to be a *shimin* (citizen) of Shanghai. If we look at the demands articulated by Shanghai groups and even the causes of conflict between Shanghai protesters and Shanghai police, we see a continual combining of class-based, generically national, and much more city-related issues. Some gatherings were called *Guomin dahui* (Assemblies of Citizens of the Nation), others *Shimin dahui* (Assemblies of the People of the City). Some protest groups included the term *guomin*, others *shimin*. And while the two terms were sometimes used almost interchangeably as referents to citizens, there was often a subtle distinction worth recapturing that is lost if they are both simply translated via use of the same English word.[34]

The mistreatment of Chinese workers by Japanese mill-owners and the killing of Chinese protesters by a foreign-run police force were seen as affronts to every worker or every Chinese person. But some aspects of the struggle were seen as especially relevant to the citizens of Shanghai (Shanghai *shimin*). For example, it was felt as a special slight to them that, even though Shanghai was their city, the foreign authorities in charge of the enclaves prevented them from coming and going within it as they wished. One goal of some actions taken by protesters was to assert their right to gather and speak out in whatever part of the city they chose. This, as well as the insertion of Shanghai-specific demands (such as the end of the Mixed Court system) into lists of grievances, led the local and the national to become inextricably entwined.

A final local May 30th phenomenon to note, as we end our look at 1925, is that many of those who played leading roles in Shanghai protests were cosmopolitan nationalists of the sort referred to in an earlier section of this chapter, in fact often the very people discussed. Some gave speeches at mass rallies; some wrote pamphlets for distribution on the streets; and some started newsletters of the sort that Ye Shengtao described the *shimin* as eagerly reading during the days of the general strike. A few cosmopolitan nationalists, such as Qu Qiubai, did all of these things. And some also took the lead in establishing new organizations. Xiang Jingyu, for example, was a leading force behind the founding of the Shanghai Women's Association, which held its first rally on June 5.

Moreover, if a memoir by Zhong Fuguang, who chaired that group's inaugural meeting, is to be believed, both partners of the city's most famous cosmopolitan nationalist couple played an inspirational role in that June 5 women's association event, even though one of them, Sun Yat-sen, had died months earlier. Zhong describes being deeply moved by catching sight of Song Qingling "sitting in the middle of the first row" on June 5. This inspired Zhong to quote a famous line of Sun's about the need to struggle for "liberty and equality" no matter how long it took to reach these goals. Zhong then went on as follows: "Now, we women from all ranks of life have united together, it is a pity that Sun Yat-sen is not with us! But we must convert our sorrow into strength and follow the last words of Sun

Yat-sen to unite and carry on the battle against the imperialists!" She "could not help crying" as she spoke and saw "tears glistening in Song Qingling's eyes."[35] We will leave May 30th here, with this vignette that resonates so powerfully with mythic visions of the time, yet is presented to us as a straightforward representation of one person's heartfelt experience.

5 1950: An in-between year

It has been an event-packed, fast-moving year since Shanghai awoke from a nightmare of oppression and took up its new life as part of liberated China. For this we owe undiminishing gratitude to our People's Liberation Army.

This has been a year of learning. We have learned about ourselves. We have learned about our city. We have learned about the future . . . What have we learned of our city?

We have found that the eyes of the nation are on Shanghai. We have become a symbol of the struggle against the dead weight of imperialism and the cynicism of bureaucratic capitalist speculation. These blights have ridden the backs of our workers and citizens almost from the very first day of Shanghai's existence. The rest of the country knows how deeply embedded is the rot of these blights [and all Chinese encourage] us as we struggle to make this a people's city . . . [During the last year] more and more people have come to believe in the new Shanghai to be. They have come to believe in the plans of the people's government. For it becomes clear to them that we can defeat imperialism and reaction. It becomes clear that Shanghai can belong to China and to our people. That is what we have learned about our city after one year of liberation.

Song Qingling, "Shanghai's New Day has Dawned," 1950[1]

As noted in the last chapter, when historians try to recapture the meaning of any particular moment, one challenge is always to take into account fully the degree to which people living through that point in history were ignorant of what was going to happen next. This was worth remembering in the case of our last snapshot year, 1925, lest we fall into the trap of assuming that Shanghailanders took for granted that the treaty-port system would soon unravel. It is equally worth remembering, though for a different reason, when thinking about 1950. In this case, the danger is that we will assume, since we know what followed in the era of high Maoism, which lasted from the mid-1950s through to the Chairman's death in 1976, that nearly everything about life in Shanghai suddenly changed when the Communists took power in 1949. And increasing the danger of falling into this trap is the fact that so much rhetoric at the time claimed that just such a complete rupture had occurred. The speech quoted above, which Song Qingling delivered on the first anniversary of the People's Liberation Army's (PLA) May 1949 arrival,

Figure 5.1 Part of a frieze in Huangpu Park commemorating patriotic and revolutionary
            events in Shanghai and China's modern history. This section shows well-to-do
            local residents welcoming the People's Liberation Army with open arms,
            smiling faces, and flowers upon their 1949 arrival in Shanghai

Source: Photograph taken by the author in 1999

was the most widely circulated 1950 text to claim that a chasm separated the new
Communist-run Shanghai from the city that existed up until the troops came in,
but it was far from the only one.[2]

The images of renewal and rebirth invoked in her speech were common in texts
of the time produced by members of the Communist Party, as well as by people
who had not joined that organization, yet welcomed the end of corrupt Nationalist
Party rule. (Song fell into this latter category: though she held various official
positions, such as "Vice Chairman, The Central People's Government"—the post
by which she was identified in Shanghai newspapers in 1950—she would not
become a CCP member until 1981.) These writers insisted that a completely new
Shanghai, not just a city ruled by a different organization, had suddenly come
into being. Meanwhile, there were in 1950 many others who hated or harbored
deep suspicions of the Communist Party and put the opposite spin on the situation.
For them, May 1949 marked not a moment of Liberation and transition from
"nightmare" into wakefulness but a descent into darkness. They spoke a language
not of rebirth but of illness and decay. An article in *Time* (a periodical owned
by Henry Luce, who had long been and remained fiercely partisan toward Chiang
Kai-shek and Song Meiling), for example, referred to Shanghai's "paralysis" under
the Communists, and presented it as a "slowly dying city."[3] And around the same
time, the headline writers at the London *Times* put the phrase "DYING CITY" (in
caps) at the top of a story about the port.[4]

Increasing this sense of the city in 1950 being separated completely from what it had been before the PLA "liberated" or "conquered" it is the fact that many people in later years would follow the lead of either Song Qingling (who by 1949 had become politically estranged from her sister, Meiling) or *Time*. Some of the post-1950 popular histories and guidebooks that elaborated on the theme of Shanghai being changed dramatically for the better and starting a glorious "new life" in 1949, transformed instantly from a depraved to a "healthy" city, will be discussed in the next chapter, so we can pass over them here.[5] But two later books that invoked contrasting imagery are worth mentioning, beginning with *Shanghai Saga*, a 1963 work by nostalgic Shanghailander John Pal, who described thus the city's sudden downward spiral:

> Steeped in a tradition of gunfire, most Shanghailanders decided to stay put [in the late 1940s] as Chiang Kai-shek was being driven out. Other Chinese leaders in the past had been driven out. Perhaps this was just another change-over . . . [But what they soon] witnessed [was] the rapid disintegration of a once proud and mighty city. Its throbbing business life all but dried up; its gay social life gave way to Red culture—lectures, propaganda, brain-washing and the firing squad.[6]

A second notable work in this vein, the title of which tells us much about its vision of 1949, much as Song's "Shanghai's New Day Has Dawned" lets us know how she views 1950, is Noël Barber's *The Fall of Shanghai*, which was published in separate British and American editions in 1979. The subtitle to the British edition, "Communist Take-Over in 1949," encourages the reader to think of the term "fall" as referring primarily to the military actions and transfer of power that had taken place thirty years before the book's publication.[7] The subtitle of the American edition, "the splendor and squalor of the imperial city of trade, and the 1949 revolution that swept an era away," encourages the reader to think of the change in much broader terms.[8] In both cases, though, to speak of Shanghai "falling" in 1949 is very different from referring to it being born anew.

Even though images of total transformation, for good or for ill, were certainly in the air at the time and have often been invoked in later re-creations of our snap-shot year, the focus here will be on the strong case to be made for seeing 1949 as something more complicated than a watershed date dividing the city that had existed prior to that year from a completely different one that suddenly came into being—and for treating 1950 as an in-between time. It was not just a year that saw the first anniversary of the inauguration of a new political order marked with parades and speeches (Song's being one of them), but also a year of continued uncertainty in many quarters about just how thoroughgoing a remake of the metropolis the Communist Party would attempt, and how soon it would try to implement some of its bolder programs. It was also a year that can be seen, in retrospect, as marked by continuities with the past as well as ruptures, whether or not these were acknowledged as such at the time.

This chapter will try to recapture the open-ended nature of 1950 and its links to preceding years by looking at several different texts. These will include newspaper articles that were published either in 1950 or, in one case, in May 1951—but that article looks backwards to survey events of the previous two years. Also discussed will be a book that the editors of the *Dagongbao* newspaper prepared in 1950, but that was not actually published until 1951, *Xin Shanghai bianlan* (A Guide to New Shanghai), as well as memoirs by two people, Shirley Wood and Lynn Pan, who look back in very different ways to their time in the city in the late 1940s and early 1950s.[9]

A year of uncertainty

One reason to think that 1950 was an in-between year is that not all Westerners had left by the time it started, and some of them stayed put while it ran its course, though as the year wore on more and more did attempt to depart. In mid-1949 and even early 1950, a fair number of Europeans and Americans, including missionaries and businessmen, seemed to think, as Pal notes, that the arrival of the Communists might trigger just a minor shift in how business was done. They had, after all, seen the end of the treaty-port system in 1943, and yet had been able, in many cases, to live much as they had before, once the Nationalists reclaimed Shanghai from the Japanese in 1945, even though there was no longer an International Settlement or a French Concession.

Just as many Westerners thought they could find ways to continue doing business in a Shanghai governed by the Communist Party, a wait-and-see attitude also seemed logical in our snapshot year to many Chinese middle-class and professional families. To be sure, some Chinese merchants and financiers and their dependants fled to Hong Kong, Taiwan, or the West in the immediate wake of the PLA's arrival—indeed some had begun to head to those locales a bit earlier, once the Communist victory on the mainland began to seem inevitable. And the city's most famous gangster, Due Yuesheng, headed to Hong Kong before May 1949 as well, assuming, no doubt correctly, that he would be better able to prosper in that British Crown Colony than in a "Red" Shanghai in which, among other things, his connections to Nationalist Party leaders would no longer protect him.[10] But other Chinese with links to capitalism, Christianity, or both of these things stayed on after May 1949 and in many cases throughout 1950 and beyond, despite the CCP's Marxist ideology and the rumors that had circulated about its antipathy to all forms of religion. And it was not uncommon for middle-class families to hedge their bets—as Hong Kong families would almost fifty years later, as that city's transition from Crown Colony to part of the PRC drew near—and have some members stay put to see what the new order would be like and protect the family's home or factory, while other members set off for other cities to try to establish connections in a new locale.

Some of those who stayed behind quickly began to regret their decision, but the gradualness with which some transformations took place late in 1949 and during the opening months of the 1950s meant that many others did not immediately feel that they had misjudged the situation. For example, while the economy certainly began to change soon after May 1949, as the Communists brought a firmer hand to the control of business, not all factories were nationalized. Similarly, though a more austere vision of appropriate lifestyles started to take hold, so that fewer luxury goods were produced and offered for sale in a city formerly known for its extravagant ways, Western-style clothing did not by any means immediately disappear from department store shelves.

Two very different memoirs—one by an American woman married to a Chinese man when the Communists took power, the other by a Chinese woman who was a small child in 1949—evoke a shared sense of the period immediately follow- ing the arrival of the PLA as a time of incremental changes. This is true even though the former, Wood's *A Street in Shanghai*, ends up celebrating the trans- formations that unfolded in the early 1950s, while the latter, Pan's *Tracing It Home: A Chinese Family's Journey from Shanghai*, looks back with regret at what was lost as the character of the city was altered. The following excerpts from the books draw attention both to this contrast in attitude and to the common emphasis on the gradual nature of the shifts taking place.

Here, for example, is how Shirley Wood ends her chapter titled "Liberation," which earlier on has traced the sense of excited anticipation with which people in her neighborhood greeted news that the PLA was heading toward and then had taken control of Shanghai:

> The day passed in quiet, and we finally went to sleep half hoping to be wakened at midnight by just a little mild excitement, but we were undisturbed and the next morning shutters were being taken off the shops and stalls set out on the sidewalks again, and even the Loochow Road market was leafing out as the more venturesome of the farmers from the suburbs trudged into town with their barrows of green vegetables. The chaotic, whirling sea which had pounded up into a mountainous crest broke with so little bubble that people sat back and blinked, almost in disappointment. Then Shanghai's citizens went back to their ordinary daily activities as they had done through a hundred years of crises.[11]

Subsequent chapters describe noteworthy developments that alter the character of daily life. Wood describes, for example, the rising importance of committees that were charged with or took upon themselves the task of "mobilizing the city's residents" for different causes and enforcing new norms of behavior related to everything from gender equality to the kinds of rents that landlords could charge.[12] Still, the dominant impression she gives is of a mixture of continuity and change, of patterns of daily life shifting, generally in positive ways in her view, but doing so bit by bit.

Lynn Pan, whose businessman father left for Hong Kong in 1948, planning to send for his wife and children to join him after getting set up there, offers us a very different take on our snapshot year and what came immediately before and after it. Where Wood welcomes the changes that the Communist Party brought, Pan laments the loss of many of the things that had made Shanghai a special place. And yet, from her account too, we get a vision of gradual as opposed to immediate and total transformation that encourages us to let go of any notion that Shanghai was a certain kind of city one day and a completely different sort of place the next. She also helps explain the mindset that led many well-to-do Chinese to stay on, at least for a time, after the PLA arrived.

Here is how she captures the mood of the city on the day of Shanghai's "Liberation" or "fall" and the weeks that followed:

> It was a Wednesday morning, May 25, after token resistance by Kuomintang troops, that soldiers of the People's Liberation Army were spotted in the streets of Shanghai and white flags were glimpsed on buildings. At the Capitol they were showing *Hamlet*, with Laurence Olivier; and at the Grand, *I Wonder Who's Kissing Her Now*.
>
> To leave or not to leave: everywhere there was talk of this, of whether the communists were the very devil or a change for the better. Those who spoke of departure and starting life anew in Hong Kong or America spoke in hushed voices—hushed because departure was at once like betrayal and surrender. Yet by no means everyone was seized by the impulse of flight. We have lived through so much, many shrugged; the worst has happened so many times; can anything appear to us as new in life, can anything appear as a surprise? If they were businessmen they thought they might strike a bargain with the new masters—what didn't they know about striking bargains? They'd done this successfully enough with the Kuomintang, with the Japanese; why shouldn't they be able to do the same with the communists?[13]

Pan makes it clear that she thinks, given what would follow, that these business-men were deluding themselves, letting the "wish to believe" that life could go on as before blind them to signs that the CCP would be different from any previous ruling group. But she also conveys how easily a combination of world-weariness, optimism that the Communists would at most be a bit harder to bribe (but surely not impossible to bribe), and a desire to hold onto property they had worked hard to obtain could combine to encourage members of the Chinese elite to stay put. So, too, could a feeling that "they could live nowhere else." She understands why, for this mixture of reasons, though her father and members of his family left: "All of my mother's family were stayers-on: her parents, her brothers and sisters." And despite her feeling that her father's choice turned out to be the right one, she admits that it has often seemed more of a conundrum for her to figure out why, while many of his contemporaries "were prepared to give communism the benefit of the doubt, he never saw it as anything other than a blight," and was convinced from the start that it would "be the ruin of lives and dreams."[14]

Pan was a very young child in our snapshot year, and she admits in her memoir that she has a hard time telling what she actually remembers of it, or rather whether the order into which she puts the things she recalls is accurate. Still, after warning her readers that what she thinks of as a single event might actually be in some cases a "palimpsest, the sum of many [scenes] slurred into one," she provides a series of evocative vignettes that together conjure up the early 1950s as experienced by a formerly privileged family adjusting to a changed order. Some of her memories are traumatic, of hearing the shots of firing squads and the angry shouts raised during campaigns that targeted members of her class as "bourgeois vermin," for example, and of passing by, while on a walk with her nanny, the corpse of a man who has committed suicide by leaping from one of Nanjing Road's tall buildings. Other memories are of alterations in what she saw or stopped seeing on the streets (rickshaws, for example, since these had been "banned by the new government as retrograde and degrading"), and in how she and people her family knew lived (large houses were divided up, for instance so that more than one family could live in them, or were transformed into "public office space"). She also describes signs of the "new puritanism" taking hold, as "the ballrooms closed," a "rounding up of the city's prostitutes" was carried out, and an increasing sameness came to characterize the way people dressed and the kinds of meals they ate.[15]

When taken together, these changes certainly add up, in Pan's mind, to a total transformation of the city she had known, but what I want to emphasize here is that she presents it as something that happened over time. She presents serious efforts to rid Shanghai of its "red-light districts" as beginning not in 1949 or even 1950 but late in 1951, and then going "on, with pauses, for a good eight years." She writes of multiple Shanghais collapsing into a solitary entity, "so that instead of each person having a Shanghai of his own, made up of sub-worlds of this or that, there was now one Shanghai for everyone." But the multiple Shanghais had not all disappeared in 1950, even if already the "familiar city receded from us, shifting further and further away every day."[16]

Survey of an in-between year

One way in which 1950 was an in-between year has to do with the mixture of old and new that characterized social conditions in the city. Trends were certainly underway during 1950 that, over time, would change a city known for the enormous gulf between "haves" and "have-nots" into one in which most people (there would always be exceptions, such as well-connected Party officials who lived in better housing, ate better food, and so on) existed in roughly similar material conditions. In our snapshot year itself, however, a divide continued to separate the lifestyles of the rich and poor; to return to Lynn Pan's memoir, as different as her childhood world became, she continued to be tended by a nanny employed by her mother. We know from miscellaneous accounts, including the best-selling memoir *Life and Death in Shanghai*, which recounts the story of one local woman with close ties to an international oil company, that a decade or more into the new era, there were some Chinese residents of the by-then clearly socialist city that still had servants.[17] It seems safe to assume that in 1950, while the city's economy had a mixture of socialist and capitalist elements (as it would again toward the end of the twentieth century, though by that later point with capitalist elements gaining rather than diminishing in importance), there were still a great many families with cooks preparing their food, housekeepers making sure their homes were clean and so on, much as had been the case during the Nationalist era and the Qing period before that.

There were also continuities in the realm of politics—and not just because the Communist leaders, like the Nationalists, believed in one-party rule. More specific forms of continuity lay in such things as the Communist Party's efforts to present itself as inheritor of the legacy of Sun Yat-sen. One British reporter claims that Sun's portrait was conspicuously absent from parades in which pictures of Mao, Zhu De, Lenin, and Stalin were carried.[18] But they were still common: in *A Guide to New Shanghai*, the photograph that opens a chapter on the new "People's Government" shows a stage decorated by two giant portraits: one of Mao Zedong, the other of Sun Yat-sen.[19]

An even more striking section of the same handbook, where issues of political continuity are concerned, is that devoted to famous sites within the city that have revolutionary or other kinds of historical significance. The second site listed here is "Mr. Sun Yat-sen's Former Residence," the house in the French Concession where the first leader of the Nationalist Party and his wife, Song Qingling (often still identified as "Madame Sun Yat-sen" in 1950), lived during the years just before the former's death. In introducing this site, the handbook begins by noting that it had fallen into disrepair during the period when the "reactionary Nationalists" held power, which the authors claimed was no surprise due to the extent to which "Chiang Kai-shek turned his back" on everything that Sun had stood for. The text goes on to stress the high priority that the Communist authorities placed on restoring the house, starting work on this project within months of assuming control of the city. Here and elsewhere, the text presents the Communists as showing true respect for Sun and other Chinese patriots of the past and struggling to get back onto the proper track the revolutionary tradition symbolized by 1911, to which Chiang Kai-shek had paid lip service but which in his actions he had perverted.[20]

There were also continuities relating to the press: not only did *Dagongbao*, the newspaper responsible for *A Guide to New Shanghai*, stay in operation, so too did the *China Monthly Review* (the direct descendant of the *China Weekly Review*, a liberal newspaper). In 1950, *China Monthly Review* continued to publish and was still edited, as it had been since World War II, by John W. Powell (son of John B. Powell, one of its founders). Not surprisingly, though, at the very end of the 1940s the periodical, which had long been critical of some aspects of the treaty-port system and during that decade had chided the Nationalist Party for its corruption, always stopping short of endorsing the CCP, modified its editorial line. It became much harsher in its attacks on the old order than it had been just a few years earlier and it celebrated the changes that had come in the wake of the Communist victory. This led *Time* to attack John W. Powell for "red" sympathies that, the magazine claimed, would have embarrassed his father.[21]

A May 27, 1950, editorial titled "The First Year" gives a sense of the new tone the periodical adopted, either due to changes in the beliefs of its writers, a desire to avoid angering Communist Party censors, or some combination of these things.

Figure 5.2 An advertisement from *Xin Shanghai bianlan* [A Guide to New Shanghai] 1951. Note the clothing and pose which would soon by labeled "bourgeois" and "decadent," also the continuity between this image and the 1901 advertisement for Western-style fashions from a guidebook reproduced in Chapter 3, p. 50.

Source: *Xin Shanghai bianlan* [A Guide to New Shanghai], p. 563 (Shanghai: Dagongbao, 1951)

It stresses that the preceding twelve months had seen Shanghai changed for the better in many ways, not the least important of which was that the hyperinflation that had been the bane of the immediate post-World War II period had ended. "For nearly four post-war years," one paragraph starts, "we lived in a whirling chaotic Shanghai in which the US dollar was the only thing possessing even relative stability." Now, by contrast, inflation was gone and the Chinese currency was stable. "If a year ago," the next paragraph begins, "someone had told us that within one year prices would remain virtually unchanged for weeks on end [and] that there would not be a rice shortage, a coal shortage, a power shortage, we would have thought them crazy." The editorial does not refer to Shanghai's "new life," but it invokes a sense of total and almost miraculous transformation for the better. "Times have changed, so much so," it says near the end, "that unless we stop and think about it a while, we find it difficult to remember just what life was like in pre-liberation days."[22] Though its ability to remain in operation speaks to continuities between the late 1940s and early 1950s, this editorial shows that its rhetoric was very much of the "new day has dawned" variety.

We can also think of 1950 as a year of carry-overs from the past as well as new trends where fashion and modes of consumption are concerned. Here, again, *A Guide to New Shanghai* is illuminating. Many chapters in it present Shanghai as having been completely transformed in 1949, but the advertisements at the back of the book tell a different story. They show men in fedoras and women in elegant apparel, models with European or American facial features, and women striking poses or with expressions that are more "come-hither" than puritanical. In one advert, we see a family grouping in which clothing is used to flag the differences between generations, with the older members of the group in "traditional" Chinese garb, the younger in Western-influenced styles.[23]

In the realm of culture and education, we again see shifts underway in 1950 that can be placed along a spectrum running from continuity to a complete alteration of familiar patterns, depending in part on how one chooses to think about them. Take, for example, the role of cinema in Shanghai, a famously movie-mad metropolis. Hollywood movies did cease to be a mainstay of the local entertainment scene after the Communist Party took power. But this did not mean that Shanghai's residents stopped being able to see foreign films. It just meant that, as in other areas, the mixture of international influences shifted, with Moscow replacing Hollywood as the place of origin of many of the features shown at local cinemas. When it came to educational institutions, meanwhile, there were certainly dramatic shifts underway. *A Guide to New Shanghai*, for example, refers to universities such as St. John's having severed their ties with America and undergone internal campaigns to rid their curriculum of the taint of Western imperialist thinking. But it also states clearly that there were still significantly more private than public institutions of higher education.

Mixed assessments and historical echoes

When thinking about the in-between nature of 1950, the uncertainty about just what this city would become with a new regime in power, it is telling that even the gloomiest 1950 reports on Shanghai by Western commentators often stopped short of saying that everything had changed, and presented some changes as needed ones that had less to do with ideology than a shift away from chaos. This is true even of the report in *The Times* whose morbid headline was quoted above. The subtitle after the reference to Shanghai as a "DYING CITY" refers to the hope of local merchants "dwindling," not having disappeared entirely. The author of the article tells of one Briton interviewed describing the despair of foreign merchants, lamenting that the Chinese middle class was being "slowly and systematically impoverished through high taxation," and mentioning that the number of beggars on the streets had grown. But the journalist also mentions some foreigners expressing ambivalence about the state of their city.

For example, one Shanghailander reported that he was sick of the incessant propaganda of the new regime, but that he nevertheless saw some benefits for China of the Communists coming to power. This Shanghailander regretted that the radio stations were running much less "entertainment," sticking largely to news and speeches, and that "all newspapers carried the same stories and interpretations of events." Moreover, "the results of the British election were not released in the Chinese Press for two days, and then a fantastic picture was painted of rigged elections and crooked practices." And yet, according to the journalist, this Briton "thought the present regime would be able to do much for the material benefit of the Chinese people," since the Communists "had the power, the drive, and the ruthlessness to push through many reforms and schemes that China should have had long ago, and which she needed if she was to become a modern and up-to-date country."[24]

It is also worth noting that we can see something familiar, linked to the past even in the rhetoric of novelty that shaped speeches such as Song's and publications such as *A Guide to New Shanghai*. The very late 1940s and very early 1950s were not the first time that local residents had been told, after all, that they were living in a completely "New Shanghai," a place completely different from the metropolis that had previously stood by the Huangpu River. We have come across references before to Shanghai being born anew (and in one case also to it being described as dying). Foreigners were fond, from almost the moment the first Shanghailanders arrived, of presenting Shanghai as having been born anew or awoken from a long slumber when it was opened to Western trade and settlement. This was, as we have seen, a theme during the Jubilee of 1893 and in the history of the city commissioned by the Shanghai Municipal Council in the early 1920s. In the previous chapter we encountered Ye Shengtao's May 30th novel, *Ni Huanzhi*, which raised the possibility that revolutionary upheaval could bring about something that might seem superficially to mean the "death" of the city, but would actually give it an invigorating new lease on life. The very term "New Shanghai" had been used before.

Some of Song Qingling's specific claims also contained historical echoes, including her insistence that a new page in local history had been turned when the Communists put an end to a long period of imperial oppression and domestic misrule. Nationalist Party publications had made the same assertion. When the Nationalists gained authority over Shanghai's Chinese-run sections in 1927, weeks before Chiang Kai-shek launched a "White Terror" aimed at all "red" elements within the First United Front, this was hailed by their supporters and spokesmen as a first step toward its gaining control of the International Settlement and French Concession as well. The imminent founding of a "New Shanghai," free of the taint of foreign domination, was proclaimed.

The Nationalist Party's efforts to overturn the unequal treaties so that the foreign enclaves would be integrated into a single Greater Shanghai did not bear fruit during the Nanjing Decade (1927–1937), in part because of Chiang Kai-shek's decision to make destroying the Communist Party his top priority. It is worth keeping in mind, though, that this period was the first during which a Chinese ruling party dreamed of remaking Shanghai into a different sort of metropolis—one that would be modern, unified, and completely under domestic control.[25]

There were also two later moments which came after the end of the Nanjing Decade but before the start of the Communist era, when local authorities spoke of Shanghai's transformation and the beginning of a glorious new epoch. One such moment, ironically, was the early 1940s, at a time when all of Shanghai was, effectively, for the first time in its history, under the control of a foreign power: Japan. All parts of Shanghai other than the International Settlement and the French Concession had fallen under the sway of the Japanese and their Chinese collaborators in 1937. Then late in 1941, right after Pearl Harbor, knowing that America would come into the war anyway, Japanese troops marched into the International Settlement. Rather than present themselves as conquerors, however, the Japanese insisted that they were liberators who had freed Shanghai from Western control.

This rhetorical stance was most pronounced in 1943, when the formal end of the treaty-port system was proclaimed and public rallies were held to celebrate the start of Shanghai's new life as a "free" city.[26] In 1945, when the Japanese military authorities and Chinese regimes that took their lead from Tokyo lost control of the metropolis and a Nationalist government loyal to Chiang Kai-shek was once more installed, yet another pre-Communist regime announced that Shanghai had been purified and liberated.

A new paper for a new China

Let us, while keeping our eye on continuities yet never forgetting that 1950 was also a time of novelty and new beginnings, turn to one of the places in which Song's "new dawn" speech was published: the inaugural issue of the *Shanghai News*. This text, we will see, has links to two previous snapshot chapters—that devoted to 1850 and that devoted to 1925. The link to the 1850 chapter is easiest to grasp: that chapter began with discussion of the first edition of a new English language publication, the *North China Herald*. In a curious parallel, which no one seems to have noted at the time or since, the *Shanghai News* went into operation almost exactly one hundred years later. Its first issue was dated June 10, 1950, and it included, along with the text of Song's speech, a report by Vice-Mayor Pan Hannian that began as follows:

> Shanghai is the biggest city in China with a population of 5 million and it is the country's economic center. In the past hundred years, the imperialists turned the city into a strong fortress that they could use in their effort to plunder China and enslave the Chinese people. The Guomindang reactionaries also used it as their key base in oppressing and controlling the Chinese people. Therefore, the liberation of Shanghai is a sign to all that the imperialist aggressors and their henchmen, the Nationalists, have been defeated. This is not only a victory for the people of Shanghai and the people of China, also for the working people of the world.
>
> As soon as Shanghai was liberated, the imperialists expected that we would fail in our effort to run the city. They sneeringly predicted that we would dig ourselves into a hole from which we would not be able to emerge . . . [But even though] the imperialists and their henchmen resorted to the intrigues of blockading and bombing our city, in an attempt to embarrass and subdue us, the Shanghai people firmly united under the leadership of Chairman Mao, determinedly overcame all the difficulties left behind by the enemy and victoriously made it through the year.[27]

It is with Song and Pan that the link to our 1925 snapshot comes in. Song was introduced in the previous chapter not just as the wife and then mourning widow of Sun Yat-sen, but also as an exemplar of the "cosmopolitan nationalist" category. And Pan was not just a leading figure in the Communist Party underground in Shanghai during the final years of Nationalist Party rule, but also a worldly and sophisticated figure who fits neatly into this category as well. One recent Chinese book on the history of coffee, for example, includes a section on Pan, near one on Picasso, claiming that both had a great fondness for cafés and the lifestyles these establishments represented. Pan, this work claims, was not just a habitué of cafés when at leisure, but used one as a favorite locale for holding clandestine political meetings with figures ranging from Zhou Enlai to Nationalist Party operatives.[28] It surely speaks to a sense of continuity with Shanghai's international past that two of the people given positions of responsibility in and made leading spokesmen for the "New Shanghai" of 1950 were not just nationalists but "cosmopolitan nationalists" of Song and Pan's type.

Having noted this link to our 1925 snapshot, it is worth asking just how much the *Shanghai News* and *North China Herald* had in common. Was there anything that linked the papers to one another, beyond the fact that they used the same language, English, to communicate with their readers? I think so, but before explaining what this was, it is important to note some of the many things that set the periodicals apart.

One crucial difference had to do with the nationalities and political stances of the people who ran them, as well as their nature as business enterprises. The *Herald* was a private concern that was originally launched by a British business-man and remained a foreign-run operation throughout its history. And it was never a government publication, even though it took on a variety of quasi-official functions (issuing in its pages the transcripts of official proceedings, for example) and even though the publishing company connected to it worked very closely with the Shanghai Municipal Council. In ideological terms, the *Herald* was consistently a supporter of the system of foreign privilege set in place by the Treaty of Nanjing. Its initial publisher and those who followed him insisted that the treaty-port system was the best thing that had ever happened to Shanghai and gave Westerners the lion's share of credit for the port's rise to greatness and international importance.

The *Shanghai News*, by contrast, was a Chinese-run operation, and, more than that, an organ of the Communist Party. It published many of the same stories that appeared in Chinese in *Jiefang ribao* (Liberation Daily), a vitally important newspaper to the Communist Party while it was in opposition (controlling not the whole country but just a small number of base areas in rural China) that shifted its operations to Shanghai soon after the Red Army took over that city.[29] And the *Shanghai News* often gave over large amounts of space to reports and speeches by local and national officials of the new regime. This group included Pan (Shanghai's Vice-Mayor) and Song.

Reflecting the politics of the CCP, one recurring theme in *Shanghai News* articles, including those contributed by cosmopolitan nationalists such as Song and Pan, was that the system of foreign privilege that the *Herald* had celebrated had been a source of great humiliation to the city's majority Chinese population. The existence of foreign-run enclaves contributed greatly to the "nightmare" period from which the Communist Party had just helped Shanghai awaken, as Song put it, though she argued that Japanese invasions and Nationalist mis-rule had also contributed to the suffering of the preceding decades. Pan, meanwhile, as we have seen, decried the "imperialists" for having "turned the city into a strong fortress," but also heaped abuse on the Nationalists for oppressing the populace.

There were many other contrasts between the newspapers, some of which simply reflect the very different moments at which they went into operation, near the start of eras in which foreigners would play widely contrasting roles. Here's one telling example: the *Herald*'s early editions often listed the names of people who had recently come from the West to do business and settle near the Huangpu; the *Shanghai News*, by contrast, sometimes provided lists of the foreigners who had just been granted exit visas.[30]

Nevertheless, despite their different political orientations and other dissimi-larities, the *Shanghai News* and *North China Herald* had some interesting things in common. Most notably, perhaps, early issues of both papers, including their first editions, were filled with sweeping statements about the transformations the city had recently undergone and bold pronouncements of what was in store for it. Another commonality is that, like the *Herald*'s first issue, the inaugural edition of the *Shanghai News* included a statement of purpose that spoke to a desire to shape not just local opinion but also international understanding of the locale. Under the headline "To Our Readers," it read in part:

> The Shanghai News . . . a paper owned and published by the Chinese . . . [aims to help] the English reading public to acquire an understanding of the new Shanghai and the new China as a whole. Inasmuch as Shanghai is one of China's largest cities and a place where contacts with foreign countries are most frequently made, many foreign nationals often come into contact with China through their contacts with Shanghai.
>
> A year has passed since the liberation of Shanghai. Within the year Shanghai, and other parts of China, underwent the greatest and most fundamental changes in their history, which will continue to advance in an accelerating tempo. The aim of this publication is to report faithfully such changes . . . to all those who are deeply concerned about the growth of the new Shanghai and the new China.[31]

What we see, then, is that in 1950 as in 1850, soon after a dramatic political shift had taken place that affected Shanghai and its relationship to foreign countries, a new periodical opened for business with the stated aim of speaking to both a local and international audience about the port and its ties to the wider world.[32]

What was newsworthy about 1950?

So far, we have tended to treat our snapshot year as a single entity, but like any year it can be broken up into smaller units, divided either evenly into months or weeks or by particularly important turning-point moments. Let us end, then, by looking at the year as a collection of successive events. And for this exercise, our guide will be a long list of "Major Events in Shanghai, May 1949–May 1951" that ran in the *Shanghai News*.[33]

The first 1950 event on the list—which begins unsurprisingly with a May 28, 1949, entry that starts "Shanghai entirely liberated"—is "Shanghai–Canton through train service restored" (January 12). The other development in 1950's first month singled out as significant is "The East China Military and Administrative Committee inaugurated" (January 27). If January was thus a month of little drama, the same could not be said for the one that followed it, for the first event listed for it is "American-made KMT planes raided Shanghai, injuring and killing more than 1,000 civilians" (February 6). The other two developments for the month speak to stability and consolidation rather than a military threat: "The Shanghai Trade Union Council inaugurated" (February 7), and "The Civil Affairs Bureau announced the results of the citywide census-taking: households: 1,019, 488: population: 4,993,217" (February 13). March was as free of drama as January, if the *Shanghai News* is to be believed, for the only events of note then were the start of the "Conference of the Shanghai Suburban Peasants Representatives" (March 10), the formation of the "Shanghai Suburban Peasants Association"

(March 14), local celebrations of "World Youth Week" (March 21), and the arrival in the city of three Soviet professors (N.I. Noozhdin, S.V. Kisehlehv, and M.F. Makarova) who were on a lecture tour (March 27). An even less eventful month followed, for the only April development that gets a mention is the opening to the public of the "Shanghai–Moscow radio-telephone service" (on the 29th).

Many of the events listed for the final eight months of the year are similar to those just detailed. Throughout the second two-thirds of 1950, new organizations continued to be established (on August 17, for example, the "Shanghai Democratic Women's Federation" was "inaugurated") and international holidays were marked (on "May Day," according to the newspaper, "600,000 people" demonstrated in "various districts" and "a review of 25,000 workers' pickets" was held "at the Race Course"). And things continued to occur that, like the lecture tour by the three Russian academics, symbolized that the city's ties to the world would now be via countries other than those such as Britain, France, and the United States that for so long had had key stakes in the metropolis. Thus, for example, one May event singled out as noteworthy is the arrival of a "Czechoslovak Trade Delegation" (on the 21st of that month), while one December development that earns a mention is the Indian government's appointment of "A.K. Sen as Indian Consul General in Shanghai" (on the 13th of that month).

There were two aspects, however, that made the months May–December different from those of January–April where what the *Shanghai News* deemed the "major events" of 1950 were concerned. One was that this period saw several celebrations linked not to international holidays but to commemorating turning points in local or national history. Included in these two categories were the giant May 27 gathering held to mark the "Shanghai liberation anniversary," the march involving "200,000 people" that was held on August 1 in honor of "Army Day" (celebrating the anniversary of the founding of the PLA), and of course the enormous rallies held on October 1 to mark National Day (the paper claimed that "750,000 people" gathered on this day).

The other feature that distinguishes the events of the second two-thirds of the year from those of January–April is a dramatic upsurge in anti-American agitation due to the outbreak of the Korean War in June. On July 15, according to the "major events" survey, the "Shanghai Branch of the Chinese People's Campaign Committee against U.S. Aggression, in Taiwan and Korea" was founded. Then, for December, significant contributions to what had come to be known as the "Resist America, Support Korea" movement are said to have taken place on five different days of the month. These included a rally by "100,000 students" on December 9. That gathering served the double purpose of expressing anger at America for aggression in Korea and attempting to draw a parallel between U.S. actions in 1950 and Japanese invasions of the 1930s, for the event also commemorated the "the fifteenth anniversary of the 'December 9th' movement," a series of demonstrations calling on the Nationalist Party to do more to stop Japan from encroaching upon Chinese sovereignty.

A final point worth noting about 1950's "major events" is that two of the last three entries for that year in the list provided by the *Shanghai News* draw our attention to the continued presence within the city of people linked to capitalism, Christianity, or in some cases doubtless both. The entry for December 16 reads as follows: "150,000 industrialists and businessmen held demonstration to pledge support for resisting U.S. and aiding Korea movement [*sic*]." Four days later, we are told, "Chinese Christians in Shanghai" gathered for a similar event.

What should we make of these two events? They could be seen, as the newspaper would like us to see them, as showing that local Chinese residents of all economic classes and followers of all creeds were united in patriotic outrage against Western imperialism, which had done so much damage to the city in the past and was now threatening a neighboring country. Or they could be seen as indications that pressure was being put on members of potentially suspect groups to show whose side they were on by taking part in loyalist rallies. The gatherings of December 16 and 20, as well as an earlier December 7 anti-imperialism rally held by "Shanghai students of Christian schools" (that also earned an entry in the listing of "major events"), should probably be understood as rooted in a mixture of spontaneous sentiment and official manipulation, with the degree to which the former or the latter was most significant varying among the participants. What seems clear, though, is that this mass movement that gathered steam just as our snapshot year ended, and would grow in intensity and be supplemented by other campaigns in the months and years immediately following, was a key factor in pushing Shanghai toward becoming less and less a constellation of separate "sub-worlds" and more and more a place where conformity was valued and expected, and a city in which public gatherings were used to show that, as Lynn Pan put it, "there was now one Shanghai for everyone."

6 1975: The East was Red

This book tells the reader about five Chinese cities—Shanghai, Hangzhou, Nanjing, Wuxi and Suzhou . . . [They] abound in a great variety of products; they have developed industries and many transportation and communication facilities. They are also noted for their scenery.

But in the years before liberation, these cities suffered greatly under the plunder and spoliation of imperialism, feudalism and bureaucrat-capitalism. Their industries were choked, their markets depressed, and they were all typical consumer cities. Since liberation, under the guidance of Chairman Mao's proletarian revolutionary line, they have undergone a profound change . . .

> *China Travel: Shanghai, Hangzhou, Nanjing, Wuxi,*
> *Suzhou,* 1975[1]

Early in the morning, as the red sun rises above the waters of the Huangpu River and brilliant sunshine floods into all of Shanghai's nooks and crannies, the melody of "The East is Red" rings out from the big clock atop the Custom House. This magnificent sound summons the people to start a new day of struggle and inspires them to push on forward from victory to ever-greater victory . . .

Nanjing Road [like the Bund], due to its many transformations since Liberation, has also undergone a profound change [*juda de bianhua*].

> *Shanghai Waitan Nanjinglu Shihua*
> (The History of the Bund and Nanjing Road), 1976

In the last chapter, we saw Shanghai at the dawn of the Communist period poised between two worlds. The year 1950 was when some of the "profound changes" mentioned in the two mid-1970s texts quoted above had already been realized: most notably, the shift to Communist control of the city's political structure. But it was also a year when some of these "profound changes" had only been partially realized. For example, although moves toward state ownership of businesses and residences had begun, most stores, factories, and houses remained in private hands in 1950. Twenty-five years later none would be. And still other changes that by 1975 would be seen as "profound" had not even begun to take shape in 1950. The city's industrial base in our last snapshot year, for example, still lay in light industry and trade, while by 1975 Shanghai had become China's leading center of heavy industry, a place where massive ships were built as well as docked.

Just as 1950 can be linked both to the treaty-port city that preceded it and the revolutionary metropolis it would become during the heyday of Maoism, 1975 can also qualify as a year poised between epochs. With the benefit of hindsight, we can see it as a Janus-faced year that looked backward to the inward-turning de-globalizing era in the city's history that peaked in the late 1960s (a time when Shanghai was shaped far less by international trends than at any previous point in its modern history) and forward to the current period of re-globalization (that has seen Shanghai touted once again, and again for good reason, as one of the most cosmopolitan cities on earth and a leader in linking China to world markets).

Here are some basic facts to keep in mind about our snapshot year, particularly where assessing Shanghai's place in global flows is concerned. Mao was still in power, physically ailing but with his personality cult going strong (shown by the constant playing of "The East is Red," a song that presented him as China's savior). Official treatments of national history remained intensely anti-imperialist and anti-capitalist, and so too did discussions of the local past, as illustrated by the way that Shanghai and neighboring cities are introduced in the 1975 English language guide for travelers quoted at the start of this chapter. There was only room within the official discourse of the time to honor a few foreign figures and events: Marx and Lenin (quotations from each of them, followed of course by a quotation from Mao, open the Chinese language popular history quoted at the start of this chapter), for example, and the Paris Commune (the 1971 centenary of which inspired celebratory speeches and posters linking French heroism in the 1870s to Chinese radicalism in the present).

Another thing to remember is that some trends that appeared powerful in 1950 had already swung into reverse, none more sharply than the positioning of the Soviet Union. If the Soviet Union was emerging in 1950 as China's model, more than a decade before the start of our snapshot year Moscow had emerged as Beijing's main enemy, despite the continued attacks on American imperialism in the Chinese press. The Sino-Soviet split—which had its roots in many factors, ranging from border disputes, to Beijing's critical attitude toward Moscow's abandonment of dreams of world revolution and efforts after Stalin's death to temper admiration for this once-revered leader, to Mao's desire not to have his country cast as "Little Brother" to its neighbor to the North—required that one of the most important new Shanghai buildings of the 1950s quickly have its name changed. This was a palatial exhibition hall, complete with turrets and a tall central spire with a star on top (and other design features that pointed to Russian architectural influences), which was built as a monument to the ties of affection between Moscow and Beijing. The phrase "close and eternal friendship between China and the Soviet Union" was incorporated into its original name, but within a few years it began to be called instead simply the "Shanghai Exhibition Center," the "Shanghai Industrial Exhibition Hall," or the "Industrial Exhibition Hall" instead. And it is telling that by the mid-1970s the photograph of the building's

Figure 6.1 The Exhibition Hall as shown in *Shanghai Huace* [Shanghai Pictorial], 1958.
The caption accompanying it reads in English "Night view of the Sino-Soviet
Friendship Building." Chinese, French, and Russian versions are also provided,
as they are throughout the book for each image.

Source: *Shanghai Huace* [Shanghai Pictorial] (Shanghai, 1958)

interior and accompanying description in *China Travel* give no hint that the
structure was once thought of as having a key international dimension, owing to its
ties to the Soviet Union. The viewer sees only Chinese people looking at displays
of machines described as linked to "Shanghai industry," under the gaze of a large

white statue of Mao, above whose head is written a slogan urging them on to quickly realize socialism.[2]

On the other hand, though Shanghai was certainly a much less global place than it had been in the past and is now again, the inward turn during the heyday of Maoism was never complete. After turning away from Moscow, China strove to present itself as a potential leader of "Third World" and non-aligned countries. The ramifications of this for Shanghai were varied. One result was that when local and national Communist Party leaders spoke in the city in the 1970s, including during our current snapshot year, they sometimes flagged this new kind of internationalism. Yu Qiuli, Vice-Premier of the State Council, certainly did in the "Address to Cadres in the Industrial and Transportation Front in Shanghai" that he delivered in January 1975—a speech that illustrates how contemporary references to the world could end up betraying special features of the time (an obsession with real and imagined ideological divisions within the Communist Party, for example, and rhetoric critical of "Soviet revisionism" and "American imperialism") while expressing enduring ideas (such as the idea that China is a country strong and rich enough to show benevolence toward smaller lands). When referring to China's "support for fraternal countries" in neighboring parts of Asia and more distant locales (such as Albania), he takes a swipe at unnamed "comrades" who foolishly criticize the Party for supporting true revolutionaries in other lands who "suffer more hardships than we do" while fighting for the same cause. He chides those who have "grumbled many times: saying that 'Korea receives nylon screens, Albania small buildings, Vietnam artillery pieces and guns, and Sihanouk a gold rice bowl; these exhaust our blood and sweat and drive us to tend sheep in the countryside.'" They are selfish and shortsighted, he claims, to begrudge support for these allies, especially our "Vietnamese comrades-in-arms," who "stand on the front line of the anti-imperialist struggle."[3]

In the mid-1970s, while visitors no longer came to Shanghai from the Soviet Union or its satellite states, some people from a range of different foreign countries did pass through, including those Yu singled out as recipients of Chinese gifts and aid, as well as Pakistan, various African states, and citizens of a few Eastern Europe countries that, like Albania, were cut off from or had strained relationships with Moscow (Romania, for example). Moreover, starting in the very early 1970s—despite the persistence of rhetoric decrying capitalism in all of its national manifestations—important preliminary moves were made that would slowly but steadily increase the city's ties to many parts of the West, laying the groundwork for Shanghai's eventual re-integration into global economic affairs. It would be more than a decade still before Shanghai's harbor would again become, as it once was, a major entry point into China for goods produced in the West (and vice versa), but cracks began to open in the barriers separating the PRC from many Western countries, including the United States.

Key in this process, of course, was the famous trip to China made by President Nixon and Henry Kissinger, who met in Beijing with Mao and Zhou Enlai but also stopped in Shanghai, staying at the Jinjiang Hotel in what had once been the French Concession. The main diplomatic outcome of this trip was the "Shanghai

Communiqué," an important first step toward the late-1970s normalization of relations between the two countries. It is interesting to contemplate the implications of prefixing the document with the name of Shanghai. The name reflects the fact that the terms were not hammered out until the end of Nixon's visit, but would it have been so readily known as the "Shanghai Communiqué" if the city in question had not been a place that, because of its past, was already associated in people's minds with a crossroads of "East" and "West"?

While this question cannot be answered definitively, we do know that some things happened in the years immediately following the "Shanghai Communiqué" that helped make the city at least a bit more of a site for East–West encounters than it had been in the 1960s. In the early 1970s, for example, a small number of Americans, including delegations of students, scholars, artists, and athletes and the occasional journalist, came through China on specially arranged visits, and Shanghai was frequently one of the places where they stopped. And during both 1974 and our snapshot year, contingents of exchange students from Australia, Western Europe, and Canada began to trickle into China for longer stays. Not all were based in Shanghai (more studied in Beijing), but some of them either took trips there while attending classes in other cities or were affiliated with Fudan University. This was one of many local schools with historic ties to the West (its founding president was a Catholic named Ma Xiangpo who had been educated in France, while one of his early successors had studied in the United States), though by 1975 these ties had been largely forgotten or were seen as embarrassing rather than as sources of pride.

The two books quoted to open this chapter, if read carefully, provide tantalizing bits of evidence of the Janus-faced nature of the period. *China Travel* is largely given over to detailing the changed nature of the city's economic base: one of its most striking shots shows an oil refinery lit up brightly at night, and several pages focus on the "Shanghai Machine Tool Plant" and the dramatic expansion of local ship-building operations.[4] It also gives the reader a sense of how politicized many aspects of local life had become: one image shows a spirited rally dedicated to criticizing Confucius (the once-venerated sage Maoists denigrated for his "feudal" ideas), and Lin Biao (the protégé of Mao's who fell from favor and died in mysterious circumstances in 1971).[5]

Even though many of *China Travel*'s pages, while detailing these features of the New Shanghai that took shape under Mao, include polemical statements harshly critical of Western imperialists, two things about the book are worth noting when it comes to anticipations of the city's re-globalization to come. First, it was designed not for Chinese but for foreign readers, especially, it seems likely, the small but growing number of Australian, British, and North American visitors (including English-speaking people of Chinese ancestry who had become residents in or citizens of other countries) who were starting to make their way to the PRC about the time of its publication. And the main nod that *China Travel* makes to Shanghai's links to the outside world speaks of Shanghai as a port that "handles trade relations with 300 ports in more than 130 countries and regions, thus strengthening the ties of friendship between the Chinese people and the people of

Figure 6.2 Photograph of an anti-Confucius, anti-Lin Biao rally of the 1970s

Source: *China Travel: Shanghai, Hangzhou, Nanjing, Wuxi, Suzhou* (Beijing: China Travel and Tourism Press, 1975)

other countries."[6] This is a global vision that transcends both the developing and the Communist worlds.

The History of the Bund and Nanjing Road, the second text quoted at the start of this chapter, is filled with often-lurid details of myriad ways that predatory foreigners and unpatriotic Chinese mistreated and humiliated Shanghai's working classes prior to 1949. But it also contains small signs of being produced at a time when the possibility of a future rapprochement with the West was in the air. For example, after pointing to the wondrous effects on the local populace of hearing the strains of "The East is Red," it speaks of how impressed by the recent improvements made to Shanghai's two most famous districts, the Bund and Nanjing Road, all open-minded foreign visitors will be—including overseas Chinese returning to see the homeland they left behind and Westerners who once spent time in the city during its decadent treaty-port incarnation.

We should not overstate the centrality of the elements of *China Travel* and *The History of the Bund and Nanjing Road* that look forward to a day when new kinds of international flows—or, rather, the mixture of revived and novel sorts of international flows—would mark Shanghai's re-globalization. *The History of the Bund and Nanjing Road* in particular resists any reading that downplays the degree to which it is shaped by a critical stance toward the West. Its strident anti-imperialism partly reflects the fact that it was produced not in Beijing (as

China Travel was) but Shanghai. Beijing had been the center of the greatest radicalism early in the Cultural Revolution. But Shanghai had become a focal point for extremists during the final stage of the Cultural Revolution proper (1966–1969) and for the first half of the 1970s a small group of radical figures (including Mao's wife, Jiang Qing) later known as the "Gang of Four" ran the city.[7]

This chapter etches some of the "profound changes" (to borrow a favorite phrase of *The History of the Bund and Nanjing Road*'s authors) that reshaped Shanghai after 1949 and especially between the early 1950s and late 1960s. By the end of the 1960s, things as basic as the way people dressed, where they lived and worked, and the meaning of major landmarks had altered dramatically, thanks to more than a decade and a half of revolutionary transformation, making the city radically unlike what it was before 1949 or even in 1950. In our current snapshot year, we see evidence of those changes. We also, though, see signs of continuities with the past in such features as the look of the local skyline (Shanghai's tallest buildings in 1975 still dated from the pre-1949 era). And it is even possible to glimpse at times hints of the new changes to come between the 1980s and the present, a period during which, as we will see in our snapshot of 2000, Shanghai's re-globalization triggered yet another reinvention of this protean metropolis.

Two views of a changed city

In a departure from previous snapshot chapters, our evocation of the "profound changes" the city underwent prior to 1975 will be carried out via a linked pair of imaginative exercises. We will conjure up the imagined experiences of two invented figures, one female and the other male, one Western and the other Chinese. We will first explore the thoughts of an imaginary British woman who went to Shanghai as a young adult in the early 1930s but then returned to London to live in mid-1941, when the Japanese invasion of the International Settlement seemed imminent. We will assume that she remained curious about the fate of her one-time "Eastern Home" throughout the following decades, but did not follow events there particularly closely and did not for some time consider it likely that she would ever see once-familiar Shanghai sights such as the buildings of the Bund. This situation began to change in 1973, when she came across two stories in *The Times* of London that first planted the idea in her mind of making a return trip before she died to see again the Chinese city that she knew best. The first of these *Times* articles was a March 12 story by one Margaret Allen, "Vivid Impressions of a First Visit" (to China), which came with a side-bar called "How to Get There" (noting among other things that visas could be tricky to secure and flight routes complex—one of the best options was to go, as the author did, from London to Addis Ababa to Shanghai via a newly inaugurated Ethiopian Airlines route). The second, also about Allen's trip (which followed a Shanghai–Beijing–Hankow–Shanghai itinerary), appeared on March 17 and was called "An Itinerary for Would-Be China Watchers." It included a hopeful note, for our former Shanghailander: "there are signs that groups will be allowed into the country" in 1974.

We will assume that, during the next two years, in order to prepare herself for the changed city, our Londoner turned Shanghailander turned Londoner would, in that pre-internet age, seek out written materials in local libraries such as that of the School of Oriental and African Studies and from the Chinese Embassy. By these means, by the end of our snapshot year, she would have consulted, among other publications, *China Travel*, as well as perhaps stories about the city that had recently appeared in British and American newspapers and magazines and in English language periodicals produced in the People's Republic.

After trying to evoke this Shanghailander's response to *representations* of New Shanghai in the Western press and English language works published in China in the early to mid-1970s (assuming that she eventually did make that trip back to her "Eastern Home," but not until a later date and hence of no special concern to us here), we will conjure up the reaction to the *actual* city of 1975 of an imagined Chinese return visitor. For the purposes of this exercise, we will make this second figure a man who was raised in Shanghai in the 1930s, as part of a family that operated small businesses in the city. We will assume that, though some members of his family left for Hong Kong late in the 1940s, he stayed on in Shanghai after the Communist take-over to manage a local bookstore the family owned on Fuzhou Road, before departing for the Crown Colony himself late in 1950. We will imagine that he had lived in Hong Kong for the next quarter-century and then made his first return trip to Shanghai in 1975. In trying to reconstruct the impression the city made on this return visitor, we will focus on things he would have seen and heard. But we will also assume that he had access to popular histories from the 1960s and early 1970s and other Chinese language materials.

A Shanghailander ponders the city from afar

> Shanghai is a comprehensive socialist industrial base in China. Most of the industries in Shanghai today have been developed since liberation by adhering to the road of independence and self-reliance. Now there are over 1.5 million industrial workers and nearly 10,000 plants and factories. Its leading industries comprise metallurgy, machine-making, electronic meters and instruments, chemicals, ship-building, construction engineering, light industries and textiles . . . The total industrial output in 1974 was about 17 times that of 1949 . . .
>
> *China Travel*, 1975, p. 19

What images of New Shanghai might have formed in the mind of our imagined London-based ex-Shanghailander as she mentally prepared herself in 1975 for a future return visit to her one-time "Eastern Home"? Let us assume she began this preparation by turning to the "Tourist Map" that begins the Shanghai section of *China Travel*. Here she would find a layout of streets and railway lines that would look familiar at first, yet on closer inspection she would be struck by differences between this map and those she remembered. The map's main boundaries would be much the same as those shown on works produced in the 1930s—the ones, that is, that paid equal attention to the Chinese-run and foreign-run parts of the metropolis (for some maps for Westerners throughout the treaty-port era only showed the International Settlement and French Concession, pushing other sections to the margins of or completely off the page, or including those districts but failing to note the names of their streets). There are two contrasts, though, that would strike her quickly. The 1975 map did not break the city up into separate administrative districts, but instead showed the metropolis as a single coherent whole (without even noting, as some tourist maps later would, which parts had once been foreign-run). And while some street names were the same or altered just a bit in spelling, others were totally different ("Avenue Joffre," for example, had become "Huaihai Road").

Examining the map more closely, another thing that might strike her as curious would be the buildings deemed important enough to have their names given, often accompanied by a sketch of the edifice. At the center of the map was a drawing of an easily recognizable building, but one that had apparently been given a new name. This was the Park Hotel, an impressive art deco building dating from 1934, now rechristened, according to the map, the "Guoji Hotel," which, though she might not know, given how little Chinese she had learned while in Shanghai, meant "International Hotel". It had been designed by one of the best-known Hungarian architects of the day, László Hudec, and upon completion become the tallest structure in the city (a title it still retained in our snapshot year) and indeed in all of Asia (a distinction it lost in the 1950s). And *China Travel* lists it as standing just west of Xizang Road ("Thibet Road" in treaty-port days) on Nanjing Road (surely, she would assume, just a new spelling of Nanking Road— but she would also note that it no longer changed its name to Bubbling Well Road once it reached the western half of the city, as it had back in the days before 1949).

Letting her eyes drift a bit to the south from the Park Hotel, she would find curious two things that were missing. Where, she would wonder, was the Racing Club, which stood very close to and was of the same vintage as the Park Hotel and was home to the second most famous clocktower in the city (the Custom House's "Big Ching" being better known still, of course)? And where was the Race Course that had been such an important local landmark? The Racing Club was not portrayed at all, while where the Race Course should have been was "Renmin Park" and "Renmin Square" ("Renmin" standing in both cases for "People's").

Continuing to scan the map, she would be struck most by the number of landmarks that had not existed or at least not been seen as special places when she lived in the city. She would likely have known that the First President of the Republic of China and the "Father of the Chinese Revolution" had once resided in Shanghai. But she would have been unaware of the precise location of his house until her eyes came across the words "Former Residence of the late Dr. Sun Yat-sen" on this 1975 map, in part of what she knew had once been the French Concession.

Letting her eye drift eastward from there, she would see a picture of a building that she might well have walked by in the 1930s, but certainly would not have thought of as a landmark then, yet which now seemed to have been elevated to a site of considerable importance. This would not seem surprising to her once she saw what the accompanying note said: "The Site of the First Congress of the Communist Party of China." Looking over at the Bund, she would be surprised to see this area devoid of sketches of landmarks (though the drawing labeled "Shanghai Mansion" just north of the district she recognized as the "Broadway Mansions" of an earlier period, a structure second only to the Park Hotel in height). She knew that some of the old buildings of the Bund must still be there (Margaret Allen's "First Impressions" article had said as much, noting that the author had stayed in one of them, the Cathay Hotel, now known instead as the "Peace Hotel"), so it would seem odd to our imagined one-time Shanghailander that there was no drawing of the Custom House or the Hongkong and Shanghai Bank. She would be pleased to note, though, that the Peace Hotel merited a mention, if not a sketch, and, having read Allen's report, been prepared to see it identified by its new name.

Flipping through the rest of the Shanghai section of *China Travel*, she would continue to be struck by things that looked familiar, things that looked completely unfamiliar, and things that looked both familiar and somehow different. In the familiar category would be the rows of houses with red tiled roofs and the old church on Thibet Road easily discernible in the bird's eye photograph of the city that takes up pages 14 and 15 of the book. In the category of the unfamiliar would be the photograph on page 34 of "A workers' residential quarter built after liberation," which shows the sun setting gently behind long rows of low-rise concrete apartment buildings, tucked behind tree-lined walking streets. Reading up on this site, she would discover that not only were workers living in newer kinds of buildings than she remembered, but were said to have gone from being exploited to being "masters of the country," with a standard of living that had "been rising steadily" in a metropolis where the problem of unemployment that had in the past plagued it had "long been solved." Another unfamiliar site would be the photograph on page 18 of a statue of the radical writer Lu Xun. Lu Xun, also romanized as Lu Hsun, is now widely considered China's greatest twentieth-century writer, but he was little known to most local Westerners while he lived in the city in the 1930s. Despite the fact that he never joined the Communist Party, preferring to remain a gadfly able to criticize folly and hypocrisy wherever he saw it, he was elevated to revolutionary sainthood in the Maoist era (two decades after his death), as our former Shanghailander would start to realize as she read the caption's claim that the Chairman himself had written out the inscription "Mr. Lu Hsun's Tomb" on the granite base of the "steel statue . . . erected in 1961, when the 80th anniversary of [the writer's] birth was commemorated."

Finally, in the category of a partially familiar yet partially strange sight, one example would be the photograph of the harbor on page 27. In the foreground of the image, which was shot from the east side of the river looking across at the Bund, are a couple of large ships, while in the background are buildings that include the easily recognizable Peace Hotel (previously the Cathay) and, if one looks very carefully, Big Ching (the Custom House clock) poking out from behind a piece of one of the ships that obscures the dome of the Hongkong and Shanghai

Bank completely from view. What is unfamiliar here is not new buildings, but a framing and sense of proportion that differ markedly from the iconography of an earlier era. Photographs with ships in the foreground and the buildings of the Bund in the background were commonly used to represent Old Shanghai on postcards and guidebook covers in treaty-port times. But in these the main focus of attention was often precisely the buildings—the Custom House and the neo-classical landmarks standing near to it—that in the 1975 guidebook's only shot of the Shanghai waterfront are (with the exception of the Cathay Hotel) nearly or completely hidden from view, are not mentioned at all in the caption to that photograph, and as noted above are not designated on the "Tourist Map" (aside, that is, once again for the Cathay Hotel).

The impressions that our imagined Londoner formed from *China Travel* would have been reinforced, with some small variations, if she had found in her researches a copy of a similar 1974 publication, once again in English, the *Tourist Guide to China*. The several pages in this book devoted to Shanghai (most containing simply photographs with shorter accompanying captions than those in its 1975 counterpart) portray some of the sites just described—indeed, in some cases, such as the portrayal of the workers' residences, the exact same photograph is used in the *Tourist Guide to China* and *China Travel*. One difference our imagined reader might note would be that in the 1974 guide there is at least one photograph in which the Custom House figures prominently. Another would be that, while the photograph of Lu Xun's tomb and statue is the same in both books, the 1974 guide uses particularly striking language to describe his political significance, and to link him to a particular ideology, even though the value of maintaining a stance of independence from allegiance to any single doctrine was a central tenet of his writing: "The great thinker, revolutionary and author Lu Hsun used the sharp ideological weapon of Marxism to produce a wealth of literature, becoming the chief commander and courageous standard bearer of China's cultural revolution."

A return visit by a former Chinese resident

> The Bund and Nanjing Road can be said to stand for modern Shanghai. Each bit of ground they contain, each of their tall buildings bears witness to the blood, sweat and tears of the Chinese workers. They stand as testaments of the way that imperialism and feudalism worked together to turn China into a semi-colonial land with a semi-feudal social order, but they also offer historical proof of unending, heroic struggles . . . The history of the Bund and Nanjing Road is the history of class struggle, and these places offer vivid lessons for learning about patriotism and socialism.
>
> This is why this has often been where foreign friends who have come to China start the Shanghai part of their visits.
>
> *The History of the Bund and Nanjing Road*, pp. 3–4.

What would make the deepest impression on our imagined Hong Kong-based return visitor, who had read Chinese language works such as *The History of the*

Bund and Nanjing Road as opposed to English language ones such as *China Travel* around the time of our snapshot year, when he arrived back in the city of his youth and young adulthood? Would he be struck most by the frequency with which the shout "Long Live Chairman Mao" echoed through the city's streets and public spaces? Or by the comparative paucity of automobiles on and disappearance of rickshaws from the streets, and even more than that the greater number of buses and bicycles in the city he came back to than in the city of his memory? Would it be the fact that so few restaurants served foreign dishes and so few bakeries offered loaves of bread for sale? Or would it be instead the disappearance of beggars, the lack of any visible signs of the sex trade?

Each of these would have marked a dramatic change from the Shanghai of the treaty-port era and the Civil War period, and even to a greater or lesser degree from the early Maoist metropolis he had left in 1950. Still, perhaps more striking to him would be superficial but telling alterations in the way people looked. Surely he would find noteworthy the surprisingly uniform way that people on the streets dressed. Even in 1950 local residents had still worn all kinds of colorful clothing, but when he looked around him in 1975, our friend would see people wearing little that was not dark blue, gray, or brown—aside, that is, from the red and gold on badges and pins.

He would also surely be struck by how similarly men and women now dressed, with a great many wearing look-alike jackets. These were cut in what the West had come to know as "Mao jackets," but which would bring to his mind Sun Yat-sen, for the Nationalist Party's founder had been the first to endorse these coats as a new national dress. Shanghai of the treaty-port era had been known as a place where women of all nationalities dressed in the latest styles according to their means. It was also known as a place with more than its fair share of dandies, a city where men of all nationalities were far from impervious to fashion concerns. The fact that apparel no longer provided ready cues to class or even gender would likely fascinate our returnee.

He would also certainly observe that other kinds of differences rooted in class and wealth—as hard to miss in Hong Kong in 1975 as they had been in Shanghai in the 1930s and 1940s—had likewise disappeared, as had ethnic diversity (gone were the Sikhs, the Europeans, the Japanese he had once encountered on the streets). Most people now seemed to live in roughly the same material conditions, with little obvious contrast between the kinds of housing and the kinds of meals that members of different occupational groups and social strata could afford. Gone were the sharp disparities in consumption patterns between rich and poor, the privileged few and the disadvantaged many, which had characterized Old Shanghai and still been noticeable when the New Shanghai of the Communists was very young. Whereas once forms of transport, for example, had divided the city in social terms, now everyone seemed to depend on public transportation and on the ubiquitous bicycles.

These kinds of contrasts with the past were not absolute. As Westerners who visited or lived in mid-1970s Shanghai have sometimes mentioned in conversations with me, even during the height of the era of Maoist sartorial conformity, some residents of that city kept alive, in subtle ways, the fashion-sense for which the metropolis was known.[8] There was always something just a bit different about Shanghai as opposed to other cities, they remember, that showed through in the way a man added a scarf to a standard ensemble or a woman snuck a bit of color into a drab outfit, and to the discerning eye, the quality of the material carried gradations differentiating workers from cadres. And in terms of lifestyles, not all forms of privilege disappeared in Shanghai (or, for that matter, in other cities). Even when the ethos of egalitarianism was being proclaimed most strongly, there were special guesthouses and restaurants frequented by those with influence and power. There were always some individuals, in these years mainly high ranking officials, who had their own drivers and even servants, and secret places where foreign movies and other things deemed decadently bourgeois and therefore off-limits to the general public were available. Still, the change in dress from the Shanghai he remembered (and the Hong Kong where he now lived) would be so great and the shift from privileged lifestyles being flaunted to being hidden would be so dramatic that our return visitor could be forgiven for thinking of these as two areas that had undergone some of the most "profound changes" between 1950 and 1975.

Many alterations in the look of local streets would strike him as almost as noteworthy as those relating to styles of dress and modes of life. In addition to the change in vehicles already noted would be the relative dearth of street corner businesses (the once omnipresent food stalls and hawkers), the storefront windows displaying so few and such uniform products (where they once showed a plethora of different ones), and a shift in advertisements: those touting goods of any sort were now nearly non-existent in public space, but those touting political campaigns were everywhere. If he asked local residents how long this had been the case in the city, they might look at him curiously, for it had been that way for more than twenty years, thanks to the government's successive mass campaigns, each of which required banners and posters to be placed throughout the city. Some might mention, though, an upsurge in the politicization of already highly politicized uses of public space during the last decade. If pressed further, a few of the more astute and forthcoming informants he encountered (perhaps people who had known him well in the past and were hence more willing to talk to him than others would be) might point out another relatively recent shift. It was not just that there were more posters and banners than in the past, but that the slogans on them had begun to change more rapidly than they had in previous decades. This was because beginning in 1966, with the launching of Red Guard activism in Beijing and then in other cities, the pace of political shifts had picked up.

Our friend might also mention how omnipresent images of Mao had become, though here more than in the case of banners and slogans, he might find it hard to convince some of those he talked to (especially, for example, young relatives who had grown up in the 1960s) that this had not always been the case in Shanghai. In 1950, to be sure, Mao's image was carried in parades and displayed on special occasions. But fairly often, as noted in the last chapter, it appeared in tandem with those of other figures, including Sun Yat-sen, Zhou Enlai, Chen Yi (the first post-1949 mayor of Shanghai), and, above all, Zhu De, a Red General second in importance during the Civil War only to Mao. The situation in 1975 was very different from what it had been in 1950 where representations of Mao's personage was concerned, for it now seemed to be everywhere one turned, often on its own, sometimes surrounded by groups of admirers who were presented less as recognizable individuals than as representatives of social groups (model workers, adoring villagers, clusters of patriotic soldiers). Images of Sun Yat-sen, as well as those of other Chinese Communist leaders, had long since disappeared almost completely from public settings: one saw everywhere the Chairman smiling benevolently out from buttons and badges, gazing down from atop giant statues, looking out sternly or beatifically from posters.

If our return visitor probed further, talking to people, reading newspapers, and exploring popular histories of and guides to the city, such as a series of volumes called *Shanghai de Gushi* (The Shanghai Story), which like *The History of the Bund and Nanjing Road* recast the local past as a tale of heroic revolutionary struggles against imperialism and Nationalist Party misrule, other things about how the city had changed might begin to strike him.[9] He might discover that migration into the city from the countryside had stopped occurring regularly, due to fixed rules that kept people bound to their place of origin, unless sent to a new locale (and then often from an urban to a rural setting, rather than vice versa) as part of a political campaign or program or unless a patriotic volunteer was heading to work to improve conditions in a remote area of the sort that residents of Shanghai would once have considered a hardship post. He might also learn that the *danwei* (work unit) had become the main shaper of individual urban lives. By 1975, work units not only provided people with jobs but also housing, social services and ration coupons, and *danwei* leaders often played the main role in communicating political directives, making sure that people took part in the latest mass campaign, and sometimes even arranging marriages for the workers under their sway.

Reading newspapers, popular histories, and guidebooks, our return visitor might come to realize that Shanghai was now regarded as distinctive in ways that differed from earlier epochs. According to these texts, it was special because it was the country's most populous city, its major industrial base and the historical center of working-class movements, the site of the Communist Party's first national congress, and a metropolis where certain forms of exploitation and national humiliation had been particularly extreme before Liberation. He would also read story after story about local residents, under Communist Party leadership, giving new life to the city's many buildings and public areas, in the process cleansing them of the stains of their semi-colonial or bourgeois origins. He would encounter in many books, for instance, the story of Huangpu Park's attainment of a *xinsheng* (new life), presented as a morality tale that encapsulated all that was wrong with Old Shanghai and all that was good and pure about the contemporary city. The "Public Garden," according to this version of the park's past, was until 1949 a space unfairly reserved exclusively for foreigners—and, adding insult to injury, had a sign at its entrance reading "no dogs or Chinese allowed," a phrase that was resented as humiliating by all Chinese. When the Communist Party took power, though, the story continued, the park was redesigned and improved, but more importantly was opened to all residents of the metropolis on an equal basis. It had been stripped of its hypocritical old name—for it hardly deserved to be called a "public" space when the vast majority of local residents were banned from entering—and become a place where Chinese of all ages engaged in physically and spiritually healthy activities, from strolling and enjoying the flowers, to doing calisthenics, to shouting out "Long Live Chairman Mao."

Moves had been underway when our returnee left in 1950 that pointed towards some of the dimensions of Shanghai *circa* 1975 just described. There were already intimations then that the city would be moving towards being one where increased ethnic homogeneity, politicization, and egalitarianism of lifestyles, as well as shifts in the uses of and meanings ascribed to public spaces, were all on the horizon. Still, he might well be shocked to see just how far what were then incipient trends had progressed.

Given all of the ways in which the city he returned to differed from that he had left, our return visitor might be taken aback the first time he ventured down to the Bund—not in this case by how much had changed but by how little. Indeed, aside from showing signs of age, many of the buildings of the Bund would have seemed unaltered. The most famous old structures were still standing, looking at first glance much as they had as far back at the late 1920s. Some modifications to the district had been made when new groups took control of what had once been the International Settlement: the Japanese had removed the statue of Sir Robert Hart from in front of the Custom House, for example, and the Communist Party had placed red flags atop all of the buildings lining the waterfront. Still, the line of structures with their pillars and distinctive roofs (the clock tower of the Custom House, the domed top of the Hongkong and Shanghai Bank building, and so on) would seem to our returnee to be, as he might think of himself, noticeably older, but otherwise little altered.

Any sense of returning to a city that had simply aged, not aged and transformed, though, would be shattered when he noticed that Big Ching was playing "The East is Red." And there were other things that had changed. The lions that had once stood guard outside the bank next door, for example, which had been totems of the British Empire and objects that could be rubbed for luck by those hoping to make a killing on a stock exchange that no longer existed, were missing. And the grand domed building they had once guarded was no longer a bank at all, but rather the headquarters of the local Communist Party authorities.

7 2000: A city in a hurry

The new Shanghai . . . as much symbol as physical city, is appearing on the far bank of the river. Facing the majestic Bund, now a popular promenade, is one of the biggest experiments in history: the new city of Pudong . . . It took a turbulent 200 years for the Western world to make the transition from a rural subsistence economy to a society that lives in flats, shops in supermarkets and gobbles fast food. In Pudong this process is supposed to take 30 years. To this end a quarter of all cranes in the world are rotating here on 22,000 building sites . . .

Ramesh Kumar Biswas, "Shanghai: Time, Tides," 2000[1]

It seems that everyone wants a biennale these days—a vast art exhibition every two years . . . But among this proliferation of biennales, which are the most interesting? Well, in terms of cultural importance, the *2000 Shanghai Biennale* certainly looks promising . . . It is fitting that such an event should take place in this city [which] has always been the Chinese [one] most ready to assimilate Western influences . . . For half a century it was left behind [but] as trade with the West has opened up again over the last decade, Shanghai has been the recipient of a Special Economic Zone, which has seen the wasteland on the east side of the Huangpu river turned into a forest of contemporary skyscrapers, including plans to build the world's tallest building. Spirits are high . . .

Emphasizing the city's desire to step forward into a new global role, the whole Biennale has been titled "Shanghai Spirit" [and] the opening week is subtitled "A Special Modernity"—suggesting an attempt to play a global game by local rules.

David Barrett, "2000 Shanghai Biennale"[2]

Shanghai at the millennium's turn was a city in a hurry. It was rushing to reinvent itself economically: it had a newly opened stock market, local financiers dreamed of their city displacing or at least once again rivaling Hong Kong as a financial hub, and information technology was taking off as an important local industry. The city was struggling to re-establish itself as a cultural hub, via hosting events such as the "vast art exhibition" alluded to above, which made the most of newly built showcase structures, including the Shanghai Museum. It was a place were old edifices were being ripped down and replaced by new ones, with low-lying neighborhoods in the central part of the city being razed at an alarming rate, sometimes to make way for totally different kinds of structures (such as towering office buildings and hotels), but in one famous case—that of the Xintiandi shopping and entertainment district (that opened in 2001)—replaced by a spruced up replica of its former self.

The latest "new" Shanghai was also a city to which and through which people were moving more speedily than ever before. This was due to several developments of the 1990s. One was the opening of a futuristic-looking international airport in Pudong, others included the construction of elevated freeways in many parts of the metropolis and the creation and then continual expansion of Shanghai's first subway system. In 2000, plans were being made as well to open the world's first magnetic levitation train line. When it went into operation soon after our snapshot year ended, it would use a technology developed in Germany to hurtle riders through part of Pudong at speeds of over 250 miles per hour, exceeding those of even Japan's famed Bullet Trains.

The city's concern with speed even showed through in its handling of chronology. Every part of the PRC is supposed to keep to "Beijing Time," meaning that clocks everywhere will be in sync with those in the capital. But when I traveled from Beijing to Shanghai in 1999, I noticed something curious. While there was no difference between the two cities where ordinary clocks were concerned, there was a contrast when it came to countdown clocks in public settings that tick off the time until a point in the future arrives. These kinds of clocks had become popular in the PRC in the mid-1990s when a giant one was set up in the center of the capital, to count down the moments until the Hong Kong handover took place on July 1, 2007. And in 1999, those in Beijing and Shanghai were ticking away the time until the new century and the new millennium began. The difference was that those I saw in the capital were set to go off on January 1, 2001, but those in Shanghai, a city impatient to enter the twenty-first century and start the millennium before its northern rival, were programmed to hit zero a full year earlier, on January 1, 2000.

This final snapshot chapter looks at various manifestations of a single phenomenon: Shanghai's turn-of-the-millennium momentum, its headlong rush to become and be seen as a city representing (as the Biennale's slogans had it) a distinctive "spirit" and a "special modernity." This desire showed itself in various exhibits that, while not always as explicitly as the Biennale, touted the city as a special place which was able to simultaneously trade upon specific past glories and showcase state-of-the-art elements of more generic types of global urbanism.

This "special modernity" was to be characterized by several things. One of its hallmarks was a rapidly changing built environment, defined by the breakneck development in Pudong flagged in the first quote at the start of this chapter— development that had been dreamed of for decades (Sun Yat-sen was the first political leader with grandiose plans for the district) and been envisioned more

Figure 7.1 Shanghai street scene in 2000. Hengshan Road which, like Huaihai Road, is located in the former French Concession and now boasts many bars and cafés

Source: Author's photograph

completely in the mid-1980s, but had only obtained official approval from the central authorities in Beijing in 1990. Another major part of this move to be seen as modern in special ways was, as the second quote highlights, Shanghai's emergence as a key site for exhibitions and displays of various kinds, which would bring to the metropolis objects and people from around the globe and draw attention to its distinctive past and ambitious dreams for the future. The "special modernity" of the city was also defined in part by the degree to which the metropolis as a whole, and especially certain sections of it, came to be seen as permanent exhibitions. That is, the city's modernity at the cusp of the twenty-first century, like that of Paris in the 1800s, was defined both by the way it worked as a site for formal displays and by the degree to which it was treated and treated itself as a place that was on display.

Before saying any more about the city as a site for exhibitions and the city as an exhibition in our snapshot year, it is worth taking stock of ways in which the city had changed since we left it at the end of the last chapter. And to do this, we again call upon a returnee to the metropolis with an image of it formed by living in Shanghai at an earlier point in time. In this case, though, we need not speculate about what *imaginary* return visitors to the city might have thought about the way the metropolis had been transformed during their absence: instead, I simply describe my own disorienting experiences in Shanghai in December 2000.

My brief stay in the city that year was filled with experiences that made me reflect upon how radically different the metropolis was from the one I got to know during my first encounters with Shanghai in the 1980s. And how it contrasted in some ways even with the city with which I had become reacquainted during my two visits to it during the preceding decade (in 1996 and 1999). Sometimes, even the most ordinary activities, such as browsing the shelves of a favorite bookstore, strolling along a street, making conversation with an old friend, or looking at the periodicals for sale at a newsstand would trigger culture shock.

Perhaps fittingly, due to how much more caffeinated in every way Shanghai seemed that year than it had during my previous visits to the metropolis, several of the memories that stand out in my mind as causing me to feel disoriented in 2000 have to do with coffee. I was struck, walking the streets, by the fact that scores of cafés had opened during the year and a half since my last trip to Shanghai. In 1986, there were none, other than those in hotels catering largely to foreigners; by 1996, there were a few; by 1999 scores; but by 2000, it seemed, there were hundreds in the central part of the city alone.

This rise of café culture was not just a Shanghai phenomenon, for new venues for drinking coffee, some linked to chains but often independents, were sprouting up simultaneously in other Chinese cities at the time, as part of a general trend—the same one that saw Starbucks open its first Beijing branches in 1999 (a time when new-style teahouse chains were also springing up in many cities). Still, in Shanghai, there was a distinctive side to the fashion, since the proliferation of cafés there was seen by many less as a pure novelty than as a return to an interrupted trajectory. Local Chinese residents I talked to about the subject often pointed out, for example, how fitting it was that many of the best cafés were located in what had once been the French Concession, the part of the treaty port that, not surprisingly, had been known as the place to head to for coffee and pastries early in the twentieth century. And the link between past and present was explicitly invoked in some of the new cafés, via their use of names that evoked "Old Shanghai" or their walls being plastered with sepia-toned or black-and-white photographs of the city *circa* 1930.

The trend also had a noticeable impact in the realm of publishing, affecting both the local Chinese language press (the newspapers and magazines I picked up during my 2000 stay contained many articles describing individual cafés and ruminating on the significance of the fashion for drinking coffee) and the offerings in bookstores.[3] In every bookstore I entered, I noticed a marked rise in the shelf space given over to what might be called guides to modern living, which offered tips on everything from the latest international styles of home decoration to understanding wine. One major subset of these books dealt with coffee, running the gamut from step-by-step handbooks for opening your own café to works that provided short accounts of the most noteworthy new cafés in various Chinese cities.[4]

The most interesting coffee-related publications I came across, which were displayed prominently at a couple of the largest local bookstores, were a trilogy of works (sold together as a package) by Zhang Yao, a globetrotting photojournalist originally from Shanghai. He had made a splash in Shanghai in the late 1990s with a pair of books (first issued in Taiwan and then re-published in mainland editions), the titles of which can be rendered into English as *Opening the Door of the Café* (a beautifully illustrated potted global history of coffee and establishments that serve that beverage) and *The Café Map* (a work also filled with lovely photographs, in this case focussing on Europe's most famous cafés).[5] The latter book opens with a prologue devoted to Shanghai, with the photographer-author pointing out that, though he has traveled the world going from café to café, his hometown also has noteworthy venues in which to order a cappuccino.[6] At the end of 2000, both books were packaged together with a third one, thrown in for free as a bonus. This one, the title of which can be rendered into English as *Café Diary*, contains a few photographs and no text other than brief captions telling where a given shot was taken. It is made up almost exclusively of blank lined pages, in which purchasers were supposed to jot down any thoughts or fantasies that came into their heads as they sat in cafés. Accompanying publicity materials explained that the book was created because one thing that is supposed to happen when you sip a cup of coffee or a cappuccino is that your mind wanders in interesting directions. This suggests the need to think about the café craze as being linked not just to the rush of caffeinated beverages and a growing interest in cosmopolitan and what until recently would have been derided in China as decadently bourgeois, but also increasing interest in individual introspection—something that also showed up via imports other than cafés, such as a fad for taking yoga classes.[7]

Seeing so many works on coffee and cafés for sale was unexpected, but the coffee-related experiences that triggered the most profound sense of culture shock were visits to a pair of local branches of Starbucks (several of these had opened during the year preceding my December 2000 visit). One of the Starbucks branches I visited was on Huaihai Road (the former Avenue Joffre that was celebrating its centenary in our snapshot year, basking in having once again become a fashionable shopping street). It stood across the street from a McDonald's (there had been none of these in Shanghai in the 1980s, but I had grown used to seeing them on my return visits in the 1990s). The other Starbucks at which I ordered a cappuccino in 2000 was in the Yu Gardens district, which had been transformed in the 1990s into a theme-parked rendition of Shanghai's pre-treaty-port past, albeit with bits and pieces of early 1900s nostalgia thrown in as well for good measure.

Upon entering the Huaihai Road Starbucks, I passed a front window in which the Golden Arches were reflected, but to enter the Yu Gardens meant one passing a site even less expected to someone whose image of the city was formed in the 1980s. Namely, there were men in costumes standing just in front of the tell-tale green logo of the Seattle coffee company, offering passersby rides in either a palanquin (if the customer wanted to pretend to be an official or even emperor of imperial times) or a rickshaw (if the customer wanted to pretend to be a foreign merchant or Chinese banker of the treaty-port era)—all this within view of one of the most famous "traditional" teahouses in Shanghai that has long stood nearby.

Even though going to these two Starbucks involved drinking a beverage and seeing some sights that had no place in the Shanghai I had come to know in the 1980s, the most disorienting parts of my visits to the first local outlets of the global

Figure 7.2 A Starbucks coffee house, 2002, located in the Portman Center, a centrally
located hotel and business complex

Source: Author's photograph

franchise were not these, but rather something I heard and something I saw inside
of each. In the Huaihai Road branch, what I heard was the manager tell me, after
I struck up a conversation with him, that his outlet and the other in Shanghai, while
outposts of an American company, were actually managed by a Taiwanese firm.
Oversight of all the local Starbucks was provided by Presidential Coffee, a
corporation that had previously shown its skills at spreading global capitalism by
bringing 7–11 stores to the Philippines. What I saw in the Yu Gardens store, which
surprised me less than it would have if I had not already learned of the Presidential
Coffee connection, was a copy of a Chinese translation of Starbucks CEO's
Howard Schultz's *Pour Your Heart into It: How Starbucks Built a Company One
Cup at a Time*, which noted inside that it was a rendition into simplified characters
of a complex character edition that had previously been published in Taiwan.

As these opening comments have indicated, the pages that follow, which dwell on the disorienting feel that the radically changed and revved up Shanghai of 2000 as opposed to the slower-paced Shanghai of the 1980s or even of the mid-1990s had for me, will have a much more personal feel than any previous snapshot chapter section. But readers should not assume that the confusion that beset me in turn-of-the-millennium Shanghai, where East met West again and East also met East in surprising ways, was unique. The city was changing so rapidly at that point that spending time there (especially in the central districts and in Pudong, where transformations were taking place at a particularly rapid rate) could be and often was a disorienting and disturbing as well as an exhilarating experience to many people. And by no means just for foreigners who, like me, returned to the metropolis after the passage of a few years and felt they no longer knew the city. Though the specific things that triggered culture shock for me were idiosyncratic, when spending time in Shanghai in 2000 (as well as in years just before and just after that one), old friends who had grown up in and continued to live in Shanghai often commented to me how strange it was for them to feel as they often now felt like strangers in their own home town.

These friends told me of feeling lost within once familiar parts of the metropolis, due to the disappearance of old landmarks and the appearance of new skyscrapers, of streets that had been associated with the sale of particular products no longer being places you could depend on finding those items for sale. They told of being pleased by some changes (some were happy, for example, that they now had shorter commute times, due to being able to take subways rather than buses), but being perplexed by others (navigating along the new elevated highways, for instance).

Works by scholars who conducted much more formal interviews with residents of the city around the same time that I made my brief turn-of-the-millennium return visits (I was there once in 1999 and twice in 2002, as well as in 2000) confirm this sense of the city *circa* 2000 as a disorienting place—even for locals. A strong sense of uncertainty and lost bearings haunts, for example, the work of ethnographer Pan Tianshu, who focusses on the shifting sense of community in one neighborhood. And the same is true of ethnographer Jos Gamble's *Shanghai in Transition*, which strives to give readers a feel for "quotidian lives" and a sense of the culture of the metropolis as a whole in the 1990s. Gamble is very effective at conveying a milieu in which not just a changing built environment but also increasing "choice, mobility, and fluidity" were "unpicking and fraying" the "texture of everyday life," as "both spatial and social" boundaries were "dismantled, fractured, undermined, and reconfigured."

One of Gamble's main themes is that the impact of the economic reforms and the re-opening to the West of the period was so unsettling that the same person could feel thrilled by the direction the city was moving one day, disturbed by it the next. He writes of reactions to the recent changes being described to him as: "like a tidal wave"; as involving shifts that "one could not have believed possible"; as "fake," a case of the foreign press being fooled by a few tall buildings going up, since really "the social and economic system has not changed"; and as "just like a conjuring trick." Then he notes that the same informant was responsible for each statement. "Responses and reactions to the changes" were continually being altered and re-thought, Gamble claims, in a way that makes sense to me given my own experiences, due to "an ongoing process of adjustment, of finding one's bearings."[8]

From 1975 to the turn of the millennium

> I want to thank our hosts. I was telling Chairman Yu that I was here in 1975 with my mother. [*Laughter*] Shanghai has finally recovered. [*Laughter*] I can't tell you what a startling difference it is—Shanghai is today than what it was in 1975 [*sic*]. It's a great testimony to the Chinese people and the leadership of Shanghai and the leadership of this great land.
>
> President George W. Bush, speaking in Pudong at the
> 2001 APEC Summit[9]

> Since 1990, and spurred on especially in 1992 [when Deng approved speeding up development in Pudong], measures have been implemented which are intended to re-create Shanghai as an international financial and commercial center. Since that time Shanghai has embarked upon one of the most adventurous and frenetic building programmes the world has ever known . . . An increasingly important private sector has re-emerged and private markets, restaurants and bars have proliferated . . . vast sums of domestic and foreign capital have flowed into the city. The first reform era joint venture was established in 1980. By the end of 1996, over 16,000 foreign-funded enterprises in the city employed nearly 60,000 people and produced 34 per cent of the city's industrial output. By early 2000, over half the world's largest 500 companies had established operations in Shanghai . . .
>
> Jos Gamble, *Shanghai in Transition*, pp. x–xi

My initial encounters with Shanghai took place during what, in retrospect, can be seen as a curiously in-between period in both Shanghai's history and that of China as a whole. The era I have in mind was one that lasted from the start of the post-Mao Reforms to the Tiananmen protests and the June 4th massacre. This decade-long stretch, running from roughly 1979 to 1989, was one when the economic innovations championed by Deng (who took power at the end of the 1970s, after a brief period following Mao's 1976 death, when the now largely forgotten Hua Guofeng, Mao's chosen successor, led the state) were just beginning to make their impact felt. The 1980s thus saw, in cities such as Shanghai, the founding of many small-scale private enterprises and some large joint venture projects involving both the Chinese state and foreign companies.

It was still not clear, though, as it would become in the rush toward an anything-goes capitalist development strategy in the 1990s, just how far the economic restructuring of society would be taken. It was also not clear whether significant reforms would transform the urban economy and urban social relations. It seemed possible that state-run enterprises would remain the dominant or at least major employers. Perhaps most significantly, it seemed unclear whether dramatic upsurges in foreign investment and the number of "joint ventures" (companies involving partnerships between Chinese and international firms) would affect many urban centers, or just the handful that had been designated "special economic zones"—a category that did not include Shanghai.

It seemed likely back then that some parts of the country would move swiftly away from a socialist economy centered around state-run enterprises: the rapidly growing metropolis of Shenzhen, for example, which the regime was trying to transform from a minor city into a competitor to nearby capitalist Hong Kong, then still a British Crown Colony. But it also seemed possible that Shanghai, with its powerful state-centered economy, would not be forced or allowed to follow a similar route toward post-socialism. And as late as 1986, Shanghai did not yet have many of the things associated with its current largely privatized and re-globalized incarnation. It had no stock market, no karaoke bars, no internet cafés, no KFC franchises. It had no new skyscrapers shooting up toward the heavens, public spaces dominated by advertisements for products rather than for political campaigns, or glossy magazines telling those with upscale aspirations how to decorate their homes and what to wear. It had no new-style gated communities (though many socialist housing developments had gates) made up of villas modeled on those of Western countries. There were no luxury apartment buildings or car dealerships.

This is not to say that the still-socialist city that I came to know in the 1980s was just the same as it had been when we left it in the last chapter. There were more Western goods in circulation by 1986, including one widely recognized symbol of American capitalism, Coca-Cola—a drink that had been consumed and advertised in early to mid-twentieth-century Shanghai but had disappeared well before the Cultural Revolution. Billboards for goods such as these, though, were still far outnumbered on the streets by posters calling for adherence to government policies, such as the limitation of births to one child per couple. And among the most common street decorations were still red banners covered with official slogans, which called on the people to rally behind the Communist Party and support one or other of the periodic campaigns that national or local authorities launched (a drive to kill rats was one of the Shanghai-specific drives initiated during my 1986–1987 stay). The festooning of streets in this manner became especially pronounced, as had been the case in earlier decades of Communist Party rule, when dates rolled around that had historical significance. The official political calendar was dotted with commemorative moments linked to global or national "red" holidays, from International Women's Day on March 8 to the anniversaries of the May 4th Movement and May 30th Movement. One break with the past, though, was that were far fewer intense political campaigns in the mid-1980s than there had been a decade earlier—and those that did take place, such as the 1987 one aimed at stemming the tide of "Bourgeois Liberalization" that occurred after a brief wave of student protests swept the city late in 1986, did not disrupt the rhythms of local life in the way that those of that the Cultural Revolution era and the late 1950s and early 1960s had done.

Another indication of partial change amidst much continuity had to do with eating out. During my first two stays in Shanghai, most restaurants were still state-run. But unlike just a few years previous to my arrival in 1986, not all of them were. There was, for example, an independently run shack selling wontons right near the Fudan campus by the mid-1980s. And every evening, at a bustling nearby market, you could find ethnic Uighurs from Xinjiang Province far to the northwest selling skewers of lamb cooked on makeshift metal barbeques on the streets.

Differences between the mid-1970s and mid-1980s as well as continuities were also noticeable on the cultural front. Though the main works on economics and philosophy sold in bookstores continued to showcase the ideas of Marxist leaders, especially Mao and Deng, for example, some publications of a sort that would have only been able to circulate in underground editions in the 1970s were being issued publicly, from new publications of Max Weber's writings to a translation of the autobiography of Chrysler executive Lee Iacocca. Occasionally, a Hollywood movie would be shown in Shanghai (it was a big event when *Superman* played in 1986); sometimes an American television show or series produced in another capitalist country would be broadcast (Disney cartoons were popular but so, too, were Mexican soap operas, which the censors of that prudish time preferred to American ones in part because of their more toned down treatment of sex); and the songs of a few Western musicians were played on the radio (John Denver was particularly popular in the 1980s, thanks largely to his having performed for Deng Xiaoping during the 1979 visit to the United States made by the Vice-Premier, his formal title which belied the fact that he was China's most powerful man).

Overall, Shanghai of the mid-1980s was not exactly like Shanghai of 1975 by any means, but neither was it a totally different place. Most local residents continued to be employed by the state in one way or another, to live in subsidized housing rented from or otherwise provided by their work unit, and to enjoy medical and retirement benefits through these same *danwei*. As in the past, virtually no family had its own telephone line and groups of neighbors often shared kitchens as well as phones. And there was virtually no variation among newspapers in the headlines they carried, editorial lines they took, or the way in which they were laid out.

In addition, and perhaps most strikingly of all, given the changes that were just around the corner, the built environment of Shanghai had changed little since the 1970s—and indeed in some central districts had changed little since the 1930s. Structures such as the Custom House and Park Hotel remained among the tallest in the city. People's Park and People's Square, two of the major urban development projects of the 1950s, still looked much as they did when first completed. And more generally, all of the city's significant landmarks continued to stand west of the Huangpu River.

Pudong seemed to many locals, as it had for more than a century, a place apart, not really a section of their metropolis at all. Many residents of Shanghai lived out their lives never venturing across the river at all. But some would occasionally go to Pudong to see relatives or to visit a park, such as the one that my wife and I were taken to by friends during our first stay in the metropolis. No one went there, though, to admire tall buildings. There were not yet luxury hotels and fancy conference centers of the sort in which George W. Bush would spend his 2001 return visit to Shanghai.

Four other important continuities between the mid-1970s and mid-1980s are worth stressing. One is that there was still very little variety when it came to not just newspapers but any form of news media. *China Daily*, the only PRC newspaper published in English, was little different in content from any of its Chinese language counterparts. There was also, in essence, just a single television station, and the state maintained nearly complete control over what sorts of entertainment as well as news came into the country from the outside world.

A second very significant continuity with the Maoist past is that most people continued to live in roughly comparable material conditions. The relatively luxurious lifestyles enjoyed by those with ties to the upper echelons of the Party were the main exception, and efforts were made to keep the special privileges that high-ranking cadres enjoyed hidden from view.

Third, while there was an increased flow of people from the countryside into the city, it was still technically illegal to leave one region for another, still less to settle permanently in the city. Most people continued to live where they were born, and Shanghai, which had been a city of immigrants from the 1840s through the 1940s, was no longer one.

Finally, control of formal state power remained firmly, as it still does today, in CCP hands. The regime was starting to be somewhat less intrusive than it had been in the past, with the more limited impact of mass campaigns being a main indication of this shift. But there was no question about who was in charge of the city and the nation and what organization had a monopoly on power.

In all but the last of these ways, the city I re-encountered in 2000 was not the same—far from it. By that point, it had gone from being a still essentially socialist city (with some room for private enterprise) to one that was capitalist in all but name, albeit still under the control of a Communist Party that was not yet, though it soon would be, welcoming capitalists into its ranks. Shanghai by 2000 was a place where, despite state efforts to control the flow of information, there were scores of options when it came to entertainment. One could buy a host of pirated as well as legally produced DVDs of Hollywood, Bollywood, Japanese, Korean, and Hong Kong movies. There were bookstores offering for sale many translated foreign works (including publications celebrating the free market and the lives of famous businessmen) and the guides to what would have been derided as "bourgeois" tastes (for coffee, fine wine, elegant home decor) alluded to above (though not works by or about Chinese dissidents or the Dalai Lama). In addition, internet cafés had sprouted up everywhere; though subject to periodic closures by a nervous state and with web browsers that could not connect to sites containing certain "dangerous" terms, such as the so-called "Three Ts" of Tibet, Taiwan, and Tiananmen, these still allowed users to access innumerable online games, hear songs popular on the other side of the world, and peruse the digital editions of many magazines and newspapers produced in other parts of Asia and the West.

Most strikingly, Shanghai had become a place where lifestyles varied enormously, with many points on the spectrum running from luxury and leisure to scrambling just to get by. Conspicuous consumption was the order of the day—for those who could afford it. At the high end, which was still largely made up of people with political connections but also included entrepreneurs who had struck it rich (and foreign managers who had come to Shanghai to work at joint ventures), people lived in high-security apartment buildings that tried to emulate those found in New York or London and in villas in gated communities named after American suburbs or trendy European locales. At various middle levels, there were professionals and workers who still lived in housing provided by their *danwei* or had just begun to rent lodgings in a more desirable locale.

At the lowest rungs of the social ladder, finally, were migrant laborers, such as the construction workers employed at the sites that kept all those cranes busy. Coming in from the countryside, they once again made Shanghai a city of immigrants (though there were also some more well-to-do newcomers, including tens of thousands who came from Taiwan to do business in the metropolis). The migrant laborers were in the city only quasi-legally, typically slept in crowded shacks, and worried about earning enough for their next meal, rather than about what to buy at the new department stores or what to eat at the city's many new fancy restaurants, concerns of the nouveau riche in Shanghai (as in scores of other cities on the rise). There were also, by 2000, beggars on the streets, as there had not been in Shanghai in the 1980s. The nostalgia craze celebrated Shanghai's resurgence to the global prominence it had *circa* 1930, but the reappearance of beggars spoke to a return of darker trends as well.

New narratives for a new city

Even though the dizzying changes that had transformed the city physically and socially during the years leading up to 2000 could make it a disorienting place for return visitors and residents alike to navigate in our snapshot year, not everything about the metropolis was more confusing then than it had been in the 1980s. Most notably, by the turn of the millennium there were much clearer storylines in play within the city—storylines that structured and in turn were reinforced by exhibitions. These narratives played up certain kind of links between the local past and the local present, and helped increase Shanghai's national and international cachet as a tourist destination.

The stories took many forms but generally converged in presenting Shanghai as a once-and-now-again global city. They treated its history as a cosmopolitan hub as an important resource for the present. They offered a vision of Shanghai as a city characterized by juxtapositions between eras (where past and present met and both collided with the future) and by juxtapositions between cultures (a place where East again met West). These new narratives shaped the displays in and of the city that helped define the "special modernity" that the organizers of 2000's Shanghai Biennale invoked in the name for the first week of their festival.

To appreciate the clarity of 2000 narratives about Shanghai, let us first go back briefly again to the 1980s when storylines, especially about the past, were much more muddied. When I first spent time in the city, two quite different sets of ideas about the treaty-port era were in circulation. One echoed the strident anti-imperialism and focus on class struggle of Mao's heyday. The other anticipated trends to come in the 1990s by seeing the treaty-port era as a mixture of positive and negative influences.

The continued influence of a Maoist storyline showed through, for example, in the Chinese language popular histories of the city offered for sale in bookstores in the 1980s. These tended to focus almost exclusively, when dealing with the treaty-port era, on inequities associated with foreign control of parts of the city, the exploitation of workers by capitalists of all nationalities, and the heroic acts of resistance undertaken by local patriots from different classes (but especially workers and to a lesser extent students) under the guidance of Communist Party organizers. Similarly, the city's historical monuments at that point still tended to celebrate revolutionary figures or decry the abuses that the masses had suffered in the past. There were multiple sites (including some small campus memorials), for example, dedicated to the heroes and martyrs of the May 30th Movement of 1925. And one of the main plaques on the Bund, standing directly across from the Peace Hotel, retold as simple fact the urban legend holding that a treaty-port era sign that humiliatingly likened Chinese to dogs had stood right there, by the entrance to the International Settlement's Public Garden, for decades.

On the other hand, though, a more ambivalent vision of the treaty-port era, as a time that should be remembered for more than forms of oppression and resistance, had begun to creep in. Guidebooks aimed at tourists, including some produced by official Chinese travel agencies, had begun to play upon the mystique of an "Old Shanghai" that deserved to be remembered as a celebrated as well as a vile place. Yes, it was wrong that the International Settlement and French Concession were under foreign control, according to these texts, but that should not lead us to forget that they were sites through which useful ideas and technologies made their way into China, and that they were characterized by excitement as well as despair, modernizing trends as well as revolutionary ones.

This modified vision of the treaty-port era did not yet have a place in formal public displays within the city, where the only museums and historic sites invoking the treaty-port past did so via commemoration of celebrated struggles (such as that of May 30th), political leaders (like Sun Yat-sen), and cultural figures (like Lu Xun). But proprietors of hotels catering to foreigners, as well as Chinese and foreign participants in joint ventures, certainly encouraged this alternative view. There were even tentative moves made by local scholars to question standard parts of the Maoist storyline. One of the deans of local history, Wu Guifang, for example, went so far as to publish a short piece on the Public Garden that, while stressing that there certainly were rules limiting Chinese access to the grounds from the 1880s through 1928 (only servants attending foreigners were allowed in for most of that period), pointed to the lack of any solid evidence that a sign directly linking native residents to dogs had ever stood by the entrance.[10] In general, while the treaty-port era continued to be treated as a troubling period in the local past, moves to tone down criticism of that period were underway, and some were beginning to acknowledge that in an era when China was seeking to re-engage with the capitalist world, there might be some parts of that early legacy worth drawing upon.

The moves toward seeing good as well as bad in Shanghai's treaty-port era encounters with international forces became far from tentative by the mid-1990s, and by the turn of the millennium it sometimes seemed that the Japanese invasions of 1932 and 1937–1945 remained the only parts of the city's past that all locals agreed should be viewed with disdain. The new narrative, firmly in place by 2000 and showcased in everything from books to the cafés trading in Old Shanghai nostalgia, was that the city had resumed in an exciting way an interrupted cosmo-politan trajectory. The most important physical manifestations of this storyline took the form of exhibits of objects from different parts of the world, which were put on display in new buildings or old ones with important historical resonances; or, in the case of the Biennale, the most prestigious exhibit of the year, in a combination of both sorts of places, for some events were held in the newly built Shanghai Museum (a large structure with state-of-the-art internal display areas erected on one edge of People's Square in 1996), while others were held in the Shanghai Art Museum (a nearby building on Nanjing Road West dating from the 1930s, which is topped by the city's second best-known old clock and began life as the Racing Club and then after 1949 was transformed into the Public Library, until the current one on Huaihai Road opened in the 1990s).

Early in our snapshot year, well before the Biennale began, the *Shanghai Star* was already alerting its readers to the increasingly prominent role of exhibitions in local life. Under the headline "Exhibitions Bring Business," a January article appeared in the newspaper that described Shanghai as a place where there had lately been a "burgeoning" of "big and small" displays of goods. According to this story, the number of exhibitions had increased at an annual rate of 17 percent ever since 1990—a watershed year for the metropolis, since it was when Pudong's development began. What sort of exhibitions had come to Shanghai up to that point? The report describes them as having involved displays of everything from "delicacies" and "flowers" and "hi-fis, to furniture and pets," and goes on to call for the exhibition "business" to be "nurtured" and expand in yet more directions in the months to come.[11] What the article does not mention—yet easily could have—is that in the previous year Chinese officials had just begun take the first tentative steps toward bringing to China the biggest exhibition of all, a World Expo (in this case, one scheduled for 2010), and that Shanghai was the city that was being touted as the logical site for that event (the bid would prove successful, though not until after our snapshot year had ended).

The year 2000 was also when displays other than formal exhibitions would proliferate in the city. Many of these again reinforced the new narrative of the local past, taking the form of nostalgic invocations of "Old Shanghai." These had begun to appear in the 1990s and continued to appear in our snapshot year, not just in and around cafés but in bars and restaurants and hotels. Some even showed up inside new malls. One glitzy shopping center I visited in 2000, for example, had special indoor "Old Shanghai" streets, which mixed real and faux treaty-port era objects (from rickshaws to streetlamps that looked as though they could have once stood by Regents Park in London) to conjure up "real" for some visitors but "faux" for most people's memories of the past (particularly the period right around 1930).

Many exhibits, formal and informal alike, spoke to the effort in 2000 to reinforce the new storyline and convince viewers that Shanghai represented a "special modernity," but none did so as elaborately as the Biennale. It was self-consciously designed to show off the city's most famous architectural landmarks, both new and old. This was why events alternated between the new Shanghai Museum and the older Shanghai Art Museum.

The overall goal of all biennales and special features of this particular one also illustrate key developments in the city *circa* 2000. All new art biennales strive to put the cities that host them on a par with renowned urban centers, such as Venice, that are already known for their gatherings of artists. Shanghai's 2000 Biennale was no different. And though it was called the "third" Shanghai Biennale, it can be seen both as continuing an established tradition and starting one almost from scratch. This is because, unlike its two predecessors of 1996 and 1998, it included, for the first time, displays created not just by artists living in China but also some based abroad, albeit in some of these cases Chinese émigrés. According to art historian Wu Hung, for example, a Paris-based artist and guest curator, Ho Hanru, "arguably contributed most" to the Biennale's "actual planning"; one of the event's conference sessions opened with the showing of a work by the American experimental filmmaker Matthew Barney; and works by Japanese artists such as Tatsuo Miyajima and Mariko Mori were displayed in the Shanghai Art Museum.[12]

Perhaps the single object that best symbolized the Biennale, though, was one by a Chinese artist that had a close tie to a major local landmark that was introduced earlier: the Hongkong and Shanghai Bank Headquarters, the great domed structure that stands beside the Custom House. The famous signature building on the Bund was not a venue for exhibits of art during the Biennale, but instead served as the inspiration for a creative act. One standout piece from the event was a scale model of that neo-classical edifice of the Bund. It was built entirely out of sand, meaning that it began to fall apart as soon as it was completed, a testament perhaps to a city in which buildings were shooting up and being torn down at equally rapid rates.[13]

Conclusion:
Ten theses on twenty-first-century Shanghai

As science fiction visionary William Gibson famously remarked, "The future has already arrived—it's just not evenly distributed." The future that almost everyone will encounter eventually is first evident in dense, economically dynamic, cosmopolitan cities. Over its erratic history, Shanghai has certainly grasped more than its share of tomorrow . . . at the beginning of the 21st century it finds itself positioned once again on the outer edge of urban possibility, opening a window onto the emerging Asian Century and basking in international fascination.

> Nick Land *et al.*, *Urbanatomy: Shanghai 2008*,
> guidebook published 2008[1]

Xiao Weiping, who lives very close to the planned route of Shanghai's high-speed "maglev" train, says there is a principle behind her decision to risk official displeasure by opposing the project.

"Development is a good thing, and as a Chinese I'm proud of Shanghai's development," the 39-year-old housewife says in her two-bedroom, walk-up apartment in the suburb of Minhang, bought five years ago for 370,000 yuan, or $51,000. "But when you're developing, you have to balance it with the lives of people" . . .

[She and others living] along the maglev's planned route are complaining about noise and electromagnetic radiation, rejecting city officials' insistence that the line would be no threat to their health.

> "Maglev Train Fuels Fundamental Change for
> Chinese Protests," January 31, 2008[2]

The years since 2000 have not seen any break with the pattern of rapid, often confusing change in the built environment and quality of local life described in the last chapter. I keep waiting to make a twenty-first-century trip to Shanghai and not feel disoriented by how different it seems from the city I last encountered. I keep expecting to return to find a city that looks basically like, and is still moving at the pace it was, when I was last there. But this has not happened yet. When I went to Shanghai twice in 2002, once in 2004, and most recently in March 2007, I felt a sense of culture shock each time. Given this ongoing breakneck pace of transformation, writers hoping to convey to readers what the metropolis is like right now face a challenge: they worry—for good reason—that as soon as they finish formulating their thoughts, the ground may shift yet again. And this is no idle concern. Consider the case of one of the best twenty-first-century volumes on the city, *Shanghai: Architecture and Urbanism for Modern China*. This richly illustrated interdisciplinary 2004 work, which includes important essays by scholars and architects and urban planners based inside and outside of China, went to press with an eye-catching cover showing the design for the twisting "Flower Bridge" that was slated to be the iconic structure of the 2010 World Expo—the answer to the Eiffel Tower of the 1889 World's Fair and the Ferris Wheel of the 1893 Chicago Columbian Exposition. By the time the book appeared, however, plans for the bridge had been scrapped, and the search had resumed for a fitting symbol for that 2010 event.[3]

The rapidity with which Shanghai has been changing and continues to change makes it difficult to predict what lies in store for it. And as the preceding pages have shown, prognostication has always been a perilous business where this shape-shifting metropolis is concerned. We have seen above various examples of predictions that turned out to be unfounded, with Hart's 1875 assertion that the treaty port would soon be eclipsed as a center of trade and the 1900 notion that this same place was destined to become China's post-Boxer capital being two notable cases in point. Still, at the risk of joining the ranks of those who have made statements they later regretted about what would happen next in Shanghai, I will close with ten propositions—in some cases intentionally provocative ones— that move between the city's past and present to reflect on its possible future. These propositions are inspired by a sense of long-term patterns in Shanghai's history. I make them based on my research on the city's past, things I have seen during my last few visits, events such as the early 2008 anti-maglev extension protests that took place in the city since I was last there (that I have followed long distance via newspaper reports, website commentaries, and e-mails from friends), and reflection on what I think may transpire between the month in which I am writing (March 2008) and the day (May 1, 2010) when the countdown clocks ticking away the seconds until the World Expo will hit zero.

There is something fitting about looking forward when dealing with the present incarnation of Shanghai. After all, it has become a city that is routinely described as looking "like the future"; by the time Paris Hilton said this about the metropolis near the end of 2007 (she was there to attend an MTV awards show), it had already become a cliché.[4] Comments about Shanghai offering a window onto urban realities to come, such as that in the guidebook quoted at the start of this chapter, have been made for more than a decade now—though they just keep increasing in frequency. And Shanghai has become a city that is now attracting not just one but two different sorts of Chinese and international filmmakers. As in the past, some go there to work landmarks of the Bund into costume dramas set in the years 1900–1949, as everyone from Steven Spielberg to Chen Kaige and Ang Lee (Li Ang) has done. But others point their cameras at the opposite side of the riverfront, as they incorporate shots of its space-age skyscrapers into action thrillers and sci-fi tales set in a futuristic present or in a period still to come.

Figure C.1 The Expo countdown clock that stands outside the Urban Planning Museum
located in People's Square in the heart of Shanghai, 2004

Source: Author's photograph

1: Shanghai's 2010 moment will be important

It is common in the West to think of World Expos and the World's Fairs from which they are descended as things whose heyday is long gone—thanks in part to some of their functions being taken over by theme parks (such as the Epcot Center in Orlando, with its discrete areas devoted to specific countries), while others are subsumed by mega-malls (where products from all parts of the world are displayed and cuisines from many lands can be sampled at food courts). Many Europeans and Americans do not spare much thought at all for Expos, unless they happen to live in or visit a city that once held one and now contains a reminder of it in the form of a landmark (the Space Needle in Seattle, for example), and view World's Fairs as events that came and went between the 1850s and 1930s (with those of 1876, 1893, and 1939 that took place in Philadelphia, Chicago, and New York, respectively, looming particularly large in the American imagination). The situation is very different, though, in Asia. The 2010 Expo is already generating enormous attention in China, with updates about new countries signing on to host pavilions showing up regularly in newspapers and on websites, while in Shanghai itself books and articles about the impact of past World's Fairs and prospects of this upcoming one have become a minor cottage industry.[5] And once the Beijing Games occur (scheduled to take place between the time I am writing and the time this book appears in print), the Chinese media will certainly ratchet up still further coverage of the planning for its Shanghai sequel. The same will be true of newspapers and television shows in places such as Tokyo and Seoul.

In addition, as an event that some are predicting will bring 70 million tourists to Shanghai and lead to yet another face-lift for its waterfront (to make room for national pavilions and provide docking space for the massive cruise ships that will bring many Expo visitors to the city), the event will be one that the international media will also cover in detail. It seems unlikely that the global media frenzy surrounding Shanghai 2010 will match that focussing on Beijing 2008, in part because World Expos are simply not as custom-made for television and do not involve the same kind of spectatorship from afar. In addition, although millions of people will come to the Expo during its six-month run (it is scheduled to close in October 2010), many of them will arrive not from the West but from other parts of the Chinese mainland, from Hong Kong, and from countries near to China, especially Japan and Korea as well Singapore and Taiwan. Still, even in terms of Western coverage, it may in the end be at least in the same general league as the Beijing Games.

Clearly, the Chinese government would like this to be the case, and both local and national authorities have begun to take steps to encourage the world to view the Olympics and the Expo as a kind of one–two punch designed to knock-out old conceptions of China—something that the Tokyo Games of 1964 and Osaka Expo of 1970 did to replace visions of Japan as a militaristic and defeated country with visions of it as a thoroughly modern and dynamic new nation. The main 2008 Olympic websites contain sections devoted to the 2010 Expo, for example, and Shanghai local officials are using the term "Economic Olympics" to refer to the event that will come to their city soon. Locally, much is also being made already of a crucial shift in the symbolic geography of Shanghai that the Expo will bring: namely, it will pull together Puxi and Pudong into more of a unified whole, since this mega-event will unfold on both sides of the river.

2: Shanghai's 2010 moment has already arrived

While the Expo will surely bring about dramatic changes to Shanghai's built environment and global image, one needs to appreciate what 2010 has *already* done for the city as well as what it will do in the months to come. The same metroppolis that was so eager to get a jump on the new millennium that its millennial countdown clocks were programmed to go off a full year before those of Beijing has not waited for its Expo year to arrive to start looking more like a metropolis that *recently held* a World's Fair than like one that is *gearing up* to host one. The linking of Pudong and Puxi, for example, has been in process for over a decade now, via the erection of bridges and tunnels that facilitate the flow of people and objects across the river. The new Maglev line, which has temporarily been put on hold, would have provided yet another method of going from Pudong to Puxi, but subway lines connecting the districts have been running for years.

One place where you can get a striking sense of 2010 having not just arrived but come and gone is at the Urban Planning Museum. Visitors to this site at People's Square, not far from the Shanghai Museum discussed in the last chapter, see an impressive scale model of the city (the largest such model of any metropolis on earth) that includes sites that will not be built full-size for another two or in some cases even twelve years. Moreover, as part of its efforts to secure the right to host the Expo and other major international events (such as the 2001 APEC Summit), and its infrastructural preparation, the Shanghai of 2008 already includes some things that are more typically left behind after than created before a World's Fair. We may not know what the iconic structure of the 2010 Expo will be, but well before it won the right to host the event, Shanghai's planners built a sky-scraper reminiscent of the Space Needle. The city also inaugurated a showy Maglev train line, with rocket-like bursts of speed that can exceed 250 miles per hour (a vehicle that awes visitors but also has generated protests by those living near proposed extensions of its route, who worry about potential health hazards and threats to their property values)—just the sort of novel form of transportation that one expects to see displayed at an Expo (e.g. the moving sidewalk was first shown to the World at the 1900 Paris Universal Exposition).

3: Visions of the city as an "East-meets-West" place are passé

It has long been commonplace both within and beyond Shanghai to talk about the city as a locale that connects Europe and America to China. This idea took hold initially during the treaty-port period, when nicknames for the city as a whole (most famously "Paris of the Orient") were used to portray the metropolis as one that had ties to both the West and the East—something that was also underscored by comparably structured shorthand phrases for specific districts or streets (e.g. when the Bund was called China's "Wall Street," Nanjing Road likened to New York's 5th Avenue, and so on) and even buildings (the best known case is the Custom House being called "Big Ching"). It is easy to trace the origin of a view of Shanghai as an East-meets-West setting, since, as we have seen, in the middle of the 1800s first Britain and then the United States and France established special enclaves by the Huangpu River. Then, later in the nineteenth century and early in the twentieth century, it became a stop on the itineraries of famous Western tourists (from General Grant to Charlie Chaplin) and a port via which Western products (from streetlights to cars, Hollywood movies to bottles of Coke, cigarettes to saxophones) made their way into China. Throughout the late 1800s and first half of the 1900s Shanghai played a dual role as at least a main window (and often *the* main window) onto the West for many Chinese, and a main window (and again often *the* main window) onto China for many Westerners. There were always cities to the south (first Canton and then even more so Hong Kong) that competed with it for the title of being the key Chinese East-meets-West location, and from the 1950s through the 1980s, the Crown Colony functioned in many ways as treaty-port Shanghai formerly had. Many claim, though, that Shanghai is now back as top claimant to the position.

As we have seen, even in the treaty-port era, it could be misleading to think of Shanghai's cosmopolitanism as simply an East-meets-West phenomenon. The city may have been a "Paris of the Orient" and a "New York of the West" (another nickname), but it was not only a place to which Europeans and American products, ideas, and people came and made their marks in a Chinese setting. There were always non-Western and non-Chinese actors playing key roles in the story of Shanghai's globalization. When the Public Garden was off-limits to Chinese other than servants, for example, it might be visited by a businessman from Korea and a family of Baghdadi Jews, who had come to listen to the Shanghai Municipal Orchestra, in which Filipinos were among the musicians, and when they entered to hear the band, they might have passed by a Gurkha constable at the gate. Most significantly, of course, among the non-Western and non-Chinese participants in Shanghai's initial rise to global city status were the many Japanese who, as investors, as tourists, as literary influences, and as invaders and then conquerors, figured prominently in shaping the history of the city throughout the first half of the twentieth century.

If Shanghai's initial globalization deserves to be treated as much more than just a tale of East-meets-West, the same holds true in spades for the city's re-globalization. The mixture of actors and influences is not quite the same, but it is once again very much an East-meets-East as well as an East-meets-West story. This is true even of some developments that seem at first to be all about the revived importance of flows to the city from America and Europe. Consider, for example, the arrival of the first Starbucks outlets in 2000. Yes, this company is based in Seattle and serves drinks, such as espresso and cappuccino, that are associated with Italy and France. But as I mentioned in the previous chapter, when the Shanghai outlets opened, they were managed by Presidential Coffee, a company based in Taiwan. And one of the Taiwanese company's goals in 2000 was to try to lure away latte drinkers in the city who had grown used to frequenting Manabe, a Japanese chain of cafés that had started operating in Shanghai in the 1990s. The re-globalization of Shanghai has been shaped by many other East-meets-East phenomena that similarly tie the metropolis to Japan. For instance, Japanese companies have been involved in creating many Pudong landmarks, including what is just now the tallest skyscraper on earth, the World Financial Center, while Puxi has many karaoke bars and giant digital display screens reminiscent of those of Tokyo. And at least several hundred thousand and perhaps even near to a million people from Taiwan currently reside and work in Shanghai, with many more living between Shanghai and Suzhou in the corridor that is the heart of the Chinese computer industry, its answer to Silicone Valley.

In addition, despite the rivalry between Hong Kong and Shanghai that is some-times stressed, the money spent on both sides of the Huangpu River by investors and tourists from the former city has played a crucial part in the resurgence of the latter metropolis. One of the city's leading entertainment and retail districts —Xintiandi (New Heaven and Earth), with its buildings that are brand new but replicate early 1900s styles—was bankrolled primarily by a Hong Kong devel-oper. In addition, one of the restaurants located there is partly owned by Hong Kong actor Jackie Chan, while a nearby clothing boutique is a branch of Shanghai Tang (a trendy clothing retailer that, despite its name, began in Hong Kong).[6] Shanghai's return to glory as a filmmaking center has been due in part to what Western directors and producers have done by coming to the city to shoot *The Painted Veil, Mission Impossible III*, and so on, but also to the Shanghai-set films shot in the city or just outside of it (in Chedun, a film studio is populated largely with replicas of key local landmarks) by directors with ties to Hong Kong (Stephen Chow of *Kung-fu Hustle* fame) and Taiwan (Ang Lee, whose 2007 film *Lust, Caution* is set in the city during the Japanese occupation).

Many other East-meets-East aspects of Shanghai's re-globalization could be cited, which is not surprising given that Japan and South Korea are now China's leading trade partners. One could point to the enormous importance of Japanese and Korean products and popular culture, including *anime* and *manga* and horror movies from South Korea, among young people in this and nearly all other East Asian cities.[7] Or to the role that authors with varying kinds of ties to South Asia, from Pankaj Mishra to Kiran Desai, Arundhati Roy to Pico Iyer, have played in the city's increasingly high profile international literary festival. Or to the business that software companies with connections to Bangalore and Singapore have done in Pudong.[8] Rather than provide an extended list of East-meets-East connections, however, I will end this section with a quick sketch of a restaurant that is as fitting a symbol for the non-Western aspects of the city's current cosmopolitanism as the many local branches of McDonald's or "M on the Bund" (an elegant haute cuisine restaurant in a refurbished Bund landmark building) are for the East-meets-West element in that cosmopolitanism. That restaurant is Dintaifeng, which features the same Shanghainese cuisine that can be bought in many of the city's eateries. It shares a signature dish, delicate *xiaolong* pork dumplings bursting with soup when one bites into them, with the best known restaurants in Yu Gardens (especially "Nanxiang Xiaolongbao," which has long lines daily made up of patrons eager to consume the product for which the shop is named, and also a near-by eatery whose name can be translated as simply "The Old Restaurant") as well as the restaurant on the eighth floor of the Peace Hotel (which has been serving the morsels since the building was known as the Cathay). The Dintaifeng chain, however, did not originate in Shanghai. It now has outlets in Beijing, Tokyo, Singapore, Los Angeles, and Hong Kong (where it competes for the custom of *xiaolongbao* lovers with an "Old Restaurant" modeled on the one in Yu Gardens), but the original Dintaifeng was not opened in any of those cities. Its original branches were all in Taiwan. The first Shanghai outlet of this Taiwanese chain, fittingly for an East-meets-East culinary tale of this sort, opened in Xintiandi, and one of its walls features a collage of the faces of Hong Kong celebrities.

4: History has influenced and will continue to influence Shanghai's burst forward

Few cities, especially those determinedly striving to be seen as futuristic, are as intensely concerned with their own past as is post-socialist Shanghai. This shows through, above all, in efforts to use the treaty-port glory days as proof that Shanghai's natural destiny is to be a global city.

What exactly is the relevance of the local past—or, rather, multiple local pasts—for Shanghai's current state and future prospects? One kind of relevance relates to patterns of tourism. Throughout the city, areas that were especially significant to different groups during the treaty-port period are seeing a boom in visitors with money to spend who are interested in revisiting sites from their youthful sojourns in Shanghai or want to see where their parents or grandparents once lived. This kind of historically minded tourism has, for example, brought Japanese and Jewish travelers alike to the Hongkou section of the city, for this was both the part of Shanghai where many people with ties to Japan once resided and the site where many of the Jews who came to the city from Europe during World War II to flee Nazi persecution clustered. The marketing of the treaty-port mystique along the Bund and in the former French Concession is done partly to attract visitors who have no personal ties to the city. But there, too, some of the Chinese and Western travelers who arrive are eager to walk along streets or gaze at buildings that were important to them in their childhoods, or became the subject of familial lore thanks to stories told to them in Hong Kong, London, New York, or Paris by parents or grandparents who once lived in or visited pre-Communist Shanghai.

This is by no means the only way in which the past has financial relevance for Shanghai's present, for the same thing that brings tourists to the city sometimes also encourages people to invest or do business in the city. There are many cases of people based elsewhere but with personal or familial ties to Shanghai who are bringing business back into the city, now that it is re-globalizing. Filmmaker Wong Kar-wai, who is Hong Kong based but was born in Shanghai, for example, has recently been shooting movies in the city of his birth.

It is hard to know just how many of the residents of Hong Kong and Taiwan who are now investing or working in Shanghai have family links to the treaty-port metropolis of old, but a significant number certainly do. This is hardly surprising, given how many members of the city's burgeoning Chinese capitalist class of the 1920s–1940s either fled to Taipei or headed to the Crown Colony just before or just after the Communist Party took control of Shanghai. The links to the city were, moreover, kept alive between 1950 and the current era of the city's re-globalization, thanks partly to a plethora of Hong Kong and Taiwan films and publications that told stories set in the treaty port by the Huangpu. So strong was the nostalgia for "Old Shanghai" that developed in Taipei and Hong Kong that many residents of those cities without any actual family ties to the mainland metropolis were predisposed to view investing in the city as natural and attractive as soon as it re-opened its doors to international business ventures.

5: The treaty-port past is not the only one that continues to shape Shanghai's future

Even though Shanghai *circa* 1930 is the focus in virtually all of the city's main nostalgia-themed restaurants and cafés, and is also the period invoked in the advertisements for boutique hotels that boast of letting visitors sleep in rooms once frequented by foreign tycoons or Chinese gangsters and their courtesans or mistresses, it is not the only historical period that is important to keep in mind. Shanghai's international tourism industry relies, albeit to a lesser degree, on sites associated with the time before the Opium War, with a full tour of the city typically including, for example, a stop at Yu Gardens, which has been remade into a theme park version of a Confucian temple complex cum "traditional" arts shopping arcade. In addition, visitors from other countries, in this as in other Chinese cities, sometimes feel that they have not really experienced it until they have bought real or faux objects linked to the Mao era, such as Little Red Books and alarm clocks containing representations of the Cultural Revolution's Red Guards. These are offered for sale in various parts of the city. One of the best places to buy them, as well as to purchase artifacts—again a mixture of the genuine article and imitations—is at a multi-story flea market that stands at the edge of Yu Gardens.

In addition, Shanghai locals in a nostalgic frame of mind have begun to pay more attention to parts of the early Mao and post-Mao periods. We can expect that, as the metropolis continues to develop in startling and rapid ways, there will be an increase in this fascination with periods such as the 1950s and 1980s. One sign of movement in this direction is that in the "Old Shanghai" sections of local bookstores, once reserved for works on treaty-port times, texts dealing with later periods, such as reproductions of a map of the city in 1956, are starting to show up.

A notable illustration of this incipient trend, which can be expected to become more pronounced in the years to come, is the success of two photography books, the English language titles for which are *A Changing Shanghai* and *A Changing Shanghai II*.[9] These books have virtually no text, but simply juxtapose black-and-white images of locales (shot in the past) with color images of the same spots (shot very recently and looking radically different, dirt lanes transformed into multi-lane highways, low-rise buildings supplanted by skyscrapers). The format is much like many previous books for sale in Shanghai that juxtaposed pre- and post-1949 images, but there are two special features of these volumes. One distinctive thing about them has to do with the photographers involved: the son of the man who took the black-and-white shots took the color ones. The other distinctive thing about them is that the seemingly long ago "then" evoked in these particular books is not the 1930s or even the 1950s, but the late 1970s, the 1980s, and sometimes even the early 1990s.

6: Shanghai is unique—but not completely so

Comparing cities is always tricky, since every metropolitan center has at least one or two features that make it not quite like any other place on earth. There are cities that have distinctive histories, unusual physical locations, or a special sort of demographic make-up. There are urban centers where the habits and beliefs of local people, the character of municipal political arrangements, or the roles the cities play in regional trade networks are highly distinctive. And there are metropolises where the nature of local architectural patterns, structure of local cultural institutions, and character of the local industrial base seem very special. Finally, there are cities such as Shanghai about which all of these things can be and have been said.

Not surprisingly, then, there have long been and continue to be people who present Shanghai as a city that defies comparison. Among many commentaries in this vein that could be cited are two written almost sixty years apart by Thomas Millard, founding editor of the *China Weekly Review*, and Zhang Zhongli, one of the leading China-based Shanghai specialists: "Shanghai is many-sided . . . unique among the cities of the world . . . almost indescribable" (Millard, 1928).[10] "Shanghai is not like London or Paris . . . She is not like New York . . . She is not even like Jakarta . . . Shanghai's development path has been unique. Shanghai is just Shanghai" (Zhang, 1996).[11]

While it is undeniable that in many specific regards Shanghai is unlike any other place on earth, in trying to understand its current state and future prospects, comparisons with other places can help. In addition, there is value for those primarily interested in other cities to contemplate some of the ways that Shanghai may be setting patterns or beginning to serve as a model for other urban centers. My next three theses make the case for different sorts of comparisons.

7: Twenty-first-century Shanghai has things in common with other re-globalizing cities

What exactly is a "re-globalizing metropolis"? How has Shanghai's status as such shaped its present and how might this feature of the city influence its future? I use the term "re-globalizing metropolis" to refer to cities that once had, subsequently lost, and are now striving to reclaim a position as one of the world's leading cosmopolitan hubs—or, in Shanghai's case, have successfully reclaimed that position, but seek to become ever more tightly enmeshed in international flows. Much of the literature on global cities, such as the very influential (and rightly so) early work on the subject by Saskia Sassen, presents these urban centers as having followed a simple trajectory, moving from being nested within a local economy, to being the center of a nation or empire, to being a key node in robustly transnational economic, financial, and cultural flows.[12] This vision of a steady movement toward figuring importantly in an ever wider arena, and ultimately beginning to have more in common with other global cities located in different countries than with any metropolis within the same geopolitical unit, works well when the urban center in question is New York, London, Paris, or Tokyo. It becomes problematic, though, in a case such as Shanghai, a city that, as we have seen, was in many ways more "global" in the first quarter than in the third quarter of the twentieth century and was more like other Chinese cities in the 1970s than it was in the 1870s. Since Shanghai is now routinely called a "global city," drawing attention to its "re-globalizing" nature can help analysts in urban studies better understand the varied routes that a metropolis can take to top tier status.

Where Shanghai itself is concerned, though, what is perhaps most valuable about the "re-globalizing" category is that it encourages observers to look for parallels between the city and some others with which it has not routinely been compared. Istanbul, for example, which is now on a similar upward trajectory and like Shanghai is staking its claim to international attention, whether from tourists or investors, on a vision of itself as becoming again the kind of cosmopolitan hub that it was roughly a century ago. One thing that cities of this sort have in common is the interest that local tourist boards and chambers of commerce show in trading on memories of a colorful past, rooting their bid for international recognition now with a vision of how famous, celebrated, even notorious and exotic their communities once were. Paris is not a re-globalizing urban center, since it has remained cosmopolitan for centuries, but, interestingly, Shanghai is not the only member of this category that was once called a "Paris of the East," for it shares this nickname with urban centers such as Bucharest, Budapest, Istanbul, and Beirut, among other places.

Looking beyond Shanghai and into the future, we can expect to see the city, due to its success at using ideas about the local past to serve its present globalizing goals, stand out more and more as a model for other urban centers that had golden ages as cosmopolitan hubs. This has happened already with Bombay (Mumbai), where some boosters have invoked Shanghai as having blazed a path that their city should follow.[13] And it is easy to imagine developers in a Havana or Hanoi of 2020 trying to figure out how to create a local counterpart to Xintiandi that would simultaneously, like that site, point to a storied past and an ambitious future. Its success at trading upon its cosmopolitan past could also be a model for some of the other Chinese cities with global aspirations, most notably other former treaty ports such as Guangzhou (Canton). But its primary mainland competitor at present, Beijing, is taking a different route—one that fits more easily into the standard move from national to international hub that other capital cities have taken en route to global city status.

8: Twenty-first-century Shanghai as a post-socialist metropolis

The category of "post-socialist" city is used here to mean simply a place where the scope for private business transactions was formerly limited and where the state closely and authoritatively dominated the economy. Not all post-socialist cities are re-globalizing, but some of the most famous ones, like Shanghai, are. Budapest and what was once East Berlin, for example, are places that are both trying to reconnect with a storied, cosmopolitan past and have recently undergone a shift away from socialism—in their cases, unlike Shanghai's, a shift that has been accompanied by the fall from power of a Communist Party.

To illustrate the usefulness of thinking about Shanghai as having much in common with post-socialist cities, especially those seeking to reconnect with a cosmopolitan golden age in the past, let me linger here briefly on some things that I have found valuable in the work of two scholars whose main focus is Budapest. One of these authors is Judit Bodnár, who wrote an excellent ethnographically informed city study of Hungary's capital at the turn of the millennium. Her book is filled with discussions of specific phenomena that can provide Shanghai specialists with food for thought while trying to come to terms with the city that fascinates and often perplexes them. One case in point is in a chapter "Urban Texture Unraveling: Fragmentation of the City," the title of which could just as easily have come from a book on Shanghai. Bodnár begins with a famous quote by Mike Davis on the rise of gated communities and other high security spaces in Southern California: "as the walls have come down in eastern Europe, they are being erected all over Los Angeles." She then adds a corrective to this notion by pointing out that while some eastern European walls (that marked political divides) have certainly fallen, "others are being erected hastily" (usually to mark social divides).[14]

The parallels with New Shanghai here are not perfect, since the most important wall to crumble in the case of Eastern Europe (that which divided "East" from "West" in Berlin) has no clear Chinese counterpart. Nor has the Communist Party yielded to a profusion of competing political forces. Still, there are things that resonate in her discussion of novel forms of fortification that have more to do with economic differentiation than with political units. I suspect that many Shanghai specialists who have returned periodically to visit friends they made in the 1980s have had experiences similar to one I had in 1999 when I went to the new apartment of a colleague who had moved from a government job into the private sector. I first met him in the 1980s at his office, and before I could see him, I had to stop at a gate and answer questions put to me by a guard employed by his *danwei* (work unit). Had I gone to his state-allocated apartment then, I would similarly have had to pass by a lightly guarded gate and tell the guard my identity and who I wanted to see. Passing these checkpoints was due more to a desire to keep track of comings and goings in order to monitor political activities than to limit burglaries.

In 1999 when I visited his privately owned apartment in a luxurious new high-rise, again there were security considerations. But these differed in being high-tech in a way that the old protected living areas were not (involving punched-in codes) and more clearly intended to limit crime (as would be the case with a similar apartment house located in New York or Budapest, as Bodnár describes the latter city).

The other Budapest specialist whose work is available in English and of obvious value to scholars concerned with New Shanghai is Ivan Szelenyi. His studies include the book *Urban Inequalities under State Socialism* and an important essay called "Cities under Socialism—and After." Each of these works, as their broad titles indicate, deals with urban centers other than Budapest. He makes it clear, though, that the Hungarian capital is the metropolis he knows best and has studied most intensively. Szelenyi's most important argument, for our purposes, serves as a corollary of sorts to what I have said above relating to intermittent moves toward global city status. He argues that in Budapest, as well as other cities that for a time were part of the Soviet bloc, we see a rise and fall in degrees of urbanism, rather than the expected steady move towards greater levels of urbanism. Building on classical works of urban theory (such as those of sociologists Wirth, Park, and Simmel), he defines urbanism as something that manifests itself largely via three things. The first is an increasing degree of social and cultural hetero-geneity within a city's border, a proliferation of difference, as people from varied places, speaking varied dialects and languages, plying varied trades, worshiping in varied ways, and cooking in diverse styles converge on a locale. The second is a rise in "positive" and "negative" expressions of marginality, the former being creative acts not constrained by tradition, the latter being criminal acts; for example, one is freer but not as safe in a fully urban setting. The third is a tendency for economic concerns to govern the use of space, especially at or near the city's center.

Szelenyi's portrait of Budapest (and also other cities such as East Berlin) moving away from and then back towards being places where a high degree of urbanism prevailed will seem instantly familiar to anyone who has spent time in Shanghai. A sense of recognition is provided by sentences such as the following: "The boredom of the socialist cities is gone, but so is their safety." The same can be said of his reference to the "rapidly increasing" number of "small shops, restaurants and street vendors" in Central European cities. And of his portrayal of Budapest as a place that is again becoming a center for the sex trade, as well as a place where organized crime and private development projects are both much more important parts of the scene than they were in the 1950s to 1970s.[15]

9: *Twenty-first-century Shanghai is a futuristic city*

It is also worth thinking of Shanghai as having entered a category made up of futuristic cities—the kinds of places that people look to when trying to figure out where, for better or worse, the world is headed. Paris and London were such cities in the 1800s, New York and Tokyo joined their ranks in the twentieth century, as did Los Angeles, and now Dubai and Shanghai are definitely such metropolises. This shows through in Shanghai's case in the kinds of films being set there, for serving as the backdrop to cinematic forays into science fiction is one sign that a metropolis fits into this category, and also in the kinds of concerns that are beginning to be expressed about and struggles that are beginning to be waged within it.

A futuristic city is one that regularly inspires dreams and nightmares, not just within but also well beyond its borders, and one that is thought of as rich in disturbing portents and also promise. It is a place that is no longer thought of as struggling to catch up with other places, as Shanghai still was in the 1990s, but seems to be setting the pace for other locales. It is the kind of city that seems just the right kind of place to hold a World Expo—an event designed to showcase state-of-the-art technologies. It is also the kind of city that inspires fears of excess, where we might expect to see, as we saw in Shanghai at the start of this year, protests break out that target symbols of modernity at the edge, like a Maglev train.

10: Twenty-first-century Shanghai is nevertheless unique—because of its mix of characteristics

In thinking about contemporary Shanghai, it is worth keeping in mind its similarities with other urban centers that belong in the three categories just sketched out above. But it is important not to let this blind us to factors—including in some cases political arrangements—that differentiate it from each of the cities I've mentioned above. Shanghai has things in common with other cities that are staking a claim to reconnecting with cosmopolitan pasts. Its social fabric is reminiscent of that of other cities that have populations that include people who remember when life within their communities was safer and duller and had a social landscape less starkly marked by chasms between rich and poor. And it has a special kinship with other cities that have been seen as representing things to come. But for better and for worse, it remains unique.

To be sure, all cities are unique. But the things that set it apart from the other great cities of the twenty-first century are sometimes overlooked. Consider, for example, a recent *Los Angeles Times Magazine* article, devoted to the rise of a "new class of 'super-cities' that includes London, New York and Shanghai," written by architecture critic Christopher Hawthorne. There is much to admire in Hawthorne's analysis, which highlights the special place of urban centers that can "set the world agenda in finance and fashion and everything in between." And there is much in it sure to provide comfort to some of the city's promoters, who have been trying since the development of Pudong began to convince international observers that their city should be seen as belonging in the same tier as London and New York, so long regarded as among an elite group of global cities par excellence. There is, however, one major flaw in Hawthorne's article when it comes to Shanghai's inclusion in the category he defines. Namely, he presents the cities within it as ones whose fates are largely determined by their mayors, who can act in ways largely independent of national authorities and take the lead in such initiatives as launching a bid to host the Olympics, as Hawthorne says "the remarkable Ken Livingstone" (who now looks a bit less "remarkable" having lost his bid for re-election) did in his successful effort to reassert London's status as a global metropolis.[16] The problem in this case is that Shanghai's mayor, though certainly capable of leaving an imprint on the city—and several recent mayors have definitely made their mark—is much less a free agent than New York's Michael Bloomberg or L.A.'s Antonio Villaraigosa, who may have to answer to an electorate down the line but in the short run can take many important initiatives with limited concern for external authorities. Shanghai, along with being a re-globalizing, post-socialist, futuristic city, is still part of a country controlled by a Communist Party. This means its mayors have to share power locally with a Party Secretary for the city, and both are part of a national bureaucracy.

What is ultimately most distinctive about twenty-first-century Shanghai is that it fits into all three of the frameworks brought into play above, while also being something else, a "controlled city," in the sense not only of being part of an authoritarian state that limits the freedom of individuals but of having less autonomy as a metropolis than those in many other kinds of nation-state. There is no other global city about which this can be said. Istanbul may be a "re-globalizing" metropolis but it is not "post-socialist," for example, while Dubai may be as "futuristic" as Shanghai but is not a "re-globalizing" city. Budapest may well be both "re-globalizing" and "post-socialist," but it is not widely seen as an urban center that gives us a foretaste of things to come, nor now, in contrast to the past, is it a "controlled city" in the sense that term is used above. Neither is Bombay a "controlled city" of this kind, something that limits in varied ways the value of the Bombay–Shanghai comparison that is sometimes floated. When it comes to expressing themselves freely in public, Shanghai residents face constraints that do not burden their Bombay counterparts (who find it easy to form labor unions and protest organizations), but officials in Bombay face constraints on their ability to remake the urban landscape in eye-catching ways that do not burden their Shanghai counterparts—at least when those Shanghai leaders get the go-ahead from the Communist Party's top leaders.

Figure C.2 (opposite) A large gold-colored revolving statue in the entrance hall of the Shanghai Urban Planning Museum. The tallest structures are, from left to right, the Jinmao Tower, the Pearl of the Orient Tower, and the at the time still only planned World Financial Center. Despite appearances, the real Jinmao Tower is taller than the Pearl of the Orient Tower, and when the World Financial Center was completed in 2007, it soared above both the other structures. It did not, however, end up looking quite as it does in this statue, for the empty circle in the design of the Japanese-financed World Financial Center was criticized by some locals as looking disturbingly like Japan's "Rising Sun" flag appearing above the Pudong skyline. When finally completed, it had a rectangular rather than circular cut-out, which has inspired some wags to dub it the "Can-Opener Building."

Source: Author's photograph taken in 2004

By fitting into so many categories, Shanghai has once again become truly, as it once was, a site with a one-of-a-kind mix of sensation and spectacle, exploitation and excitement, which is a magnet for international capital and international tourists, a cinematic city and a global trading hub. As for what will happen next, only one thing is clear: Shanghai's protean transformations will continue, and it will continue to re-invent itself as a complex city of the future best understood in light of its past.

Suggestions for further reading

One goal of the preceding pages has been to make readers curious to learn more about a variety of topics associated with Shanghai. Before singling out various places to turn to for additional information about, and sometimes also contrasting approaches to, the topics I have covered, a general caveat is in order. The literature on Shanghai's modern period, especially the first decades of the twentieth century, has grown exponentially during the last decades. Shanghai studies was just a minor subfield as recently as the early 1980s, with most of the work in it being done within the city itself. Now, it is a booming cottage industry. Important work on a host of topics has been done and is being done by gifted and hard-working scholars and freelance writers based near the Huangpu River (with the Shanghai Academic of Social Sciences, or "SASS" for short, standing out as the most important local center for academic work on the subject), as well as in cities located far from Pudong and Puxi. There are currently Shanghai specialists based in the United States, Japan, Germany, Australia, France, Canada, and the United Kingdom, to name just the first countries that come to mind.

This means that even if one limits discussion primarily to English language works, as I will below, there are many choices when it comes to directions in which to point the reader. It also means that, inevitably, given the format I have chosen of providing only limited footnotes to individual chapters and also my desire to keep this section brief, many valuable works will go unmentioned. Suffice it to say that, without the boom in Shanghai studies, which has not only been decidedly international but also decidedly interdisciplinary (with everyone from anthropologists to urban geographers contributing), this book would have been impossible to write.

General surveys

There is still no satisfying English language introduction to Shanghai history that provides a detailed narrative of the period stretching from the Opium War through the 1990s or into the early years of the twenty-first century. In French, there is Marie-Claire Bergère's excellent *Histoire de Shanghai* (Paris: Fayard, 2002), as well as a wonderful visually driven work, produced by Christian Henriot and Zheng Zu'an, *Atlas de Shanghai* (Paris: CNRS, 1999), that is given over largely to maps and graphs, but provides a useful quick sketch of the city's history via the introductions to those materials. In Japanese, there is the fascinating and nicely produced collective overview *Shanhai shi* [The History of Shanghai] (Tokyo, 1995), by Takashi Kosuke and Furuya Tadao *et al.* In Chinese, there are many options; one of the best and most up to date is *Shanghai: yi zuo xian dai hua du shi de bian nian shi* [Shanghai—A chronological history of a modernizing city] (Shanghai: Shanghai shudian, 2007), edited by Xiong Yuezhi and Zhou Wu.

One option for readers of English looking for a different sort of overview of the entire period of time covered by this book than the one I provide is to take a mix-and-match approach. In other words, begin with one of the several lively introductions to the treaty-port era that are available. My favorites include *In Search of Old Shanghai* (Hong Kong: Joint Publishing, 1986), which is by Lynn Pan (writing then as Pan Ling), a wonderfully readable work that is based on a thorough grounding in the details of the local past, and geographer Rhoads Murphey's classic, *Shanghai: Key to Modern China* (Cambridge, Mass.: Harvard University Press, 1953). Then finish with a work that focusses mostly or exclusively on post-1949 developments, such as Brian Hook's edited volume, *Shanghai and the Yangtze Delta* (Oxford: Oxford University Press, 1998).

Alternatively, there are several recent books in English that move across the 1949 border in interesting ways, albeit not providing the sort of decade-by-decade narrative found in the surveys in French, Japanese, and Chinese cited above. Two notable examples are a pair of lavishly illustrated publications with an architectural focus that use consideration of buildings and urban planning to engage with many other issues. These are Seng Kuan and Peter G. Rowe's wide-ranging edited collection *Shanghai: Architecture and Urbanism for Modern China* (Berlin: Prestel, 2004) and Edward Denison and Guang Yu Ren's *Building Shanghai: The Story of China's Gateway* (Chichester, Sussex: John Wiley and Sons, 2006). Another work that moves between the treaty-port era and the present in an intriguing way (despite the years flagged in its subtitle, its final chapter engages with very recent developments) is Yeh Wen-hsin's *Shanghai Splendor: Economic Sentiments and the Making of Modern China, 1843–1949* (Berkeley: University of California Press, 2007)—a book whose copious notes to recent scholarship in Chinese, incidentally, provide readers of that language with a very nice sense of where to turn to sample the good work being done by scholars based at SASS and other local institutions.

Also worth mentioning here are two places to turn that focus on the pre-1949 period but include some material on the era of Communist Party rule: *Shanghai: Electric and Lurid City* (Hong Kong: Oxford University Press, 1998), an anthology edited by Barbara Baker, and *Historic Shanghai* (http://www.historic-shanghai. com/?page_id=2), a new website. *Historic Shanghai* complements an excellent pre-existing site, "Tales of Old Shanghai" (http://www.earnshaw.com/shanghai-ed-india/tales/tales.htm), devoted to treaty-port times, which has full-text versions of some of the best old guidebooks.

Shanghai before the 1911 Revolution

Several of the best English language essays on this period are by Mark Elvin; originally published in varied journals and edited volumes, they are gathered together in his *Another History: Essays on China from a European Perspective* (Sydney: Wild Peony Press, 1996). For a quick tour of late Qing developments (and also early Republican ones), F.L. Hawks Pott's *A Short History of Shanghai* (Shanghai: Kelly and Walsh, 1928) remains useful and easy to read, even though it focusses very heavily on the activities of the foreign community. More scholarly and more focussed on the Chinese community, but stopping just before 1860, is Linda Cooke Johnson's *Shanghai: From Market Town to Treaty Port, 1074–1858* (Stanford: Stanford University Press, 1995).

Valuable examinations of the city as it was shaped by and revealed through the local Chinese language press are provided by Rudolf G. Wagner's edited volume *Joining the Global Public: Word, Image, and City in Early Chinese Newspapers* (Albany: SUNY Press, 2007), and Barbara Mittler's *A Newspaper for China? Power, Identity and Change in Shanghai's News Media (1872–1912)* (Cambridge, Mass.: Harvard University Press, 2004). See also Ye Xiaoqing's *The Dianshizhai Pictorial: Shanghai Urban Life, 1884–1898* (Ann Arbor: University of Michigan Center for Chinese Studies, 2003), which is filled with reproductions from one of the periodicals analyzed by Wagner *et al.*

Other kinds of useful windows onto the period are offered by Bryna Goodman's *Native-Place, City, and Nation: Regional Networks and Identities in Shanghai, 1853–1937* (Stanford: Stanford University Press, 1995), which concentrates on an especially significant kind of mutual aid society, and Theodore Huters' *Bringing the World Home: Appropriating the West in Late Qing and Early Republican China* (Honolulu: University of Hawaii Press, 2005), which deals largely with Shanghai novels of the time. In addition, though also covering events of the Republican era, many important nineteenth-century and early-twentieth-century phenomena are illuminated in various chapters contributed to Frederic Wakeman and Yeh Wen-hsin's edited volume *Shanghai Sojourners* (Berkeley: Institute of East Asian Studies, 1992).

The Republican era (1912–1949)

In addition to works already mentioned that deal with the end of the Qing but also this period, the following studies provide scholarly yet accessible introductions to major issues relating to this period. On the local foreign community, for a general overview, see Nicholas R. Clifford's *Spoilt Children of Empire: Westerners in Shanghai and the Chinese Revolution of the 1920s* (Hanover, New Hampshire: New England University Press, 1991); for a stylish and imaginative look at the same topic, which brings the Western experience in Shanghai to life via the story of a single policeman, see Robert Bickers' *Empire Made Me: An Englishman Adrift in Shanghai* (New York: Columbia University Press, 2003).

For crime and law enforcement, two important subjects, see Frederic E. Wakeman, Jr., *Policing Shanghai, 1927–1937* (Berkeley: University of California

Press, 1995), Brian Martin's *The Shanghai Green Gang: Politics and Organized Crime, 1919–1937* (Berkeley: University of California Press, 1986), and Lynn Pan's *Old Shanghai: Gangsters in Paradise* (Hong Kong: Heinemann Asia, 1984), as well as Gail Hershatter's *Dangerous Pleasures: Prostitution and Modernity in Twentieth-Century Shanghai* (University of California Press, 1997), which focusses on many aspects of sex work, including its criminalization. For the lives of ordinary women workers, see Emily Honig's *Sisters and Strangers* (Stanford: Stanford University Press, 1986), and for labor activism, see Elizabeth J. Perry's *Shanghai on Strike* (Stanford: Stanford University Press, 1993) and S.A. Smith's *Like Cattle and Horses: Nationalism and Labor in Shanghai, 1895–1927* (Durham: Duke University Press, 2002).

For popular culture and literary trends, see Leo Lee's *Shanghai Modern* (Cambridge, Mass.: Harvard University Press, 1999). For the music scene, see Andrew F. Jones's *Yellow Music: Media Culture and Modernity in the Chinese Jazz Age* (Durham: Duke University Press, 2001). For fashion and design and related issues, see Lynn Pan's *Shanghai Style: Art and Design Between the Wars* (San Francisco: Long River Press, 2008). For patterns of quotidian existence among ordinary Chinese, see Lu Hanchao's *Beyond the Neon Lights: Everyday Shanghai in the Early Twentieth Century* (Berkeley: University of California Press, 1999). For the Communist Party's struggle to maintain a presence in the city during the period of Nationalist Party rule, see Patricia Stranahan's *Underground: The Shanghai Communist Party and the Politics of Survival, 1927–1937* (Lanham, Maryland: Rowman and Littlefield, 1998). For a lively look at department stores and other sites of consumption, see Sherman Cochran's edited volume *Inventing Nanjing Road: Commercial Culture in Shanghai, 1900–1945* (Ithaca, New York: Cornell University East Asia Program, 2000). For the role that networks of disparate kinds played in keeping the city working, see Jean Oi and Nara Dillon's edited volume *At the Crossroads of Empires: Middle Men, Social Networks, and State-Building in Republican Shanghai* (Stanford: Stanford University Press, 2007). For Shanghai's role as a center of cinema, see Zhen Zhang's *An Amorous History of the Silver Screen: Shanghai Cinema, 1896–1937* (Chicago: University of Chicago, 2005). For the period of the Japanese occupation of Shanghai, see the various contributions to Yeh Wen-hsin's edited volume *Wartime Shanghai* (London: Routledge, 1998) and to the collection that she and Christian Henriot co-edited, *In the Shadow of the Rising Sun: Shanghai Under the Japanese Occupation* (Cambridge: Cambridge University Press, 2004), as well as Frederic Wakeman's *The Shanghai Badlands: Wartime Terrorism and Urban Crime, 1937–1941* (Cambridge: Cambridge University Press, 2002), and Bernard Wasserstein's *Secret War in Shanghai* (New York: Houghton Mifflin, 1999). For the Civil War era, see Suzanne Pepper's *The Civil War in China: The Political Struggle, 1945–1949*, revised edition (Lanham, Maryland: Rowman and Littlefield, 1999).

Many memoirs and works of fiction are available in English that provide insights into life in Republican Shanghai. Among works written during the Republican era itself, see Yokomitsu Riichi's *Shanghai* (Ann Arbor: University of Michigan Center for Japanese Studies, 2001), translated by Dennis Washburn; André Malraux's *Man's Fate* (New York: Vintage, 1990), translated by Haakon M. Chevalier; Mao Dun's *Midnight* (Beijing: Foreign Languages Press, 1979) and also his *Rainbow* (Berkeley: University of California Press, 1992), translated by Madeleine Zelin; and Eileen Chang (Zhang Ailing), *Written on Water* (New York: Columbia University Press), translated by Andrew F. Jones and edited by Nicole Huang; and John Espey's *Minor Heresies, Major Departures: A China Mission Boyhood* (Berkeley: University of California Press, 1994). Two particularly interesting works of fiction written after the fact are J.G. Ballard's *Empire of the Sun* (New York: Simon and Schuster, 2005), which first appeared in 1984 and is based on his experiences as a child living in war-torn Shanghai, and Bo Caldwell's *The Distant Land of My Father* (New York: Harvest Books, 2002).

The city since 1949

A good general introduction to Shanghai's post-1949 transformations is provided by the previously mentioned edited volume *Shanghai: Architecture and Urbanism for Modern China*. See also the treatment of Shanghai in various contributions to edited volumes such as John R. Logan's *The New Chinese City: Globalization and Market Reform* (New York: Wiley and Blackwell, 2002) and *Urban China in Transition* (New York: Blackwell, 2008), as well as Wu Fulong's *Globalization and the Chinese City* (London: Routledge, 2006).

For an introduction to the city during the final years of Nationalist Party rule and the first part of the Maoist era, see the chapters by Frederic Wakeman, Nara Dillon, Elizabeth J. Perry, and Sherman Cochran in Jeremy Brown and Paul G. Pickowicz's edited volume *Dilemmas of Victory: The Early Years of the People's Republic of China* (Cambridge: Harvard University Press, 2008), a book that came out too late to be drawn upon in my chapter above on 1950. See also, for two intriguing personal views of the same period, Shirley Wood's *A Street in China* (London: Michael Joseph, 1958) and Lynn Pan's *Tracing it Home: A Chinese Family's Journey from Shanghai* (New York: Kodansha, 1993). For fictional accounts of the time, see Wang Anyi's *The Song of Everlasting Sorrow* (New York: Columbia University Press, 2008), translated by Michael Berry and Susan Chan Egan, and also Chou Er-fu's *Morning in Shanghai* (Beijing: Foreign Languages Press, 1981), translated by A.E. Barnes.

For good treatments of key issues of the first two decades of the Maoist era, see the chapters dealing with Shanghai by Lynn White and others in John Lewis's important early edited volume *The City in Communist China* (Stanford: Stanford University Press, 1971). See also, for this same period and also developments in the 1970s, Christopher Howe's *Shanghai: Revolution and Development in an Asian Metropolis* (Cambridge: Cambridge University Press, 1981). For the Cultural Revolution in particular, see Elizabeth J. Perry and Li Xun's *Proletarian Power: Shanghai in the Cultural Revolution* (Armonk, New York: M.E. Sharpe, 1997). Shanghai in the 1980s has yet to receive much attention in English language works, but one important topic relevant to this period, campus activism, is addressed in the final chapter of my *Student Protests in Twentieth-Century China: The View from Shanghai* (Stanford: Stanford University Press, 1991). For the 1990s, see Pamela Yatsko's *New Shanghai: The Rocky Rebirth of China's Legendary City* (New York: John Wiley, 2001) for a breezy overview; James Farrer's *Opening Up: Youth Sex Culture and Market Reform in Shanghai* (Chicago: University of Chicago Press, 2002), for an ethnographic look at a particular social group; and Jos Gamble's *Shanghai in Transition* (New York: RoutledgeCurzon, 2003), for a broader ethnography of the city.

Shanghai's twenty-first-century transformations are too new to have become the focus of much scholarly writing, but several guides to the city as a whole or to particular sections of it do an unusually good job at mixing eye-catching images of the metropolis with efforts to place recent developments into perspective. See, for example, Nick Land *et al.*'s *Urbanatomy: Shanghai 2008* (Shanghai: Urbanatomy, 2008); *Lonely Planet Shanghai City Guide* (Victoria, Australia: Lonely Planet Publications, 2008); and Peter Hibbert, *The Bund: China Faces West* (Hong Kong: Odyssey Books and Guides, 2007). For an eerie visual take on the contemporary city, see Greg Girard's *Phantom Shanghai* (Toronto: Magenta, 2007), which fittingly, given how often the city is now linked to science fiction, comes with a "Foreword" by William Gibson.

Notes

Introduction

1 For Shanghai's early history, some sources to turn to are Cao Juren, *Shanghai chunqiu* [Shanghai annals] (Shanghai, 1996), pp. 4–8; Linda Cooke Johnson, *Shanghai: From Market Town to Treaty Port, 1074–1858* (Stanford: Stanford University Press, 1995); Zhang Zhongmin, *Shanghai: cong kaifa zouxiang kaifang, 1368–1842* (Kunming, 1990); *Shanghai tan yeshi* [An informal history of Shanghai] (Shanghai, 1993); FL. Hawks Pott, *A Short History of Shanghai* (Shanghai: Kelly and Walsh, 1928); C.A. Montalto de Jesus, *The Rise of Shanghai* (Shanghai: Shanghai Mercury, 1906).

2 For background on the histories of Hangzhou and Suzhou (and their relationship with Shanghai both before and after its rise), a good place to start is with Linda Cooke Johnson, ed., *Cities of Jiangnan in Late Imperial China* (Albany: SUNY Press, 1993), especially the following chapters: William T. Rowe, "Introduction: City and Region in the Lower Yangzi" (pp. 1–16); Michael Marmé, "Heaven on Earth: The Rise of Suzhou, 1127–1550" (pp. 17–46); and Susumu Fuma (translation by Michael Lewis), "Late Ming Urban Reform and the Popular Uprising in Hangzhou" (pp. 47–80).

3 Publications of local history were a major part of this anniversary celebration. See, for example, Shanghai yanjiu zhongxin and Shanghai renmin chubanshe [Shanghai Research Center and Shanghai People's Publishing], compilers, *Shanghai 700 nian, 1291–1991* [Shanghai's 700 Years] (Shanghai: Shanghai renmin chubanshe, 1991).

4 *The Jubilee of Shanghai* (Shanghai: North China Herald, 1893); see also, for discussions of the Jubilee as an event and the texts associated with it, Kerrie L. MacPherson, *A Wilderness of Marshes: The Origins of Public Health in Shanghai, 1843–1893* (Hong Kong: Oxford University Press, 1987); Jeffrey N. Wasserstrom, "Comparing Incomparable Cities: Postmodern L.A. and Old Shanghai," *Contention*, vol. 5, no. 3 (1996), pp. 69–90; and Bryna Goodman, "Improvisations on a Semi-Colonial Theme, or, How to read a Celebration of Transnational Urban Community," *Journal of Asian Studies* (November 2000), pp. 889–926.

5 One of the best sources for population figures remains Zou Yiren, *Jiu Shanghai renkou bianqian de yanjiu* [Research on Changes in the Population of Old Shanghai] (Shanghai: Shanghai renmin chubanshe, 1980). Throughout this book, I rely on that source, as well as on Christian Henriot and Zheng Zu'an, *Atlas de Shanghai—Espaces et représentations de 1849 à nos jours* (Paris: CNRS, 1999).

6 A sample authoritative work that uses 1292 is Shanghai tongshe, ed., *Shanghai yanjiu ziliao* [Historical research materials on Shanghai] (Shanghai, 1984: a reprint of a 1936 collection of essays by a Nationalist Party-run official research unit), vol. 1, p. 363. A recent work that ignores the significance of 1291 and cites 1074 as the most important year in Shanghai's early history is Kai-iu Fung, Zhong-min Yan, and Yue-min Ning, "Shanghai: China's World City," in Yue-man Yeung and Xu-wei Hu, eds, *China's Coastal Cities: Catalysts for Modernization* (Honolulu, 1992), pp. 124–152.

7   The Shanghailander tendency to downplay urbanization that occurred before the city was transformed from a Chinese-run community into a multinational treaty port is treated in detail in later chapters; citations to primary sources are given there. Two scholarly works that analyze well the mindset I have in mind, which Robert Bickers aptly dubs "mudflat-ism," are Kerrie MacPherson, *A Wilderness of Marshes: The Origins of Public Health in Shanghai, 1843–1893* (Oxford, 1987); and Robert Bickers, "History, Legend and Treaty Port Ideology, 1925–1931," in *idem*, ed., *Ritual and Diplomacy: The Macartney Mission to China, 1792–1794* (London, 1993), pp. 81–92.

8   Robert Fortune, *Three Years' Wanderings in the Northern Provinces of China* (London, 1847), pp. 121–122; quoted in Robert Eng, "The Transformation of a Semi-Colonial Port City: Shanghai, 1843–1941," in Frank Broeze, ed., *Brides of the Sea: Port Cities of Asia from the 16th–20th Centuries* (Honolulu: University of Hawaii Press, 1989), pp. 129–151.

9   Robert Bickers, "History, Legend, and Treaty Port Ideology."

10 Works in which one or all of these tropes occur include *Xin Shanghai bianlan* [A Handbook to New Shanghai] (Shanghai: Shanghai Dagongbao, 1951); *Shanghai de gushi* [The Shanghai Story] (Shanghai: Shanghai renmin chubanshe, 1963); Song Qingling, "Shanghai's New Day has Dawned," a 1950 speech reprint in *idem*, *The Struggle for New China* (Beijing: Foreign Languages Press, 1952), pp. 245–249.

11 Tsung-yi Michelle Huang, *Walking Between Slums and Skyscrapers: Illusions of Open Space in Hong Kong, Tokyo and Shanghai* (Hong Kong: University of Hong Kong Press, 2004), pp. 19 and *passim*.

12 George Lanning and Samuel Couling, *The History of Shanghai, Volume 1* (Shanghai: Kelly and Walsh, 1921), p. 274.

13 Jean Cocteau, *Tour du monde en 80 jours* (Mon Premier Voyage) (Paris: Gallimard, 1936). This quotation is taken from the English translation by Stuart Gilbert, first published in 1937 and recently reissued as *Round the World Again in 80 Days* (London: Tauris Parke, 2000), p. 163. As a side note, the French director's sightseeing in Shanghai was partly done in the company of the silent film stars Charlie Chaplin and Paulette Goddard.

14 Michael Sorkin, "See You in Disneyland" in *idem*, ed., *Variations on a Theme Park: The New American City and the End of Public Space* (New York: Hill and Wang, 1992), pp. 205–232.

15 See the title essay in Chen Danyan, *Shanghai sela* [Shanghai Salad] (Bejing: Zuojia chunbanshe, 2001), pp. 15–17, which treats this cosmopolitan dish as a fitting symbol for a cosmopolitan city.

16 On the city as a hub of radical activity early in the twentieth century, see the translations of Chinese scholarly articles in Jeffrey N. Wasserstrom and Elizabeth J. Perry, eds, *Shanghai Social Movements, 1919–1949*, a special double issue of *Chinese Studies in History*, Fall/Winter, 1993–1994; on the Cultural Revolution era, see Elizabeth J. Perry and Li Xun, *Proletarian Power: Shanghai in the Cultural Revolution* (Boulder, Colorado: Westview Press, 1997).

17 A revised version of that thesis was published as *Student Protests in Twentieth-Century China: The View from Shanghai* (Stanford: Stanford University Press, 1991); one major difference between the dissertation (that was filed in 1989) and the book was that only the latter included an extended discussion of events of the 1980s, including the 1986 demonstrations I observed.

18 Mark Twain, *Innocents Abroad; or the New Pilgrim's Progress* (New York: Author's national edition, 1869).

19 For more on this theme, see Jeffrey N. Wasserstrom, "Traveling with Twain in an Age of Simulations," *Common Place* (April 2004), no pagination (an online journal), a revised version of which can also be found in *idem*, *China's Brave New World—And Other Tales for Global Times* (Bloomington: Indiana University Press, 2007).

20 Several Western accounts of Shanghai in circulation abroad by the 1860s will be discussed in a later chapter.

21 English language editions of all of these novels are available: Mao Dun, *Midnight* (Beijing: Foreign Languages Press, 1957), translation by Xu Mengxiong; Mao Dun, *Rainbow* (Berkeley: University of California Press, 1992), translation by Madeleine Zelin; Malraux, *Man's Fate* (New York: Vintage reissue edition, 1990), translation by Haakon M. Chevalier; and Yokomitsu Riichi, *Shanghai: A Novel* (Ann Arbor: University of Michigan Press, 1993), translation by Dennis C. Washburn.

22 One of the earliest of these is *The Hotel Metropole's Guide to Shanghai and Environs* (Shanghai: Hotel Metropole, 1903).

23 For citations to some sample works of this sort, see the notes to Chapter 1.

24 On Samuel Clemens' aborted plans to visit China, see Harriet Elinor Smith and Richard Bucci, eds, Lin Salamo, assoc. ed., *Mark Twain's Letters, Volume 2, 1867–1868* (Berkeley: University of California Press, 1990), pp. 187–188 and 230n7.

25 *North China Herald*, August 3, 1850.

26 Maurine Karns and Pat Patterson, *Shanghai High Lights, Low Lights, Tael Lights* (Shanghai: Tridon Press, 1936); see http://www.earnshaw.com/shanghai-ed-india/tales/library/high/t-high.htm (accessed December 11, 2006), for an online version.

27 *New York Times Sunday Magazine*, February 18, 1996.

28 The "miracles" section was part of the following website when I accessed it several times in 2003: http://www.expo2010china.com/. The website has since been revamped and no longer had a "miracles" subsection when accessed December 11, 2006.

29 For Chinese press accounts celebrating the coming of the 2010 Expo, see also http://www.expo2010china.com/ (accessed December 11, 2006).

30 For "Paris, the Capital of the Nineteenth Century" and other of his essays on France's capital city, see *Walter Benjamin: Selected Writings, Volume 3, 1935–1938* (Cambridge, Mass.: Harvard University Press, 2002), translated by Edmund Jephcott, Howard Eli, and others, edited by Howard Eli and Michael W. Jennings.

31 Christopher Isherwood and W. H. Auden, *Journey to a War* (London: Faber and Faber, 1939), p. 237.

32 Mike Davis, *City of Quartz: Excavating the Future in Los Angeles* (New York: Vintage, 1990).

33 Mian Mian, "The Illusionary City that Belongs to the World," *Time Asia*, September 27, 1999, accessed at http://www.time.com/time/asia/magazine/99/0927/shanghai.html (last visited on June 2, 2004).

34 Ray Huang, *1587: A Year of No Significance: The Ming Dynasty in Decline* (New Haven: Yale reprint edition, 1982).

35 See, for example, the discussion of "archaic globalization" and related topics in C.A. Bayly, *The Birth of the Modern World, 1780–1914* (Oxford: Blackwell, 2004).

36 See, for example, the reference in *Shanghai 700 nian*, p. 142, to Shanghai's reputation as "Little Suzhou."

37 On this novel, see Jonathan Spence, *The Chan's Great Continent: China in Western Minds* (New York: Norton, 1998), pp. 129–133. Spence has fascinating things to say about the novel itself and its connection to an earlier work by Oliver Goldsmith, which portrays the adventures of an imaginary Chinese immigrant to England.

38 An English language translation is Jules Verne, *The Tribulations of a Chinaman in China* (Amsterdam: Fredonia Books, 2001, reprint of an 1880 edition), translator's name not given; the protagonist's progressive outlook is stressed on p. 40.

39 *North China Herald*, February 22, 1881, p. 168; the same theme is emphasized, and the same rhetorical device of imagining the reactions upon his return of an early settler is used, in a May 27, 1881 editorial in the same newspaper, pp. 497–498.

40 See, for example, on Shanghai's place vis-à-vis one or both of its Southern rivals, Carolyn L. Cartier, *Globalizing South China* (Oxford: Blackwell, 2001), which includes a valuable long-term perspective on the issues; and David R. Meyers, *Hong Kong as a*

Global Metropolis (Cambridge: Cambridge University Press, 2000), which is strongest on the situation in the 1990s.

41 The earliest example I have come across is *North China Herald*, June 3, 1854, p. 174.

42 See *North China Herald*, March 22, 1881, p. 273; for more on this planned exhibition, see Chapter 7.

43 John Gittings, "Fortress Shanghai Awaits Bush," *The Guardian*, October 16, 2001 (accessed Dec. 7, 2006, at http://www.guardian.co.uk/china/story/0,,574853,00.html).

44 Quoted in the *Economist*, no. 343, March 23, 1850, p. 310.

45 See "The Exhibition Plague," *Punch – Or the London Charivari*, Vol. 19, 1850, p. 191.

1 1850: The birth of a newspaper

1 The relative unimportance of 1850 as a year is explicitly noted in one of the earliest English language histories of the city, J. W. McLellan, *The Story of Shanghai: From the Opening of the Port to Foreign Trade* (Shanghai: North China Herald, 1889), which contains the following line (on page 27): "The only noticeable event which occurred in 1850 was the falling in of the roof of the newly built Trinity Church, on the morning of the 24th of June." The same text then does go on to mention that a few other things did happen during that year, one of which was the founding of the *Herald*.

2 For basic information on this newspaper, including what its Chinese name was ("Tzu Lin Hsi Pao") and its circulation figures (which "peaked at 7,817 copies"), see Pan Haixia, "Witness to History," *Shanghai Star*, November 20, 2003. Pan describes it as having been "the most influential foreign newspaper of the time in Shanghai, and even in all China." Not every local resident viewed the launch of the newspaper as the most important development of the year, of course, as an article that ran in the *Times* (London) under the heading "The Church in China" indicates. Published on May 14, 1850 (p. 5), this piece includes the following lines extracted "from a letter from an Episcopal missionary clergyman at Shanghai": "But the great event to us was the opening of our large new church, in the very midst of the Chinese city . . . The Bishop began with the consecration service adapted to the circumstances, and then a young Chinese convert (who is also a candidate for the ministry) came forward and read aloud a petition, stating that one Mr. Appleton, of America, who honoured God, and had heard that the people of Shanghai worshipped idols, had sent $5,000 to build this house . . . The people seemed to be very much struck by the whole of this service, and if you consider that this was done in the midst of a city of 200,000 inhabitants, all hitherto given to idolatry, and that one of the most frequented shrines or temples was actually within hearing of our voices, you may judge the striking novelty of the scene." For more on this church, see McLellan, *Story of Shanghai*, p. 21, where it is described as a "small chapel" built near the "North Gate" to the old walled city to serve the needs of "the native converts, of whom there were a good number living in the Settlement, and foreign Catholics." The reference to a "good number" of Chinese Catholics living in the Settlement is intriguing, though not explained, given that the only Chinese supposed to be residing there at this time were servants working in the houses of foreigners.

3 Robert Bickers, *Britain in China: Community, Culture and Colonialism, 1900–1949* (Manchester: Manchester University Press, 1999), p. 125.

4 The prevalence of the term "eastern home" is attested to by its incorporation into the "Jubilee Song" written for and performed by children during the 1893 celebrations of the passage of half a century since the founding of the enclaves (an event alluded to in the preceding chapter). See *The Jubilee of Shanghai* for the complete lyrics. An early use of the term appears in the *North China Herald*, December 28, 1850, p. 86.

5 Shanghailanders of the sort just described clung to what Richard Feetham, in his famous analysis of Shanghai politics and history, *Report of the Hon. Mr. Justice Feetham, CMG, to the Shanghai Municipal Council*, three volumes (Shanghai, 1931), referred to as a "historic" interpretation of life in the Settlement. This took literally the original

founding terms of the Settlement, under which the only ones allowed to live within its borders were foreigners and Chinese living in their homes as servants. In contrast to this view, other Shanghailanders embraced over time a "civic" view of the situation, which held that once Chinese were living in the Settlement, they could claim some rights within it.

6 The best single-volume introduction to the new scholarship that emphasizes the diversity of treaty-port foreign communities is Robert Bickers and Christian Henriot, eds, *New Frontiers: Imperialism's New Communities in East Asia, 1842–1953* (Manchester: University of Manchester Press, 2000). Though it deals with the region as a whole, many chapters focus on Shanghai. For the variation in views—toward Shanghai politics and many other issues—within the local British community, see Robert Bickers, *Britain in China*, esp. pp. 67–114. This work also provides citations to and a useful direct critique of the literature from an earlier time that fostered the image of foreigners in Shanghai as homogeneous in their outlook. He points the reader as well to some significant studies that appeared in the 1980s and 1990s that tried, as he does, to move beyond stereotyped visions of Shanghailanders as either uniformly myopic, parochial and bigoted or as uniformly enlightened and broadminded.

7 See, for example, C.A. Montalto de Jesus, *Historic Shanghai* (Shanghai: Shanghai Mercury Limited, 1909), p. 102), in which a local Westerner, presumably from Britain, is quoted as having said the following to the leading local British official *circa* 1855. "You, as Her Majesty's consul, are bound to look to national and permanent interests— that is your business. But it is mine to make a fortune with the least possible loss of time . . . In two or three years at the farthest, I hope to realise a fortune and get away; and what can it matter to me, if all Shanghai disappear afterwards, in fire or flood?" He further referred to his time in Shanghai as time of "exile" in an "unhealthy climate"— a far cry indeed from time spent making an "eastern home" worthy of prolonged affection and loyalty.

8 On the American community, see James Huskey, "Americans in Shanghai: Community Formation and Response to Revolution, 1919–1928," Ph.D. thesis, University of North Carolina, 1985; Nicholas R. Clifford, *Spoilt Children of Empire: Westerners in Shanghai and the Chinese Revolution of the 1920s* (Hanover, New Hampshire: New England University Press, 1991); and Mark Wilkinson, "The Shanghai American Community, 1937–1949," in Bickers and Henriot, *New Frontiers*, pp. 231–249.

9 See Marcia Ristaino, *Port of Last Resort: The Diaspora Communities of Shanghai* (Stanford: Stanford University Press, 2001), and various contributions to Bickers and Henriot, *New Frontiers*, including Chiara Betta, "Marginal Westerners in Shanghai: The Baghdadi Jewish Community, 1845–1931" (pp. 38–54); and Christian Henriot, "'Little Japan' in Shanghai: An Insulated Community, 1875–1945" (pp. 146–169).

10 A comprehensive history of Shanghai's multilingual foreign press has yet to be written, but it would make a colorful tale to say the least. See Ristaino, *Port of Last Resort*, p. 131, for interesting comments on the variation within one subset of newspapers (those that addressed Shanghai Jews) and pp. 340–341 for a list of the broad array of newspapers in different languages she consulted when researching her book. See Samuel Couling, *History of Shanghai, Volume 2*, pp. 450–453, for some interesting tidbits on several English and French language periodicals that were founded in the second half of the nineteenth century. Some of these publications, Couling notes, went on to have long and impressive runs, as was the case with *L'Echo de chine* ("founded in 1895, and still [in the early 1920s] one of the most important French papers of the Far East"). Others almost immediately went out of business, as happened with a very short-lived "serio-comic" monthly, *The Shanghai Chronicle of Fun, Fact, and Fiction*, which the *Herald*'s publishing office started in 1859. For more systematic discussion, see Ma Guangren, ed., *Shanghai xinwenshi (1850–1949)* [A history of the press in Shanghai, 1850–1949] (Shanghai: Fudan University Press, 1996). And for sample issues of more obscure Western and Asian language local newspapers of the early 1900s, see the 60

plus reel microfilm series of Shanghai Municipal Police files held by various libraries. These contain either clippings from or translations of articles that appeared in many papers.

11 An excellent study of Hong Kong newspapers, which focusses on Chinese language ones but discusses English language ones in passing, is Elizabeth Sinn, "Emerging Media: Hong Kong and the Early Evolution of the Chinese Press," *Modern Asian Studies*, 36, 2 (2002), pp. 421–465. See also Ma, *Shanghai xinwenshi*, pp. 21 and 99, and John King Fairbank, *Trade and Diplomacy on the China Coast: The Opening of the Treaty Ports 1842–1854* (Stanford: Stanford University Press, 1964, a one-volume reprint of a 1953 two-volume Harvard University Press work), p. 160.

12 For the Chinese language Shanghai press in general and *Shen Pao* in particular, the most important work in English has been done by Rudolf G. Wagner, Barbara Mittler and other scholars based at Heidelberg University's Sinological Institute. The findings of this group are showcased to good effect in Rudolf G. Wagner, ed., *Joining the Global Public: Word, Image, and City in Early Chinese Newspapers* (Albany: SUNY Press, 2007); see also Mittler, *A Newspaper for China? Power, Identity and Change in Shanghai's News Media (1872–1912)* (Cambridge, Mass.: Harvard University Press, 2004).

13 For details, see Ma, *Shanghai xinwenshi*, and Couling, *History of Shanghai, Volume 2*, p. 451, which gives 1879 as the year when the first two important English language competitors to the *Herald* and the *North China Daily News* (the *Celestial Empire* and the *Shanghai Evening Mercury*) were established.

14 See, for example, the novel *Morning in Shanghai* by Zhou Erfu, translated by A.C. Barnes (Beijing: Foreign Languages Press, 1962), pp. 572 and *passim*.

15 Ma, *Shanghai xinwenshi*, pp. 11–12.

16 In what follows, I rely heavily upon general works such as the following: Zhang Zhongli, ed., *Jindai Shanghai chengshi yanjiu* [Researches on the modern history of the city of Shanghai] (Shanghai, 1990); *Shanghai 700 Nian*; Bergère, *Histoire de Shanghai*, pp. 17–44; Fairbank, *Trade and Diplomacy*; George Lanning and Samuel Couling, *The History of Shanghai: Part I* (Shanghai: Kelly and Walsh, 1921); de Jesus, *Historic Shanghai*; and Shanghai tongshe (Society of Shanghai Natives), eds, *Shanghai yanjiu ziliao* [Historical research materials on Shanghai] (Shanghai, 1984: reprint of 1936 collection of essays); Rhoads Murphey, *Shanghai: Key to Modern China* (Cambridge, Mass.: Harvard University Press, 1953). Particularly valuable, where the era around 1850 is concerned, is Linda Cooke Johnson, *Shanghai: From Market Town to Treaty Port* (Stanford: Stanford University Press, 1995), in which the appearance of the inaugural issue of the *Herald* is also treated as a noteworthy local turning point (see p. 248).

17 Mark Elvin, "Market Towns and Waterways: The County of Shanghai from 1480–1910," in G. William Skinner, ed., *The City in Late Imperial China* (Stanford: Stanford University Press, 1977. This article was later reprinted in Elvin, *Another History: Essays on China from a European Perspective* (Canberra: Wild Peony, 1996), pp. 101–139. Chinese pirates also caused problems; see de Jesus, *Historic Shanghai*, p. xv.

18 Paul Xu and other early local converts to Christianity are discussed in many works; the presence of a foreign priest is less commonly mentioned, especially in Chinese works of scholarship. Some recent exceptions include *Shanghai 700 Nian*, p. 246,

19 D.E. Mungello, *The Great Encounter of China and the West, 1500–1800* (Lanham, Maryland: Rowman and Littlefield, 1999), p. 42.

20 *The Chinese Repository*, vol. 19, no. 8 (August 1850), pp. 462–463.

21 Zhu Hua *et al.*, *Shanghai: Yibainian* [Shanghai: One Hundred Years] (Shanghai: Shanghai renmin chubanshe, 1999), p. 13; Charles Maybon and Jean Fredet, *Histoire de la concession française de Shanghai* (Paris: Plon, 1929).

22 de Jesus, *Historic Shanghai*, p. 47.

23 Ma, *Shanghai xinwenshi*, p. 14.
24 On Shanghai's early population and the difficulty of estimating it, see Zou, *Jiu Shanghai renkou*, and de Jesus, *Historic Shanghai*, p. xxvii.
25 On this enduring complaint, the best analysis can be found in Bickers, *Britain in China*.
26 *North China Herald*, August 3, 1850, p. 2.
27 "To Our Readers," *North China Herald*, December 28, 1850, p. 86.

2: 1875 Putting the city on the map

1 Catherine Vance Yeh, "Representing the City: Shanghai and Its Maps," in David Faure and Tao Tao Liu, eds, *Town and Country in China: Identity and Perception* (New York: Palgrave, 2002), pp. 166–202.
2 Marie-Claire Bergère, *Histoire de Shanghai* (Paris: Fayard, 2002). Another strong candidate for best general survey is Takashi Kosuke and Furuya Tadao *et al.*, *Shanhai shi* [The History of Shanghai] (Tokyo, 1995), a work co-authored by several Japanese Shanghai specialists and one Chinese Shanghai specialist. One thing that makes these two works unusual is that, unlike most comparable works in Chinese, English and Japanese, they include detailed discussion of both the treaty-port era and the Communist one. *Shanhai shi* has a much more detailed chronological appendix than does *Histoire de Shanghai*, and comments on the following pages lean heavily on that section of it.
3 Bergère, *Histoire de Shanghai*, p. 503.
4 On Major, see Rudolf Wagner, "The Role of the Foreign Community in the Chinese Public Sphere," *China Quarterly*, 142 (June 1995), pp. 423–443; various contributions to Rudolf G. Wagner, ed., *Joining the Global Public: Word, Image, and City in Early Chinese Newspapers* (Albany: SUNY Press, 2007), especially *idem*, "Joining the Global Imaginaire: The Shanghai Illustrated Newspaper *Dianshizhai huabao*," pp. 105–174; and Mittler, *A Newspaper for China?*
5 In addition to works already cited, see Natascha Gentz, "Useful Knowledge and Appropriate Communication: The Field of Journalistic Production in Late Nineteenth Century China," in Wagner, *Joining the Global Public*, pp. 47–104.
6 See "Chinese Newspapers," *North China Herald*, August 28, 1875, cited in Wagner, "Joining the Global Imaginaire," p. 162, note 41. Wagner also points out there that the *Illustrated London News* had "a Shanghai subscription price printed in each issue."
7 On the *Dianshizhai huabao*, in addition to various contributions to Wagner, *Joining the Global Public*, see Ye Xiaoqing, *The Dianshizhai Pictorial: Shanghai Urban Life, 1884–1898* (Ann Arbor: University of Michigan Center for Chinese Studies, 2003).
8 Wagner, "Joining the Global Imaginaire," pp. 112–113.
9 Takashi and Furuya, *Shanhai shi*, p. 16 (of the appendix, which is separately paginated).
10 Takashi and Furuya, *Shanghai shi*, appendix p. 15.
11 Xiong Yuezhi and Zhou Wu, eds, *Shanghai: yi zuo xian dai hua du shi de bian nian shi* [Shanghai: A chronological history of a modernizing city] (Shanghai: Shanghai shudian, 2007), pp. 633–634.
12 See Wagner, "Joining the Global Imaginaire," p. 112.
13 H. Lang, *Shanghai Considered Socially: A Lecture* (Shanghai: American Presbyterian Mission Press, 1875).
14 S.T. Wang, *The Margary Affair and the Chefoo Agreement* (New York: Oxford University Press, 1940).
15 Pott, *Short History of Shanghai*, p. 108.
16 For an extended quote from the Hart memorandum, see Pott, *Short History of Shanghai*, pp. 101–102; local reactions to it are discussed later in this chapter.
17 *North China Herald*, March 11, 1875, p. 223, and *North China Herald*, May 29, 1875, p. 521.

18 "Retrospect of 1876," *North China Herald*, February 10, 1876, pp. 105–106, and *North China Herald*, February 17, 1876, pp. 129–130.

19 See "Retrospect of 1876," p. 105, which says that trade has been slow, and that when "trade is dull, things generally are, of course, dull in Shanghai," and p. 106, for the Hongkong and Shanghai Bank headquarters being "the only new public building of importance that has been opened during the year."

20 Yeh, "Representing the City."

21 On the Chinese Catholics, see J.W. MacLellan, *The Story of Shanghai: From the Opening of the Port to Foreign Trade* (Shanghai: North China Herald, 1889), p. 21.

22 The results of this census are provided in H. Lang, *Shanghai Considered Socially*, pp. 61–63. Much of the increase in the Chinese population came soon after 1850, since some "twenty thousand Chinese" came into the Settlement in 1853—see C.E. Darwent, *Shanghai: A Handbook for Travellers and Residents* (Shanghai: Kelly and Walsh, 1920), p. 182. According to *Shanghai 700 Nian*, p. 193, more than 100,000 Chinese sought refuge in the various foreign-run areas between 1853 and 1862, but some left after the crises passed.

23 Lang, *Shanghai Considered Socially*, p. 61.

24 Lang, *Shanghai Considered Socially*, p. 62.

25 On the persistence of this vision of the relationship between districts on the part of some foreigners, and its reflection in maps and guidebooks, see Yeh, "Representing the City"; see also Robert Bickers, *Britain in China*.

26 *Shanghai 700 Nian*, pp. 207 and *passim*.

27 The use of the male pronoun here is again done with a purpose: many more men than women came to Shanghai as migrants in this period. See Henriot and Zheng, *Atlas de Shanghai*, p. 95, for the claim that, in 1870, within the combined Chinese and foreign population of the Settlement as a whole, men outnumbered women three to one, and that in the Chinese-run parts of the city, the ratio of males to females was even higher. On the gradual shift to more balanced gender ratios over the course of later decades in the Settlement, see the chart in Takashi and Furuya, *Shanhai shi*, p. 77.

28 Sojourners from Ningbo and Canton were particularly numerous in Shanghai, and in part as a result of this each had unusually active native-place associations; see *Shanghai 700 Nian*, pp. 193 and 206–210, as well as Bryna Goodman, *Native Place, City and Nation* (Berkeley: University of California Press, 1995), the most comprehensive English language study of Shanghai *tongxianghui*. See also, for a good discussion of native-place associations of various sorts, Bergère, *Histoire de Shanghai*.

29 It is worth noting that, while many Chinese guildhalls were located in the old walled district, some were not. A useful map, which gives a sense of the geographical spread of *tongxianghui* throughout all parts of the city, is provided in Takashi and Furuya, *Shanhai shi*, p. 49. Note the location of the Ningbo guild right on the border between the Chinese district and the French Concession. This proved a source of conflict when at a different point the French authorities sought to run a road through the guild's cemetery.

30 "Inevitable meeting place of world travelers" was one phrase used for the city in the guidebook *All About Shanghai: A Standard Guidebook* (Oxford: Oxford University Press, 1983: reprint of a work originally issued in Shanghai by the University Press in 1934–5), p. 1.

31 My comments are based on reading the Routledge reissue (in facsimile form) of the 1873 original text; this is volume 3 in a four-volume series called *The History of Tourism: Thomas Cook and the Origins of Leisure Travel* (London: Routledge, 1998).

32 Cook, *Letters from the Sea and Foreign Lands*, pp. 31, 98, and 100.

33 The edition of Jules Verne's *Around the World in Eighty Days* on which I have relied is the Oxford World's Classic edition, edited and translated by William Butcher (Oxford: Oxford University Press, 1995). On Fogg's near miss of Shanghai, see pp. 114 and *passim*; on the various possible sources of inspiration for *Around the*

World in Eighty Days, including Cook's account of his tour, see "Appendix A," pp. 203–206.

34 "SHANGHAE," entry in *Encyclopedia Britannica*, eighth edition (Boston: Little, Brown & Co, 1860), vol. XX, p. 91

35 Cook, *Letters from the Sea*, p. 32.

36 Verne, *Around the World in Eighty Days*, p. 96.

37 "Mr. Hart's Memo. on the Future of Shanghai," *NCH*, May 1, 1875, p. 409. The *Herald* criticizes Hart (later Sir Robert) for having dared to suggest that, due to problems with its harbor, Shanghai would soon lose its commercial viability. This was nonsense, the editorial claimed: Shanghai had rapidly become "the entrepôt for Central and North China" and would continue to rise.

38 Verne, *Around the World in Eighty Days*, pp. 96–97. In light of the prevalence of references to Shanghai's rise as resulting from a "magical" process (as noted in a previous chapter, for example, one contributor to *Jubilee of Shanghai* wrote that the city had grown "as by enchantment"), it is interesting to mention the way the Hong Kong passage cited above is rendered in an alternate translation of Verne's novel to the one I have been citing. In the translation by George Makepeace Towle (New York: Bantam, 1984), p. 74, the transfer of a Kent or Surrey town to the antipodes is said to be the work of some "strange magic."

39 According to Samuel Couling, *History of Shanghai, Volume 2* (Shanghai: Kelly and Walsh, 1923), regular Shanghai vs. Hong Kong cricket matches were even being played by this point.

40 *Jubilee of Shanghai*, p. 1.

41 On efforts to replicate features of British towns, see Bickers, *Britain in China*, and also Frances Wood, *No Dogs and Not Many Chinese: Treaty Port Life in China, 1843–1943* (London: John Murray, 1998), pp. 18–33 (a chapter entitled "Early Days at Shanghai"). On the early days of the police force, see K.J. McEuen, "Police," in Arnold Wright, ed., *Twentieth Century Impressions of Hong Kong, Shanghai, and Other Treaty Ports of China* (London: Lloyds Greater Britain Publishing Company, 1908), pp. 409–412. According to this text, the force had originally been made up of 30 people (when it was founded around 1853), but by 1870 had one officer, in charge of 32 foreign constables and 84 Chinese ones; by 1875, our snapshot year, the number of foreign constables had declined to 30, but the number of Chinese ones swelled to 105.

42 Couling, *History of Shanghai, Volume 2*, p. 204.

43 Robert Bickers, "'The Greatest Cultural Asset East of Suez': The History and Politics of the Shanghai Municipal Orchestra and Public Band, 1881–1946," in Chi-hsiung Chang (chief ed.), *Ershi shiji de Zhongguo yu shijie* [China and the world in the twentieth century] (Taibei: Institute of History, Academia Sinica, 2001), vol. 2, pp. 835–875.

44 Both quotes are from *NCH*, March 11, 1875, p. 223; on the Cathedral's opening, see *North China Herald*, May 29, 1875, p. 521.

45 E.K. Laird, *The Rambles of a Globe Trotter* (London: Chapman and Hall, 1875), vol. 1, Page 306.

46 Laird, *Rambles*, vol. 1, p. 286.

47 Laird, *Rambles*, vol. 1, pp. 242 and 284.

48 M. Le Baron de Hubner, *A Ramble Round the World, 1871*, translated by Lady Mary Elizabeth Herbert (New York: Macmillan, 1875), p. 446; all subsequent quotations come from this same work, pp. 445–470.

3 1900: A year of fire and sword

1 All of these developments, except the bicycle, are mentioned in Pott, *Short History of Shanghai*. Additional new technologies that arrived in or around 1900 are mentioned on pages 16–18 of the chronology of Shanghai that serves as an appendix to Takashi and

Furruya, *Shanhai shi*. See also, for references to many of the developments listed here, as well as comments on the 1900 local comings and goings of leading Chinese intellectuals and revolutionaries (including Sun Yat-sen), the detailed month-by-month account in Xia Dongyuan *et al.*, *Ershi shiji Shanghai da bolan* [English title given as Chronicle of the 20th Century of Shanghai] (Shanghai: Wenhui chubanshe, 1995), pp. 1–13. Electric lighting only gradually replaced the gas lighting that had been in use, according to MacLellan, *Story of Shanghai*, p. 63, since 1866. Major developments relating to public health also occurred in this period; see Kerrie L. McPherson, *A Wilderness of Marshes: The Origins of Public Health in Shanghai* (Oxford: Oxford University Press, 1987). Worth a mention as well are trams—another new mode of transport whose appearance made the foreign-run parts of Shanghai look more like European and American cities. They went into operation a few years into the new century. On bicycle use in 1900, see the letter to the editor (signed simply "A Resident") in the *North China Herald*, August 29, 1900, which claims that the city had "hundreds of more or less enthusiastic cyclists" by that point. The best general look at Shanghai in 1900 in English remains a short piece by Robert Bickers, "Chinese Burns: Britain in China 1842–1900," *History Today*, 50 (2000), pp. 10–17, which mentions several of the developments alluded to above.

2 James Ricalton, *China through the Stereoscope: A Journey through the Dragon Empire at the Time of the Boxer Uprising* (New York: Underwood & Underwood, 1901), pp. 73–74.

3 Xiong Yuezhi, "The Image and Identity of the Shanghainese," in Tao Tao Liu and David Faure, eds, *Unity and Diversity: Local Cultures and Identities in China* (Hong Kong: Hong Kong University Press, 1996), pp. 99–106, quotations from p. 100.

4 Ye Xiaoqing, p. 65.

5 "A Trip to Pootung," *North China Herald*, June 6, 1900, p. 1035.

6 On economic trends at the turn of the century, see Zhang, *Jindai Shanghai chengshi yanjiu*, pp. 274–277, 315–336 and *passim*. See also "The Beginnings of an Industrial Revolution," in Hawks Pott, *Short History*, pp. 132–136; and Bergère, *Histoire de Shanghai*, pp. 64–74.

7 According to *ibid.*, p. 141, the Settlement grew from 2.75 square miles to 8.35 square miles when this extension took effect.

8 The map is from Henriot and Zheng, *Altas de Shanghai*, p. 28.

9 Zou, *Jiu Shanghai renkou*, p. 90, lists the population of the two enclaves rising from just under 300,000 to just under 450,000 between 1895 and 1900. He does not give any figure for the Chinese-run districts for any years between 1866 and 1909, but during that period he claims the population there rose from just over 540,000 to just over 670,000. This suggests that the city reached the million mark around the turn of the century.

10 I have not found any source for the enclave as a whole, so this comment on male–female ratios in the Settlement relies on two documents, one of which deals with Chinese and the other with foreign residents. For Chinese residents, see the table in Zou, *Jiu Shanghai renkou*, p. 122, which shows the ratio slipping from more to less than two to one between 1895 and 1900. For foreigners, see "The Census of Shanghai," *North China Herald*, July 12, 1895, p. 49. This notes that the number of foreign adult males had "only grown from 1,811 in 1890 to 2,068 in 1895," while the "number of adult females" had risen "from 979 to 1,227." The number of foreign children had also risen dramatically, in part simply because of the increased presence of women. The *Herald* speculated, though, that there might be another reason: fewer Westerners were sending their children home to be educated. This was due partly to economics (they could not afford to do so). But it was partly, the *Herald* claimed (never missing an opportunity to boast), a testament to the fact that "the healthiness of Shanghai has so greatly improved under fifty years of enlightened municipal government" and the local educational institutions had become so much better.

11 See, for example, William Crane Johnstone, Jr., *The Shanghai Problem* (Stanford: Stanford University Press, 1937), p. 128: "Administration of justice in Shanghai has proved to be one of the most complicated and controversial of the problems confronting the municipal and consular authorities." This statement comes at the beginning of a chapter on the Mixed Courts in which Chinese and Western judges jointly presided. One of the best sources on the Court remains A.M. Kotenev, *Shanghai: Its Mixed Court and Council* (Shanghai: North China Daily News and Herald, 1925). An end to the Mixed Court—and a call for Chinese to be tried in purely Chinese courts—was included in many lists of grievances drawn up by protesters during the May 30th Movement. Though there was division among different groups when it came to some demands, e.g. whether a right to strike should be included in lists of grievances, dislike of the Mixed Court seems to have transcended class boundaries. See its inclusion in both the more radical list of "17 Demands" and less radical list of "13 Demands" circulated in 1925; *Wusa yundong shiliao* [Historical Materials on the May 30th Movement], vol. 2 (Shanghai: Shanghai renmin chubanshe, 1986), pp. 252–253 and 280–282.

12 *North China Herald*, May 23, 1900, p. 913.

13 Just what percentage of local foreign residents could vote varied over time, but it was often one-in-ten or less, due to the requirement that one be a land-holder and pay a certain level of rates. Johnstone, *The Shanghai Problem*, p. 56, notes that in 1935, for example, there were 3,852 qualified voters out of a total foreign population in the enclave of 38,915. How many of those 38,915 were children is unclear, but Zou, *Jiu Shanghai renkou*, p. 127, says that in 1935, in the combined Chinese and foreign population of the Settlement (of a bit over a million), 22 percent were 15 years old or under. If we limit consideration to adult foreign males, therefore, we might assume that roughly 30 percent could vote by that point. As we will see below, that is not so different from what the *Herald* estimates was the case in 1900. In contrast to the editors of the *Herald*, though, who thought this an expansive enough suffrage to make the term "oligarchy" inappropriate, Johnstone, in many ways a quite moderate commentator on the situation, saw no problem with employing it. By linking the franchise to property values, he wrote (p. 53), "it was easy to perpetuate the 'taipan oligarchy'" in the Settlement. It is interesting to note that no one, at least in any of the commentaries on SMC elections that I have come across in newspapers and the like from the early 1900s, ever mentioned the possibility of women voting. This silence continued even after 1911 when some calls for and experiments with female suffrage took place in Chinese-run parts of the country. I have also seen no sign that British or American women's suffrage movements made an impact on Shanghai discussions of voting rights.

14 C.B., "The Franchise at Shanghai," *North China Herald*, March 21, 1900, p. 522. I have taken it for granted that C.B. was a man (though women frequently wrote to local papers in this period) for a simple reason: he mentions seldom attending (but being able to attend) the "annual meeting of ratepayers," and these were all-male affairs.

15 "The Franchise at Shanghai," *North China Herald*, March 21, 1900, p. 494.

16 For a longer excerpt from this particular *Shen Pao* editorial, as well as quotations from other related ones, see Mittler, *A Newspaper for China?*, pp. 365–367.

17 "The Future Capital of China," *North China Herald*, August 29, 1900, pp. 434–435; this article concluded that the choice of Shanghai as capital city was unlikely, but did take seriously the possibility.

18 One of the better popular histories to speak of a unified foreign response is E.O. Hauser, *Shanghai: City for Sale* (New York: Harcourt Brace and Co., 1940); it describes the solemn thanksgiving ceremony that took place that August but does not mention the controversy over public parades and illumination.

19 "No Compromise," *North China Herald*, August 29, 1900, pp. 453–454.

20 "How to Treat China," *North China Herald*, August 29, 1900, p. 451. For readers today, the main thing that sticks out about the more bloodthirsty letters in that issue is the wide

range of appallingly racist sentiments they express. These are especially hard to stomach by those who know that a violent, often "barbarous," foreign campaign of revenge, during which many Chinese who had never been Boxers were killed and many Chinese women were raped, was beginning as those epistles were written. It is worth noting, though, that some of even these letter-writers worried about the ordinary Chinese bearing too much of the brunt of reprisals. And this indeed came to pass: a deal was struck that allowed the Qing ruling house to stay in power—even though the Dynasty had supported the Boxers in the end.

21 The term "natives" was used routinely by all types of Shanghailanders around this time; and, as we will see, many different kinds of writers could and did use not just colonially tinged but directly dehumanizing language when referring to at least some local Chinese.

22 The letter containing this phrase is dated August 23 and signed F.R. Graves. A letter referring to it (dated August 24), signed "Englishwoman," appeared two letters down. Presumably both had appeared in the *North China Daily News* on successive days. Englishwoman's letter (pp. 451–452) tells us that Graves, whose letter it endorses, was the local Bishop. Both letters stress, among other things, that there was still some doubt as to whether all foreigners in Beijing were safe. This made holding celebrations seem premature as well as unseemly.

23 Letter dated August 24, *North China Herald*, August 29, 1900, p. 452.

24 *North China Herald*, August 29, 1900, p. 452.

25 *North China Herald*, August 29, 1900, p. 452. Other evidence of the *Herald*'s support for the proposed celebrations comes from a pair of editorials found elsewhere in that same issue. The first is "Let Us Rejoice" (p. 434), which is dated August 25 (presumably when it appeared in the *North China Daily News*) and argues against allowing the "wet blanket of solemnity" upon a community that deserves to express its joy at the passing of a crisis. The second is "A False Step," which is dated August 28 and laments the decision made to postpone (as it turned out indefinitely) all celebratory activities. I say more about the latter editorial below.

26 *North China Herald*, August 29, 1900, p. 452. One more thing to note about this letter is that in it L.H.K. takes issue specifically with Bishop Graves, though without mentioning him by name. The letter refers to an earlier writer's claim that local residents owed "more than an empty illumination" to the victims of Boxer violence. But L.H.K. chided this writer (Graves) for failing to tell readers what exactly should be done instead.

27 *North China Herald*, August 29, 1900, pp. 452–453.

28 *The Royal Visit to Shanghai* (Shanghai: Shanghai Mercury, 1890).

29 *Ibid.*, quotations on pages 14–16.

30 *Ibid.*, p. 18.

31 The information just provided comes from *Jubilee of Shanghai* (Shanghai: North China Daily News, 1893), pp. 36–45, and *1843—Shanghai—1893. The Model Settlement—Its Birth. Its Youth. Its Jubilee* (Shanghai: Shanghai Mercury, 1893), pp. 49–72. For more on the Jubilee, see Ye Xiaoqing, "Shanghai before Nationalism," *East Asian History*, no. 3 (June 1992), pp. 33–52; and Goodman, "Improvisations on a Semi-Colonial Theme."

32 See, for all of this, the following two books on Grant's travel: John Russell Young, *Around the World with General Grant* (Baltimore: Johns Hopkins Press, 2002), an abridged edition (edited by Michael Fellman) of the original 1880 publication; and L.T. Remlap (a pseudonym for Loomis T. Palmer, based on his name spelled backwards), *General U.S. Grant's Tour Around the World* (Chicago: J. Fairbanks and Co., 1880), pp. 235–238. For more on Young's book and the former President's travels, see the chapter "Around the World with Grant and Li," in Wasserstrom, *China's Brave New World—And Other Tales for Global Times*.

33 The most important English language work on the Ningbo native-place society in

general and the 1874 and 1898 riots in particular is Bryna Goodman, *Native Place, City and Nation: Regional Networks and Identities in Shanghai, 1853–1937* (Berkeley: University of California Press, 1995).

34 On this riot, see Robert Bickers, "Ordering Shanghai: Policing a treaty port, 1854–1900," in David Killingray, Margarette Lincoln, and Nigel Rigby, eds, *Maritime Empires: British Imperial Maritime Trade in the Nineteenth Century* (Rochester, New York: The Boydell Press, 2004), pp. 173–194.

35 Pott, *Short History of Shanghai*, pp. 128–129.

36 "A False Step," *North China Herald*, August 29, 1900, p. 435.

37 "The End of the Century," which appeared on page 11 of the January 2, 1901 issue of the *North China Herald* (presumably it was written for and appeared in the last 1900 issue of the *North China Daily News*).

4 1925: A city in the streets

1 In rendering these passages into English, I have relied heavily on A.C. Barnes's version, *Schoolmaster Ni Huan-chih* (Beijing: Foreign Languages Press, 1958), pp. 278 and 281, but altered it at various points. I changed "clamour of bells" to "ding-ling-ling," for example, to retain the onomatopoeic sense of the original, and "Western-style" to "European-style" (again to stay truer to Ye). For these changes, the Chinese edition I used was Ye Shengtao, *Ni Huanzhi* (Hong Kong: Sanlian, no date), pp. 184 and 186–187. One chapter was dropped in some PRC editions, so those pages appear in Chapter 21 in the Barnes edition but Chapter 22 of the Hong Kong one. I am grateful to Daniel Fried for ideas about Ye Shengtao that he shared with me in Taiwan; for an insightful reading of works of fiction from the time, see his "A Bloody Absence: Communist Narratology and the Literature of May Thirtieth," *Chinese Literature: Essays, Articles and Review*, 26 (2004).

2 Though both authors wrote their May 30th novels (Mao's was *Rainbow*) years later, each immediately published short eyewitness accounts. These are reprinted in Yu Zhi and Cheng Xinguo, eds, *Jiu Shanghai fengqing lu* [Famous impressions of Old Shanghai] (Shanghai: Wenhui chubanshe, 1998), vol. 2, pp. 2–5 (Mao Dun) and 6–9 (Ye Shengtao).

3 Yeh Sheng-tao (Ye Shengtao) (Barnes translation), *Schoolmaster Ni Huan-chih*, p. 293; as modified in light of Ye Shengtao, *Ni Huanzhi*, pp. 193–194.

4 Bergère, *Histoire de Shanghai*, p. 505.

5 For details on this (such as that the Chinese team beat the Japanese one), see Xia, *Ershi shiji Shanghai da bolan*, p. 307.

6 On population, see Zou, *Jiu Shanghai renkou*, p. 90. On warfare and refugees, see Hawks Pott, *Short History*, pp. 274–284. On the *Herald*'s anniversary, see *NCH*, August 8, 1925. And, on *Xin Qingnian*, which was founded in Beijing but then soon moved to Shanghai, see Rigby, *May 30th*, p. 238; as he notes, by 1925, this journal had abandoned its original ideological eclecticism and become a CCP organ.

7 Zou, *Shanghai renkou yenjiu*, p. 145. In 1900, the Japanese population of the Settlement was still well under a thousand, and in 1910 there was still a much larger number of Britons (4,465) than Japanese (3,361) living in this enclave. By 1925, however, there were 5,879 of the former, but 13,804 of the latter. It is also worth noting, as scholars inside and outside of Japan have stressed, that a divide emerged within the local Japanese community that was much like that Robert Bickers describes for the local British community. On the one hand, there were Japanese "settlers" (to follow the terminology Bickers employs, in *Britain in China: Community, Culture and Colonialism 1900–1945* (Manchester: Manchester University Press, 1999) and else-where) for whom Shanghai was a new home. There were also, however, many for whom it was just a temporary stopping-off point. I am grateful to Paul Cohen for drawing my attention to this point.

8 Wang Min, ed., *Shanghai xuesheng yundong dashiji, 1919–1949* [A Chronology of the Shanghai Student Movement, 1919–1949] (Shanghai: Xuelin chubanshe, 1985), p. 73.
9 For Sun and Song's Shanghai lifestyle, see Marie-Claire Bergère, *Sun Yat-sen* (Stanford: Stanford University Press, 1998), trans. by Janet Lloyd, pp. 276–277; see also, for a fictional account that sticks closely to known facts where the 1920s are concerned, Ping Lu, *Love and Revolution: A Novel about Song Qingling and Sun Yat-sen* (New York: Columbia University Press, 2006), translated from the Chinese by Nancy Du.
10 On Russell's visit, see Zhang, *Jindai Shanghai*, p. 1053.
11 For fascinating personal histories of the lives early CCP activists led in Shanghai in the 1920s, see S.A. Smith, *A Road is Made: Communism in Shanghai, 1920–1927* (Richmond, Surrey: Curzon, 2000). The information provided above is taken largely from pp. 18–19, 49 and 60–61 of this work.
12 Zhang, *Jindai Shanghai*, p. 1053.
13 Hesen [Cai Hesen], "Bei waiguo diguo zhuyi zaige bashi nian de Shanghai" [Shanghai's 80 years of exploitation at the hands of foreign imperialists], *Xiangdao Zhoubao*, no. 46, November 16, 1923, pp. 352–353.
14 Sun Zhongshan, "Zhongguo neiluan de yuanyin" [Reasons for China's internal chaos], *Sun Zhongshan xuanji* [Sun Yat-sen's Collected Works] (Beijing: Renmin, 1956), vol. 2, pp. 899–911.
15 On crime and the French Concession, see Brian Martin, *The Shanghai Green Gang: Politics and Organized Crime, 1919–1937* (Berkeley: University of California Press, 1986); and Frederic E. Wakeman, Jr., *Policing Shanghai, 1927–1937* (Berkeley: University of California Press, 1995). See also, for a wonderfully readable but scholarly, solid work on the subject, Lynn Pan, *Old Shanghai: Gangsters in Paradise* (Hong Kong: Heinemann Asia, 1984).
16 Jonathan D. Spence, *The Search for Modern China*, second edition (New York: Norton, 1999), pp. 303 and 344.
17 Joshua A. Fogel, "The Other Japanese Community: Leftwing Japanese Activities in Wartime Shanghai," in Wen-hsin Yeh, *Wartime Shanghai* (London: Routledge, 1998), pp. 42–61, with the reference to Lu Xun on p. 45. Fogel's main focus in that essay is, as the title of the book it appears in suggests, the last decades of the Republican era, during which Japan was fighting to control or had taken over part or all of Shanghai. It nevertheless provides a very good sketch in its opening pages of Shanghai's Japanese community or rather, as he aptly stresses, its Japanese *communities* in the late 1800s and, the era that interests us in this chapter, the first quarter of the twentieth century. Fogel tells us, for example, that well before the Settlement fell to Japan, the Hongkou section of it had already become a place with "Japanese clubs, bathhouses, restaurants and bars, beauty salons, and inns." He also tells us that, by the start of the 1920s, there was a Japanese Chamber of Commerce in Shanghai and three separate Japanese language newspapers were being published in the city. So, too was the *Jiangnan zhengbao*, a Chinese language newspaper controlled by Japanese interests that began operation in 1918. One thing he does not mention (but might have as another sign of the Japanese cultural presence) is that one of the Settlement's English language papers, the *Shanghai Times*, tended to influenced by and sometimes under the control of Japanese interests.
18 For a biting discussion of the state of various Lu Xun sites as of the 1970s, and a scathing commentary on the unsuitability of the CCP's moves to transform an iconoclastic figure into a one-dimensional Maoist saint, see Simon Leys, *Chinese Shadows* (New York: Viking, 1977), pp. 93–94. Based on my 2004 visit there, I can say that Lu Xun's former residence is now in much better shape than it apparently was in the 1970s, with objects displayed that give a fuller sense of some of the varied contours of this complex individual's life and work.

19 Several people have told me, however, that the town of Mao Dun's youth, which lies not far from Shanghai, has been restored and is well worth a visit.

20 My debt in this section to Leo Lee's *Shanghai Modern* (Cambridge, Mass.: Harvard University Press, 1999) is great, as any reader of that book will soon realize.

21 Lu Hanchao's *Beyond the Neon Lights* reminds us, correctly, that the majority of Shanghainese never went to nightclubs or wore imported clothes. But many middle-class Chinese did. How fashionable one item of foreign apparel (straw hats from Japan) became is attested to by the stress protesters put on eschewing it during the anti-Japanese protests of 1919; see my *Student Protests in Twentieth-Century China*, p. 63.

22 Rigby, *May 30th*, p. 207, note 19, refers to Kotenev as a "generally reliable author." Kotenev's most widely read book was probably his more general one on China, *New Lamps for Old* (Shanghai: North China Herald, 1931), which also contained some information on the May 30th Movement. On Chengyan, which Rigby describes as directly supported by the Shanghai Municipal Council, see *May 30th*, p. 73, which also details efforts local radicals, including Qu Qiubai, made to combat that supplement's influence on the city's Chinese population.

23 Zou, *Jiu Shanghai renkou*, pp. 145 and 146; for a comprehensive look at White Russians within the enclaves, see Ristaino, *Port of Last Resort: The Diaspora Communities of Shanghai* (Stanford: Stanford University Press, 2001).

24 See Richard Rigby, "Sapajou," which I consulted at www.talesofchina.com on July 16, 2002; this piece originally appeared in *East Asian History*, 17/18 (June/December 1999).

25 Ibáñez, *A Novelist's Tour of the World* (New York: Dutton, 1926), pp. 191 and 193.

26 I am grateful to Robert Bickers for urging me to consider Kounin's work as in part an assertion of Shanghailander status. He encouraged me to do this after reading an unpublished conference paper of mine on the 1893 and 1938 jubilees, which I presented at Berkeley's Center for Chinese Studies in 1994. I.I. Kounin, *Diamond Jubilee of the International Settlement of Shanghai* (Shanghai, 1938).

27 Pan Ling, *In Search of Old Shanghai*, p. 38.

28 Gao Da, ed., *Waitan jinxi* [English title: The Bund Then and Now] (Shanghai: Shanghai huabao chubanshe, 1996), p. 52. Text throughout in both Chinese and English.

29 See, for example, Wu Jiang, *Shanghai bainian jiangong shi, 1840–1949* [The History of Shanghai Architecture, 1840–1949] (Shanghai: Tongji Daxue chubanshe, 1997), p. 133.

30 Wu, *Shanghai bainian*, p. 116 and *passim*.

31 Cohen, *History in Three Keys*.

32 *Schoolmaster Ni Huan-chih*, p. 293; *Ni Huanzhi*, p. 194.

33 See Emily Honig, *Sisters and Strangers* (Stanford: Stanford University Press, 1986) Elizabeth J. Perry, *Shanghai on Strike* (Stanford: Stanford University Press, 1993); Chen Weimin, "Zhongguo gongchandang jianli chuqi de Shanghai gongren yundong pinggu" [An evaluation of the Shanghai labor movement in the early years of the Chinese Communist Party], *Shilin*, vol. 4, no. 11 (1988); and S.A. Smith, *Like Cattle and Horses: Nationalism and Labor in Shanghai, 1895–1927* (Durham: Duke University Press, 2002).

34 A good sense of the overlapping yet separable contemporary meanings of these terms can be gleaned from the detailed June 12, 1925 *Xinwenbao* article on a *Shimin dahui* reproduced in Shanghai Academy of Social Sciences, *Wusa yundong shiliao* [Historical Materials on the May 30th Movement], volume 2 (Shanghai: Shanghai shehui kexue yuan, 1986), pp. 290–297.

35 Zhong, "My Propaganda Activities during the May 30th Movement," in Elizabeth J. Perry and Jeffrey N. Wasserstrom, eds, *Shanghai Social Movements, 1919–1949*, a double-issue (Fall–Winter 1993/94) of *Chinese Studies in History*, translations by Zhu Hong, pp. 110–112.

5 1950: An in-between year

1 The full text of the speech can be found, most easily, in Song Qing Ling, *Struggle for New China* (Peking: Foreign Languages Press, 1953), pp. 245–249.

2 Song's speech appeared in many newspapers, and in fact in her *Struggle for New China*, just below the title on p. 245 comes the following wording: "Issued to the Shanghai newspapers on the first anniversary of the city's liberation." One place where it appeared was the June 10, 1950 (inaugural) edition of the English language *Shanghai News*, p. 3, a newspaper discussed further below.

3 "China: Paralysis in Shanghai," *Time*, April 2, 1950, p. 32. The unnamed author of this article claims that the "early enthusiasm which sent daily parades of workers and students into the streets" had "worn thin" by the spring of 1950, and quotes a local Briton as saying that a "general paralysis is setting in, a paralysis of commerce and spirit." The phrase "slowly dying city" is used to describe the impression of Shanghai given by "83 Shanghailanders (including four U.S. citizens)" who had recently arrived in Hong Kong. On Luce's high opinion of Chiang Kai-shek (whom he once described as a Christ-like figure) and Song Meiling (referred to in *Time* as the "Christian Miss Soong"), see T. Christopher Jespersen, *American Images of China, 1931–1949* (Stanford: Stanford University Press, 1996), pp. 29–38 and *passim*; the Generalissimo and his wife shared *Time*'s "Man of the Year" title in 1937.

4 "Shanghai 'Dying City,'" *The Times* (London), April 14, 1950.

5 A nicely distilled version of this vision of Shanghai as reborn, cleansed, and made "healthy" can be found—in four different languages: Chinese, French, English, and Russian—on the opening pages of *Shanghai huace* [Shanghai Pictorial] (Shanghai, 1958).

6 John Pal, *Shanghai Saga* (London: Jarrolds, 1963), p. 22.

7 Noël Barber, *The Fall of Shanghai: The Communist Takeover in 1949* (London: Macmillan, 1979).

8 Noël Barber, *The Fall of Shanghai: The Splendor and Squalor of the Imperial City of Trade, and the 1949 Revolution that Swept an Era Away* (New York: Coward, McCann & Geoghegan, 1979).

9 *Xin Shanghai bianlan* [A Guide to New Shanghai] (Shanghai: Dagongbao, 1951); Shirley Wood, *A Street in China* (London: Michael Joseph, 1958); Lynn Pan, *Tracing it Home: A Chinese Family's Journey from Shanghai* (New York: Kodansha, 1993). I am grateful to John Gittings for bringing *A Street in China* to my attention.

10 On Due Yuesheng's life and career as a crime boss, see Brian G. Martin, *The Shanghai Green Gang: Politics and Organized Crime, 1919–1937* (Berkeley: University of California Press, 1996), and Lynn Pan, *Old Shanghai: Gangsters in Paradise* (Singapore: Cultured Lotus, 1999).

11 Wood, *A Street in China*, p. 39

12 See, for example, the discussion of the "Family Women's Organisation" in the chapter titled "Organise, Babe O' Mine," pp. 102–124 (the quoted phrase comes from p. 109).

13 Pan, *Tracing it Home*, p. 109.

14 Pan, *Tracing it Home*, pp. 110–111.

15 Pan, *Tracing it Home*, pp. 117–131.

16 Pan, *Tracing it Home*, p. 131.

17 See, for example, Nian Cheng, *Life and Death in Shanghai* (New York: Penguin, 1988). And also the excerpt from Dympha Cusack's 1958 book, *Chinese Women Speak*, excerpted in Barbara Baker, *Shanghai: Electric and Lurid City* (Hong Kong: Oxford University Press, 1998), pp. 215–231, which describes an interview the author conducted with members of a former "capitalist's family" who had become reconciled to the new regime quite quickly. Though focussing on changes since 1949, it mentions in passing that the family still had a servant to wait on them and their guests (in this case, the interviewer) several years after the Communists came to power.

18 "Shanghai: 'Dying City,'" London *Times*, April 14, 1950.

19 *Xin Shanghai bianlan*, p. 15.

20 *Xin Shanghai bianlan*, p. 426.

21 Randall Gould, "Dream Street, Shanghai," July 17, 1950.

22 "The First Year," *China Monthly Review*, May 27, 1950, pp. 218–219.

23 For a fascinating discussion of clothing trends and other details about life, attitudes, and new international influences in Shanghai in 1950, see the two-part series on "Marxist Shanghai," which ran in *The Economist*, September 16, 1950, pp. 484–485 (I), and September 23, 1950, pp. 517–518 (II). These articles are much more sensitive to the complexities of the year than the articles from *Time* and the London *Times* cited above.

24 "Shanghai 'Dying City,'" *The Times* (London), April 14, 1950. All passages that I have placed in quotation marks are the reporter's phrasing (not direct quotations for the interviewee), though presumably much of what he is doing is paraphrasing comments that he heard.

25 On Nationalist Party plans for the city's transformation, and the reasons that they came up short, see Christian Henriot, *Shanghai, 1927–1937: Municipal Power, Locality and Modernization* (Berkeley: University of California Press, 1993).

26 On efforts by Chinese collaborators and the Japanese to represent themselves as having "liberated" Shanghai from foreign imperialism, see Jeffrey N. Wasserstrom, *Student Protests in Twentieth Century China: The View from Shanghai* (Stanford: Stanford University Press, 1991).

27 "Work of the Shanghai People's Gov't During the Past Year," *Shanghai News*, June 10, 1950. The original Chinese version of Pan's speech can be found in, among other publications, *Shanghai jiefang yinian, 1949–1950* [One year of liberated Shanghai, 1949–1950] (Shanghai: Jiefang ribao chubanshe, 1950); my quotation is based on the *Shanghai News* version, but has been modified slightly in light of the Chinese original. Also in that same inaugural issue of *Shanghai News* is a speech by Guo Moruo, yet another cosmopolitan nationalist (he not only studied in Japan but married a woman from that country), which is entitled "Mankind Demands Peace." Still other headlines from that issue include one that refers to Stalin's seventieth birthday and one that reads "40,568 Visitors at Hungary Exhibition, Fickert Honoured." These kinds of articles helped show that the CCP's commitment to anti-imperialism did not require a disengagement with the world but rather a shift in the parts of the outside world to which the Chinese people should look.

28 Wu Wenhu, *Baifenbai jiafei* [Everything about Coffee] (Guangzhou: Guangdong yuyou chubanshe, 2001), pp. 131–133. Wu lists specific people Pan met in cafés between 1927 and 1949 (Zhou Enlai, famous writers, etc.) and specific places he went to drink coffee and talk (the upper floor of the famous "Gongfei" Café on Sichuan Road in the International Settlement, for instance).

29 On *Jiefang ribao*, see Patricia Stranahan, *Molding the Medium: The Chinese Communist Party and the Liberation Daily* (Armonk, New York: M.E. Sharpe, 1991).

30 One such list, "Exit Permits Granted to 53 Persons," appears just to the right of the "To Our Readers" notice in the June 10, 1950, inaugural issue of the *Shanghai News*.

31 *Shanghai News*, June 10, 1950.

32 On Pan's cosmopolitan tastes and fondness for Shanghai cafés (and Hong Kong cafés when he was operating there) as a member of the Communist Party underground, see Wu Wenhu.

33 "Major Events in Shanghai," *Shanghai News*, May 28, 1951, p. 3.

6 1975: The East was Red

1 *China Travel: Shanghai, Hangzhou, Nanjing, Wuxi, Suzhou* (Beijing: China Travel and Tourism Press, 1975), pp. 13, 27, 34.

2   *China Travel*, pp. 20–21, which identifies the structure as "The Shanghai Industrial Exhibition" and says it is a "centre where new products of Shanghai are displayed and new techniques exchanged." Contrast this with the photograph in *Shanghai huace*, unpaginated text (roughly a quarter of the way into the book), which shows the building from the outside (something that accentuates the international influence on its architecture), lit up at night, and gives as its English language name (the text is in Chinese and three foreign languages), "The Sino-Soviet Friendship Building."

3   A translation of this speech appears as "Yu Ch'iu-Li's Address to Cadres in the Industrial and Transportation Front in Shanghai," in *Issues and Studies*, vol. 11, no. 8 (August 1975), pp. 90–92.

4   *China Travel*, pp. 24, 26, and 30–31.

5   *China Travel*.

6   *China Travel*, p. 26.

7   For background on these factional struggles and general information about the city during the Cultural Revolution, see various contributions to Christopher Howe, ed., *Shanghai: Revolution and Development in an Asian Metropolis* (Cambridge: Cambridge University Press, 1981); Elizabeth J. Perry and Li Xun, *Proletarian Power: Shanghai in the Cultural Revolution* (Armonk, New York: Westview Press, 1997); and Roderick MacFarquhar and Michael Schoenhals, *Mao's Last Revolution* (Cambridge, Mass.: Harvard University Press, 2006).

8   I am grateful to China specialist Harriet Evans, who studied in Beijing in the mid-1970s, for first bringing this to my attention in the late 1990s in a personal communication. Since then, I have talked about the phenomenon with a variety of Westerners who spent time in China during that same period, as well as Chinese colleagues and acquaintances who grew up in the PRC, and all have confirmed her impression.

9   *Shanghai de gushi* [The Shanghai Story] (Shanghai: Shanghai renminchubanshe, 1963).

7   2000: A city in a hurry

1   Ramesh Kumar Biswas, "Shanghai: Time, Tides," in *idem*, ed., *Metropolis Now! Urban Culture in Global Cities* (New York: Springer, 2000), pp. 15–25 (quotation taken from page 20). Note: in the book, the number 22,000 appears without a comma: I added one to avoid confusion.

2   David Barrett, "2000 Shanghai Biennale: A Day-by-Day Eyewitness Account," in Wu Hung, ed., *Chinese Art at the Crossroads: Between Past and Future, Between East and West* (London: New Art Media Ltd., 2001), pp. 223–244; quotation from pp. 223–225.

3   One of the most interesting examples is the wide-ranging exchange about cafés between two local academics that ran in the May 2000 issue of the Shanghai edition of *M Magazine*, "Kafeiguan yu Shanghai yu Wo" [Cafés, Shanghai, and Me], pp. 48 and 50.

4   One of the most beautifully produced and textually interesting of the works I saw displayed was Wu Meidong, *Yu Bijiasu he kafei* [Drinking coffee with Picasso] (Shanghai: Shanghai wenyi chubanshe, 1999). It is a book of many parts, including a potted history of global coffee drinking (where the limited popularity of the drink in China throughout most of its history is stressed), but also provides tips on the meaning and preparation of different espresso beverages. In addition, as its title indicates, it has much to say about Picasso's love for cafés, and one of his striking paintings of a woman, with a delicate china cup filled with coffee added, makes for an eye-catching cover. See also the previously cited Wu Wenhu, *Baifenbai kafei*, which was published in Guangzhou and describes and shows photographs of new coffee-related venues in various PRC cities, but in its section on famous coffee drinkers (where Picasso is mentioned) the only Chinese individual discussed is one-time Shanghai Vice-Mayor Pan Hannian.

5 Zhang Yao (text and photographs), *Dakai kafeiguan de men* [Opening the Door of the Café] (Shanghai: Dongfang chuban zhongxin, 1999); and *Kafei ditu* [Café Map] (Shanghai: Dongfang chuban zhongxin, 1999). These works first appeared in 1997 in Taiwan editions issued by China Times Publishing.

6 I have not seen the original Taiwan edition, so I am not sure if the prologue about Shanghai was added specially for the 1999 mainland edition. For details on Zhang Yao, see his website, http://www.zhangyao.com/english/home.htm (accessed April 18, 2008).

7 *Kafei biji* [Café Diary—or Coffee Diary, as the term kafei can be translated either way] (no date or place of publication given); publicity materials seen by the author in Shanghai Shucheng (Shanghai City of Books), Fuzhou Road, December 2000. I am grateful to Kate Merkel-Hess for pointing out the link to yoga classes, an example of a point emphasized in the next chapter: the need to think in terms of East meets East as well as East meets West varieties of cosmopolitanism in treaty-port era Shanghai but even more so contemporary Shanghai.

8 Jos Gamble, *Shanghai in Transition: Changing Perspectives and Social Contours of a Chinese Metropolis* (London: Routledge Curzon, 2003), pp. xi and 17–18; see also Pan Tianshu, "Neighborhood Shanghai: Communist Building in Bay Bridge," unpublished dissertation (Harvard, Anthropology Department, 2002).

9 Quotation provided by "The American Presidency Project," a resource associated with the University of California, Santa Barbara; the full text of his speech is available at http://www.presidency.ucsb.edu/ws/index.php?pid=63185 (accessed October 3, 2007).

10 Wu Guifan, "Songgu mantan (san)" [An informal discussion of old Shanghai (part 3)], *Dang'an yu lishi* (Archives and History), vol. 2, no. 1 (1986), pp. 80–82.

11 *Shanghai Star*, January 25, 2000.

12 Wu Hung, "The Third Shanghai Biennale," in Wu, ed., *Chinese Art at the Crossroads*, pp. 220–222, quote from page 221. My other comments on the Biennale are based on, along with Wu's short essay and Barrett's diary, "2000 Shanghai Biennale," these other contributions to Wu, *Chinese Art at the Crossroads*: Regi Preiswerk, "Letters from Shanghai (pp. 245–250), Wang Nanming, "The Shanghai Art Museum Should Not Become a Market Stall in China for Western Hegemonism" (pp. 265–268); and Wu Hung, "The 2000 Shanghai Biennale: The Making of a 'Historical Event' in Contemporary Chinese Art" (pp. 275–285).

13 For an image and description of this work of art, "Bank of Sand or Sand of Bank," see Wu, *Chinese Art at the Crossroads*, p. 230.

Conclusion: Ten theses on twenty-first-century Shanghai

1 Nick Land, editor, *Urbanatomy: Shanghai 2008* (Shanghai: Urbanatomy, 2008).

2 Published by *Cossacks Breaking News*, http://cossacks.org.uk/business/maglev-train-fuels-fundamental-change-for-chinese-protests/ (accessed March 27, 2008); note some small oddities of spelling and punctuation have been corrected to improve the flow.

3 Peter G. Rowe and Seng Kuan, eds, *Shanghai: Architecture and Urbanism for Modern China* (Berlin: Prestel, 2004).

4 On Paris Hilton's visit, see http://shanghaiist.com/2007/11/23/paris_hiltons_s.php (accessed March 23, 2008).

5 See, for example, Li Dajian and Jiang Fuming, editors, *Shibohui dui Shanghai to ying xiang he duice* [Planning for the World Expo's Impact on Shanghai] (Shanghai: Tongji, 2004), which includes some thirty academic pieces that look at the prospects for 2010 from different disciplinary and topical angles. Tongji University, which published this book, has emerged as a major center of "Expo Studies"—a counterpart to the "Olympic Studies" that has taken shape as an academic subfield on campuses in several cities that have hosted the Games, including Sydney's University of New South Wales.

6 The Hong Kong links of Xintiandi are mentioned in many local guidebooks, as well as newspaper and magazine articles, but for a recent publication that discussed these connections and also provides a potted history of Shanghai Tang, see Leo Ou-fan Lee, *City Between Worlds—My Hong Kong* (Cambridge, Mass.: Harvard University Press, 2008).

7 For an insightful discussion of this general phenomenon, see the following article in Japan Focus (http://www.japanfocus.org/products/details/2660, accessed May 15, 2008): Nissim Kadosh Otmazgin's "Japanese Popular Culture in East and Southeast Asia: Time for a Regional Paradigm?" I say "nearly all" rather than all East Asian cities due to North Korea's urban centers standing apart from the trend.

8 On this issue, see Andrew Ross, *Fast Boat to China: Corporate Flight and the Consequences of Free Trade—Lessons from Shanghai* (New York: Pantheon, 2006).

9 Xu Xixian and Xu Jianrong, *Baibian Shanghai* [English title: A Changing Shanghai] (Shanghai: Shanghai People's Fine Art Publishing House, 2004), and Xu Xixian and Xu Jianrong, *Zuiyi she Jiangnan II* [English title: A Changing Shanghai II] (Shanghai: Shanghai People's Fine Art Publishing House, 2006).

10 Thomas Millard, *China: Where It is Today and Why* (New York: Harcourt Brace, 1928), pp. 249–250

11 Zhang Zhongli *et al.*, *Dongnan Yanhai chengshi, yu Zhongguo jindaihua* [Southeastern port cities and China's modernization] (Shanghai: Shanghai renmin chubanshe, 1996), p. 38. For citations to many additional quotations stressing Shanghai's unique features, see Jeffrey N. Wasserstrom, "Is Global Shanghai 'Good to Think'?: Thoughts on Comparative History and Post-Socialist Cities," *Journal of World History*, vol. 18, no. 2 (June 2007), pp. 199–234.

12 Saskia Sassen, *The Global City: New York, London, Tokyo* (Princeton: Princeton University Press, 1991); for further discussion of this topic, see Wasserstrom, "Is Global Shanghai 'Good to Think'?"

13 See Rama Lakshmi, "Bombay Moves to Push Out the Poor," *Washington Post*, May 8, 2005, p. A20, http://www.washingtonpost.com/wp-dyn/content/article/2005/05/07/AR2005050701004.html (accessed April 18, 2008), and Siddharth Srivastava, "Can Mumbai Become India's Shanghai? Not So Fast," *Pacific News Service*, April 17, 2005, http://news.pacificnews.org/news/view_article.html?article_id=d5ba5a408fa73cfbc2eee2e094d26670 (accessed April 18, 2008).

14 Judit Bodnár, *Fin de Millénaire Budapest: Metamorphoses of Urban Life* (Minneapolis: University of Minnesota Press, 2001), pp. 157–182, quotations from p. 157. The quotation from Mike Davis is from his seminal study, *City of Quartz: Excavating the Future in Los Angeles* (New York: Vintage, 1992), a book that has considerable influence on the way that I think about many urban centers, including Shanghai. For a fascinating study of East Asian cities, including the one of primary interest here, which draws heavily upon Davis, see Tsung-yi Michelle Huang, *Walking Between Slums and Skyscrapers: Illusions of Open Space in Hong Kong, Singapore and Shanghai* (Hong Kong: Hong Kong University Press, 2004).

15 Ivan Szelenyi, "Cities under Socialism—and After," in Gregory Andrusz, Michael Harloe, and Ivan Szelenyi, eds, *Cities after Socialism: Urban and Regional Change in Post-Socialist Societies* (Oxford: Blackwell, 1996); see also Ivan Szelenyi, *Urban Inequalities under State Socialism* (Oxford: Oxford University Press, 1983).

16 Christopher Hawthorne, "The Gridlock Kid: Can the Mayor Find His Way Out of a Jam and Lead the City to Global Glory?" *Los Angeles Times Magazine*, March 2, 2008, pp. 24–26.

Index

Lightning Source UK Ltd.
Milton Keynes UK
16 November 2010

162962UK00003B/19/P